Doing Business with Jordan

towards golden opportunities

Jordinvest offers you fully rounded investment banking services in Jordan and the region. Brought to you by outstanding professionals, who cater for your investments objectives based on intensive research and a good eye for exceptional opportunities.

Jordinvest Your Ultimate Investment Guardian...

Capital Markets & Asset Management
Corporate Finance
Research & Analysis
Brokerage & Trading

Jordinvest
Jordan Investment Trust P.L.C

For inquiries:P.O.Box: 911447 Amman 11191 Jordan, Tel: 962 6 5508888, Fax: 962 6 5508899, e-mail: information@jordinvest.com.jo

Doing Business with
Jordan

SECOND EDITION

Consultant editor:
Philip Dew

Associate publisher :
Abdullah J Wallace

Forewords from:
Suhair Al-Ali
Minister of Planning and
International Cooperation, Kingdom of Jordan

James Watt
British Ambassador,
to the Kingdom of Jordan

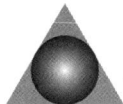

GMB

Publisher's note

Every possible effort has been made to ensure that the information contained in this publication is accurate at the time of going to press and neither the publishers nor any of the authors, editors, contributors or sponsors can accept responsibility for any errors or omissions, however caused. No responsibility for loss or damage occasioned to any person acting, or refraining from action, as a result of the material in this publication can be accepted by the editors, authors, the publisher or any of the contributors or sponsors.

Users and readers of this publication may copy or download portions of the material herein for personal use, and may include portions of this material in internal reports and/or reports to customers, and on an occasional and infrequent basis individual articles from the material, provided that such articles (or portions of articles) are attributed to this publication by name, the individual contributor of the portion used and GMB Publishing Ltd.

Users and readers of this publication shall not reproduce, distribute, display, sell, publish, broadcast, repurpose, or circulate the material to any third party, or create new collective works for resale or for redistribution to servers or lists, or reuse any copyrighted component of this work in other works, without the prior written permission of GMB Publishing Ltd.

GMB Publishing Ltd.
120 Pentonville Road
London N1 9JN
United Kingdom
www.globalmarketbriefings.com

525 South 4th Street, #241
Philadelphia, PA 19147
United States of America

This edition first published 2007 by GMB Publishing Ltd.

© GMB Publishing Ltd. and contributors

Hardcopy ISBN 1-84673-054-6   ISBN-13 978-184673-054-2
E-book ISBN 1-84673-055-4   E-ISBN-13 978-184673-055-9

British Library Cataloguing in Publication Data

A CIP record for this book is available from the British Library

Typeset by David Lewis XML Associates Ltd

Printed and bound by the Oriental Press Ltd, The Kingdom of Bahrain

Contents

Foreword

Living in a highly competitive global economy, Jordan understands that the requirements of integrating into this economy and enhancing the country's growth are large. Therefore, Jordan continues to do its utmost to create a viable state with substantial potential for growth and prosperity.

Jordan has placed political, social and economic reforms at the core of its development agenda. This is evident in many of the recent policies and programs that aim at creating an enabling economic environment through increased openness and integration into the global economy, adopting an export-led growth strategy, and implementing monetary and fiscal reforms.

For many years, Jordan has been adopting structural, economic, legal, administrative and social reform programs. Many elements of these programs have been successfully implemented and others are still in progress. Extensive efforts have also been undertaken to further enhance the regulatory environment in order to attract direct investments. Our reform efforts have clearly corresponded to the evolving global trends, and success has been attained in molding a lucrative investment climate, in which businesses can thrive by tapping into the vast world market. These efforts have succeeded in opening the door for foreign investors to come and invest in Jordan. Our commitment to attract foreign direct investment is coupled with a comprehensive public sector reform program, including legislative, administrative, and judicial reforms to improve the efficiency of the public sector, enhance investment environment, and ensure strict and transparent implementation of the rule of law.

To strengthen Jordan's economic base and improve the competitiveness and efficiency of Jordanian enterprises, an export-oriented policy was adopted. This was reflected in joining a series of initiatives of international and regional free trade arrangements. We have also worked towards developing export platforms that offer world class investment infrastructure, free access to major regional and international markets, and lucrative investment incentive packages.

A large number of laws and regulations were amended and investment related laws were streamlined. The legal regulatory environment seeks to open and improve integration, reduce bureaucracy, simplify procedures, as well as facilitate services offered to local, Arab, and foreign investors to come and invest in Jordan. An increase in foreign direct investment flows and portfolio investments was witnessed over the past couple of years. In 2006, foreign direct investment scored over US$2.5 billion, primarily coming from the Gulf countries. However, the Government of Jordan remains committed to further enhance the investment climate in Jordan and work towards introducing new measures related to starting a business, dealing with licenses, registering property, employing workers, and enforcing contracts.

The privatization program was accelerated through the adoption of a multi-track approach that included divestitures of shares, sales to strategic investors, and management contracts. The privatization program succeeded in creating a competitive market, enhancing the efficiency of privatized firms, as well as attracting investments.

It is worth noting also that the Jordanian economy has managed to achieve positive results at the macroeconomic level and demonstrated resilience to the challenges that it has been facing, including the increase in the international oil prices and the regional political and economic instability. Jordan was able to achieve a GDP real growth rate of 6.4% in 2006. A marked increase in foreign direct investments and other inflows of private capital was also witnessed along with an increase in official foreign currency reserves to US$6.4 billion (providing around six months of import cover).

We remain committed to continue the thrust of our reform agenda and realize the vision of His Majesty King Abdullah II for building a model of economic vitality, peace, regional cooperation, and social stability. Transforming Jordan from a lower-middle income country into a modern knowledge-based economy with increased productivity and employment continues to be at the core of Jordan's long-term development agenda. This is emphasized in the Kuluna al Urdun (We are all Jordan) initiative, which is a framework for Jordan's future plan for reform and development in all sectors that was developed through a public-private partnership.

I would like to take this opportunity to extend my appreciation for the team of experts who prepared this book, and I hope that it provides you with the needed information that enables you to explore the investment opportunities available in Jordan.

Suhair Al-Ali
Minister of Planning and International Cooperation

Foreword

Jordan has long been a close friend and regional partner of the United Kingdom. The two Kingdoms have enjoyed flourishing political and commercial relationships over many decades. Those ties continue to grow as Jordan extends its reputation for political stability and modernisation. Jordan is a gateway to Iraq, with Amman playing host to numerous international and Joint Venture companies managing their regional business from this thriving city.

Jordan's economic growth in 2006 was strong at 6.4%, with a similar rate forecast for 2007. The last few years have seen a marked improvement in the economy. In 2004 Jordan graduated from a strict IMF regime through progressive liberalisation and deregulation of the economy. These policies have helped control Jordan's historical difficulties with debt service and budget and balance of payments deficits. These challenges persist but so does Jordan's commitment to continued reform. At the end of 2006 Jordan's external debt stood at 51.1% of GDP, down from 52% in 2005 and 65.5% at the end of 2004. The IMF forecast is that it will drop to 43.9% by the end of 2007 and dip to 39.2% by 2010.

A key objective of the Jordanian Government is attracting foreign investment. This has met with considerable success in the last couple of years, with extensive FDI inflows, particularly in the property and construction sectors. FDI in 2007 is expected to reach US$2.9 billion, mainly from the Gulf.

A wide range of large projects are in progress ranging from residential and tourist complexes in Aqaba, to the central Amman Al Abdali urban regeneration project and several Dead Sea hotel projects. A number of these have British consultants and architects working on them. The construction and infrastructure sectors are booming, but there are also promising opportunities in tourism, energy and healthcare.

In addition to the Aqaba Special Economic Zone, Jordan has also Qualified Industrial Zones (QIZs), which enjoy duty/quota free access to the US market, and has established a further Special Economic Zone at **Mafraq** in the North of the country.

British companies are in an excellent position to benefit from emerging opportunities in Jordan. I look forward to welcoming you to Jordan in the near future. If you are planning to visit, please do not hesitate to contact my commercial team in Amman on +962 6 590 9200 or amman.comm@fco.gov.uk for a more detailed briefing on Jordan's potential for your business.

James Watt

British Ambassador to the Hashemite Kingdom of Jordan

reaching greater heights through partnership

Being the sole integrated telecom operator in Jordan, we have the means to enhance and sustain your success. Allow us to act as your communications partner and showcase your achievements.

& jordan telecc
group

List of Contributors

Abdoun Real Estate is owned by Wael AlJaabari, General Manager, who established the business in 1988. Abdoun Real Estate is a turnkey company for all real property needs, whether it is commercial or residential, lease or purchase, long term or short term. The company is the biggest and most advanced real estate service provider in Jordan and has 20 employees. **Mrs. Alma Alic AlJaabari** is Head of Relocation and Area Orientation.

Abdullah Arar, PhD is Director, Arar Establishment for Water & Agriculture Technology. Amman and has an MSc and a PhD from U.K. and German Universities respectively. For seven years he was Senior Land Reclamation Engineer, Development Board of Iraq and for 27 years (1964-1990) FAO Senior Regional Adviser in Land and Water Development for FAO Near East Region. He has also held leading positions on different Irrigation, effluent re-use and soil reclamation missions with FAO, WHO, UNDP, World Bank and ICARDA. Since his retirement from FAO he has operated as a freelance land and water development consultant as well as running a 230 dunums irrigated farm in the Jordan Valley producing asparagus, barhi and medjool dates and seedless grapes.

Abdullah Jonathan Wallace is a consultant publisher with Global Market Briefings with responsibility for titles on the Middle East. He was, from 1965, the editor in chief and latterly chairman of the Middle East Economic Digest (MEED) Group, which he sold to the UK publishers EMAP in 1987. Since then he has worked as Middle East editor in chief for United Press International (UPI), as publisher for the Arab Bankers Association and as a consultant to a number of Arab and European companies. He is now based in Bahrain, where he is setting up an Institute of Journalism.

Dr. Ahmad Niyasat is Managing Director of National Electric Power.

Amman Chamber of Industry (ACI) was established in 1962 as a non-profit organisation that groups manufacturing firms varying in size from large to the medium and small under one umbrella. ACI, whose membership totals 8000 firms, includes those engaged in mining, energy, fertilizers, chemicals and pharmaceuticals and is run by 12 Board Members, elected for a four-year term by the Chamber's General Assembly.

The Chamber serves as a forum for the views and opinions of the country's industrial sector, with the aim of promoting economic development in Jordan. It conducts studies, surveys and builds data banks to serve the industrialists, investors and researchers. It cooperates closely and maintains regular contacts with all government ministries and departments that are involved in the country's economic planning.

There are fourteen consulting committees, representing various industrial sub-sectors. They are elected for a two-year term to coordinate with the Board on all issues relevant to the sectors they represent.

The ACI also co-operates with the Government in enacting laws and regulations relevant to the needs of industry. It sponsors panel discussions and seminars on various economic issues relating to industry. It also organises and participates in trade fairs. Furthermore, the Chamber serves on a number of national, regional and international bodies including: The Arab Labour Organization, The International Labour Organization, The International Organization of Employers, The General Union of the Chambers of Commerce, Industry and Agriculture for Arab Countries, the Social Security Corporation, the Vocational Training Institute and the Jordan Industrial Estates Corporation.

Amman Stock Exchange was established in March 1999 as a non-profit, private institution with administrative and financial autonomy. It is authorized to function as an exchange for the trading of securities.

Aqaba Development Corporation (ADC) was launched in 2004 with the objective of unlocking the potential of the Aqaba Special Economic Zone by accelerating its economic growth and development. Today ADC owns Aqaba's seaport, airport and strategic parcels of land as well as the rights to development and management of these assets and key infrastructure and utilities.

ADC is mandated to develop ASEZ through building new or expanding existing infrastructure and the required superstructure, creating business enablers for ASEZ and managing or operating its key facilities. ADC also has responsibility for implementing the ASEZ Master Plan so as to ensure integrated development and the transformation of Aqaba into a leading business and leisure hub on the Red Sea.

Aqaba Special Economic Zone Authority (ASEZA) is the financially and administratively autonomous institution responsible for the management, regulation and development of the Aqaba Special Economic Zone.

Asem Haddad is audit & tax partner with **Deloitte & Touche (Middle East)**. Academically and professionally qualified from USA and Jordan with more than eighteen years of experience in auditing and tax consultancy services to clients in different industries. Functioned as a member of many national economic committees and participated in different business and economic forums and conferences and has an in-depth knowledge of business laws and regulations of Jordan. He has also intensive and specialized training skills with multi-national expertise and extensive experience in the following areas: business advice and counselling due diligence studies and diagnostic studies business appraisal tax consultancy training and research international and US accounting and auditing standards

Central Bank of Jordan is the country's central banking organisation tasked with the supervision of banks the definition and implementation of monetary policy, including credit policy the conduct of exchange rate policy the holding and management of official international reserves the promotion, regulation and oversight of the smooth operation of payments and settlement system the performance of the tasks of banker and financial agent of the government and the participation as a member in international monetary and economic organisations.

Capital Investments is a newly formed entity within the Capital Group, which itself came into being in 2006 having commenced business in 1996 as Export and Finance Bank.

Faris Sharaf is Deputy Governor of the Central Bank of Jordan. Prior to joining the Central Bank, Faris was the Managing Director for Investment Banking and Capital Markets at the Export & Finance Bank in Jordan. He also held positions as an investment analyst with the International Finance Corporation in Washington D.C. and as an economic researcher with the Amman Financial Market. Faris holds Masters degrees in Money & Banking and Economics, and a Bachelor's degree in Economics and Political Science.

IDEA JWT. One of the best associations achieved in recent years. JWT was the first advertising agency in the world, founded in 1864 and is the premier worldwide agency network with 312 offices in 150 cities in 87 countries across the four major regions, including in the Middle East, Gulf, and North Africa, where it has 11 offices and 3 associates covering 19 countries. IDEA/MJ being one of the first agencies in Jordan, founded in 1976 and a previous associate of DDB, is one of the strongest advertising agencies in the country housing some of the best brand names in the world such as Toyota, OKI, NEC, Panasonic, brother, NOKIA, and i-mate, as well as some of the best trade names in Jordan including Central Trade and Auto, Events Unlimited, empretec Jordan, King Abdullah Design & Development Bureau, SOFEX, Jerash Festival, British Embassy, Amwal Invest and Jordan River Foundation.

Eng. Issam Qabbani is the Head of Petroleum Studiesat the Natural Resources Authority

Jalil Tarif is the Chief Executive Officer of the Amman Stock Exchange (ASE), a position he has held since the creation of the ASE in March 1999. During this period the ASE has implemented an electronic trading system and all of the rules and regulations required to run the ASE. The ASE has also started remote trading, allowing brokers to trade from their offices instead of the stock exchange floor and completed the infrastructure of the ASE

Prior to his work at the ASE, Mr. Tarif was the Deputy Director General of the Amman Financial Market (AFM) where he oversaw Jordan's entire capital market. During his six years as Deputy Director General, Mr. Tarif assisted in writing the new securities law that implemented the three separate entities that make up Jordan's Capital Market today. He also supervised all of the regulatory and operational aspects of the AFM. He has also published several works including External Debt and Economic Development of Jordan, Obstacles of Attracting Foreign Investment in Jordan and The Legal Structure of Arab Stock Exchanges. In addition to those, Mr. Tarif was awarded a certificate of merit from the International Development Centre of Japan (IDCJ). In 1995, he earned the certificate of distinguished delegate in the alternative structure for securities markets conference that was held at Georgetown University, U.S.A.

Mr. Tarif is the Chairman of NSC-Unix users Group (Countries using the French Trading System), Atos - Euro Next. Mr. Tarif is also the Chairman of the Technical Committee of the Federation of Euro-Asian Stock Exchanges (FEAS) He received his undergraduate degree and Masters Degree in economics from the University of Jordan and began his career in 1978, as an Assistant Director at the Central Bank of Jordan.

Jamal Abdul Rahim Itani is Chief Executive Officer of Abdali Investment and Development PSC. He has an extensive background in general contracting, construction management and civil engineering which have enabled him to undertake development projects of impressive size and function throughout his career.

Before joining Abdali PSC, Mr. Itani occupied the position of President of the Council for Development and Reconstruction (CDR) for the development of post-war Lebanon, a post for which he was elected by the Late Prime Minister, Rafic Hariri. Over the ensuing 3 years, Mr. Itani managed and operated the planning and development of all the sizable projects in Lebanon, ranging from schools and hospitals to infrastructure works including: roads and highways dams and water distribution networks the power sector and airports and ports. Most importantly his responsibilities included the critical task of securing all the financing for the government of Lebanon from different International sources like the World Bank, European Investment Bank and the different Arab Funds.

Mr. Itani has also worked with various international firms drawing on his experiences in the field of Civil Engineering and consultancy. At Mawarid Holding Company located in the Kingdom of Saudi Arabia, Mr. Itani was appointed Advisor to the owner Prince Salman Bin Khalid bin Abdulrahman AlSaud with responsibity for developing different businesses in the Gulf and Europe.

Mr. Itani holds a Bachelor of Science in Civil Engineering from Washington University and a Masters from Pennsylvania State University.

Jordan Free Zones Corporation was established under the terms of The Free Zones Corporation Law No. (32) of 1984 to carry out the following tasks and duties: To establish free zones to establish warehouses, stores and any other establishments necessary for managing and developing the free zones in such a manner that ensures their growth and expansion, including joint venture free zones to manage, invest and develop free zones and gear them to serve the national economy, promote international trade exchange, transit trade and export oriented industries to implement the conditions and provisions relating to customs control, foreign exchange control and set up any establishments necessary for this purpose registering establishments and companies at any free zone issuance of licences and approvals related to exercising economic activities at the free zones in accordance with the provisions of the law, regulations and instructions issued in this regard protecting and preserving the environment in the free zones and ensuring continuous development in accordance with standards and foundations to be determined pursuant to a regulation to be issued for this purpose, provided that the level of such standards and foundations are no less than that applicable elsewhere in the kingdom. For this purpose the Corporation shall exercise the power of the Ministry of Environment and the Minister shall exercise the power of the Minister of Environment in accordance with the in-force Protection of Environment Law.

Jordan Insurance Federation The Association of Insurance Companies was established in 1956 as the first authority for regulating the business of the insurance sector in Jordan and presided over by several pioneer members of the Jordanian insurance industry of that time. Then, in 1987, the Unified Insurance Office was created for the insuring of motor vehicles and started its work under the control of this Society which remained in business until 1989 when a Royal Decree was passed for the establishment of the Jordan Insurance Federation followed by the definition of its basic bylaws.

Jordan Investment Board. The Investment Law of 1995 established the Jordan Investment Board as a governmental body enjoying both financial and administrative independence and as a result of the government's realization of the importance of increasing foreign direct investment to Jordan in a bid to create new job opportunities and the need for the transfer of technology.

Jordan Tourism Board was officially launched in March 1998 as an independent public – private sector partnership committed to utilizing marketing strategies to brand, position and promote the Jordan tourism product internationally as the destination of choice.

Juma Abu-Hakmeh was formerly the Director General of the Amman Chamber of Industry. His career has included the planning and development engineer for Jordan Fertilizer Industry, Amman Head of Anodizing, Paint and Water Treatment Section and Production Manager at Arab Aluminium Industry (Aral), Amman Production Manager and Assistant Managing Director, Advertising Publicity & Decoration Products Manufacturing Co. Ltd., (Electro Decor), Electro Décor, Jeddah Partner, Palestine Drug Store, Amman General Manager, Rum Metal Mfg Co.

Dr. Maen F. Nsour is the Chief Executive Officer of Jordan Investment Board, a position he has held since May 2005. Prior to this he was Senior Advisor at the Regional Bureau for Arab States at the UNDP in New York and Coordinator of the Arab Human Development Report 2003. Before joining UNDP in 2001 Dr.Nsour was Director of the Policy Planning Department at the Ministry of Planning in Amman. He has taught at George Mason University in Fairfax, Va and at the University of Jordan and was a researcher at the United States Institute of peace (USIP) in Washington DC between 1995 and 1998. He holds a PhD from George Mason University in political economy.

Mahmoud Quteishat is Director General of The Free Zones Corporation having previously been a Consultant at the Council of Ministers and Director General of the Customs Department. His other roles include Chairman of Aqaba Special Economic Zone Customs Committee and membership of the boards of directors of the Free Zones Corporation, Jordan Investment Board, Jordan Institution for Economic Projects Development, the Syrian-Jordanian Industrial Free Zone and the Jordan Industrial estates Corporation. He has a BA in Business Administration and Economics and an Honorary PhD in Economics & Business Administration from the Royal Collage for Specialized Technology-.

Mark Timbrell has been in the Hotel business for 25 years, graduating with a Higher National Diploma in Management from Ealing Hotel and Catering College, he worked for 10 years in Central London at various five star properties including The Dorchester, The Stafford, Brown's, The Westbury and Grosvenor House. Ten years ago he moved to Jordan to pursue his career overseas and but for a brief 2 year stint at the Regency InterContinental in Bahrain, he has been working in Amman. Currently he is Resident Manager of the InterContinental Hotel in Amman.

Marwan A. Kardoosh is a Jordanian national who read Economics in London, England. He is currently acting as Director of Research at the Jordan Center for Public Policy Research & Dialogue in Amman. His fields of specialization are international trade (including in the area of services), macroeconomics and the political economy of Jordan.

Naim Khoury is a former Chairman of the Jordanian Association of Certified Public Accountants (JACPA), a member of the Higher Commission for the Audit Profession in Jordan, author of many articles on accounting and auditing and a partner in **Saba & Co. Deloitte & Touche (Middle East)**, Jordan.

National Electric Power Company (NEPCO) is responsible for electricity transmission and control activities, besides responsibility for interconnection with neighbouring countries.

Natural Resources Authority (NRA) was established in 1965. Since 1985, The Minister of Energy and Mineral Resources has been the President of NRA which is entrusted with the following responsibilities:- Suggesting policies to investigate, develop and exploit energy and mineral resources exploring and prospecting for mineral resources in the form of executing geological, geophysical, geochemical, technical, and economical studies adopting plans and programmes to administer laws and regulations in various fields of mineral resources issuing permits and licenses for prospecting explorations, mining, quarrying and mineral rights certificates coordinating cooperation with various international entities supervising all hydrocarbon activities within the borders of Jordan including granting concession, exploration and exploitation agreements and whatever other duties are assigned to it by the Council of Ministers, such as investment promotion activities in mining.

Noor A. Jundi, Associate, Rajai K.W. Dajani & Associates, was born in 1979. Education: University of Jordan (LL.B.). Member: Jordanian Bar Association. Languages: Arabic and English.

Philip Dew owns and manages his own business development consultancy, has worked and resided in the Middle East for over 30 years, is an

xx   Doing Business with Jordan

Arabic speaker and has undertaken many assignments for clients from across the world. He has been Consultant Editor on seven titles in the Doing Business series, namely those on the United Arab Emirates, Bahrain, Iran, Oman, Qatar, Jordan and Cyprus has authored a number of business books on the Middle East, including 'Saudi Arabia: Restructuring for Growth' 'The Kingdom of Bahrain: The Financial Capital of the Middle East' and "Jordan: Shaping the Future" and has also written a number of books on major banks and industries in all of Bahrain, Kuwait, Saudi Arabia and the UAE.

Rajai K.W. Dajani & Associates. The senior partner, Rajai K. W. Dajani, established the firm in 1990 in Amman with the aim of creating a high standard law firm that serves a diverse range of specializations. The firm offers comprehensive legal services in effect meeting the needs of clients and acts for a multitude of domestic and international clients that are engaged in a wide spectrum of activities on local and international levels.

The firm collaborates and cooperates with law firms worldwide. The practice's members, paralegals and counsels are geared towards the rapidly developing legal sector worldwide. Our team of lawyers and associated offices in Amman and through out Jordan possess highly valuable experience and provide qualified services within the practiced aspects of the law. The areas covered include Civil Law, Commercial Law, Corporate Law, Government, Telecommunications, Media, E-Commerce, Contracts, International Trade, Construction Law, Foreign Investment, Insurance Law, Taxation, Banking Law, Franchise and Distribution, Agency Law, Intellectual Property, Marine Insurance, Maritime Law, Securities, Immigration, Citizenship, Mergers and Acquisitions, Labour Law, Aviation Law. Litigation before all courts and Arbitration.

Sana Abdallah is a Jordanian journalist based in Amman. She is the correspondent for United Press International, a Washington-based news service, and for the Middle East International, a London-based biweekly publication.

Shereen S. Said, Associate, Rajai K.W. Dajani & Associates, was born in 1980. Education: National University of Amman (LL.B.). Member: Jordanian Bar Association. Languages: Arabic and English.

Subhi A. Ramadan has an MSc in Sanitary/Civil Engineering from Syracuse University, USA and a BSc in Civil Engineering from Al-Hikma American University of Baghdad, Iraq. He has many years experience mainly in management, construction & environmental projects, including operation & maintenance. Tendering, assessments, health aspects, water quality management and pollution prevention. He has undertaken many consultancy and evaluation assignments on projects related to the World Bank-IFC, CIDA and IDRC of Canada, UN, WHO, RSS of Jordan and others.

For ten years he been a self-employed consultant based in both Jordan and Canada performing environmental consulting, environmental Studies, impact assessments of projects and business activities, mainly in the water, environmental and EIA fields including undertaking management, quality, pollution control, monitoring and resources studies.

Suleiman I. Matouk. Founding Partner and the Managing Director of one of Jordan's fastest growing advertising agencies. A born entrepreneur and the mastermind of the first merger in the advertising industry in Jordan. A visionary who believes that hard work and honesty actually pay off.

A graduate of Economics, Suleiman always believed in the power of advertising and marketing in growing the economy. After a successful career with Arthur Anderson & Co. in Dubai, Abu Dhabi and Damascus, Suleiman moved back to Jordan, a country he believed in. In late 1996, Suleiman followed his life long dream and founded IDEA Advertising, an agency that would reshape the advertising scene in Jordan. In less than a year, he managed to sign his first association agreement with the world's most creative agency, DDB. In late 1999, Suleiman started negotiations with Modern Jordanian Advertising Agency, one of the first agencies in Jordan, and the number one local agency at the time, to finally complete the first ever merger in the industry by March, 2000. The outcome of which was known as DDB Jordan.

Last year, Suleiman succeeded yet again in attracting a new association with the world's first advertising agency, JWT. A difficult decision to make the move that soon proved to be the right one. With the new association, IDEA JWT is now part of the JWT group, the strongest agency in the region with the biggest number of brand names earning it the "House of Brands" title.

The Philip Dew Consultancy Limited celebrated 25 years in business in February 2007, having been founded in 1982 to support local and international principals in the comprehensive development of their businesses in the Middle East. The basic services provided include: identification, investigation and evaluation of market opportunities market research and feasibility studies identification of partners, principals and associates development of marketing and business strategies and on-the-ground support and assistance to market entrants, including the provision of background and cultural information.

Yousef S. Khalilieh, (Member) born Jordan, 1969 admitted to bar, 1995, Jordan. Education: University of Westminster (LL.B., Honours, 1992) University of London (LL.M., International Business Law, 1993). Member: Jordanian Bar Association the ad hoc Jordanian Copyright Law Review Committee, 1995. Languages: Arabic and English. E-mail: ykhalilieh@dajanilaw.com

Dr. Ziad S.Hamarneh is Director of Projects Development and Investment at the Natural Resources Authority.

Company profiles

Where would you like to **GROW** ?

Over 400 branches in 29 countries spanning 5 continents

Jordan, Lebanon, Palestine, UAE, Qatar, Bahrain, Yemen, Egypt, Morocco, Algeria, Oman, Saudi Arabia, Tunisia, Syria, Switzerland, Germany, Austria, U.K, France, Italy, Cyprus, Spain, USA, Singapore, China, South Korea, Kazakhstan, Australia, Turkey.

البنك العربي
ARAB BANK

www.arabbank.com

ARAB BANK

البـنك العـربي
ARAB BANK

Introducing Arab Bank
In 1930, Arab Bank was established as the first private sector financial institution in the Arab World with the vision of creating a financial institution to serve as a driving force in advancing Arab economies through financing strategic infrastructural projects across the Middle East.

The Arab Bank Group has an unmatched Arab Banking branch network, the largest worldwide, consisting of over 400 branches in 29 countries spanning 5 continents including key markets and financial centers such as London, Singapore, New York, Zurich, Dubai, Bahrain, Paris and Sydney.

The Group has had unprecedented financial performance over the past few years, receiving high ratings from the most internationally recognized rating agencies, further emphasizing the Bank's financial strength and stability.

History
Abdul Hameed Shoman, whose vision and ambition led him to establish a bank that would play a significant role in shaping the lives of nations and their economies. With a startup capital of 15,000 Palestinian pounds, Arab Bank began its operations in Jerusalem in 1930.

The Bank's Headquarters were moved to Amman, Jordan in 1948 after the British Mandate Authority withdrew from Palestine. All deposit claims by customers who fled the country were redeemed in full upon the Shomans' insistence, winning the Arab Bank a reputation of commitment from the Bank towards its customers, as well as an enormous loyalty from customers towards the Bank, both of which still prevail today.

The decades following were a period of rapid expansion; during the 1940's and 1950's, the Bank expanded its branch network in the

Arab World. By carefully investing in a wide range of new industries and public projects, the Arab Bank acted as a catalyst for Arab economic development in the days when no one was willing to take the risk. In Jordan, the Bank's loans created jobs and its loans for new cement, textile and food processing plants enhanced the country's growth rate.

The 1960's were characterized with a wave of nationalization which swept the Arab World as country after country gained independence from British and French colonial rule. In a period of ten years, Arab Bank lost a total of 25 branches. Undaunted, the Bank continued to expand, and in 1961 established its first international presence, establishing a sister institution, Arab Bank Switzerland, and becoming the first Arab financial institution to open in Switzerland.

The 1970's focused on the newly emerging oil economies of the Gulf while steadily expanding its new home base, Jordan.

Abdul Majeed Shoman became the Chairman and General Manager of the Arab Bank after the death of his father in 1974. Determined to expand the Bank's activities, he set out to open new branches across the globe, opening branches in Frankfurt, London, Australia, New York, Singapore and other locations.

Parallel to growing in size, Arab Bank expanded its products and services into new areas of business. Previously concentrating on trade and small scale construction finance, the Bank undertook a leading role in large scale project finance, both directly and through participation in syndicated loans. By the 1990's, Arab Bank added investment banking to its established services.

With over 30 years of banking experience, Abdel Hamid Shoman, the founder's grandson, became CEO in May of 2000. Upon Abdul Majeed Shoman's death on July 5, 2005, Abdel Hamid was elected Chairman.

In 2005, the Arab Bank reopened operations in Syria and made necessary preliminary arrangements to begin activities in Iraq, circumstances permitting. In 2006, the Bank was given the green-light to establish Europe Arab Bank (EAB), a London-based, fully-owned subsidiary. It also acquired 50% of MNG Bank in Turkey, and

50% of Al Nisr Al Arabi Insurance company in Jordan, thus introducing Bank Assurance to its product variety. The Bank also has 60% in AB Capital based in Dubai, which will now serve as the Bank's investment arm in the Gulf area.

Profile

The Bank's founding mission has been the driving force behind the significant role we play in advancing Arab economies through financing strategic infrastructural projects across the Middle East /North Africa region (MENA).

Headquartered in Amman, Jordan, the Arab Bank is the first private sector financial institution in the Arab world, and currently the largest financial services institution in the MENA region by equity.

The Arab Bank is rated amongst the largest international financial institutions, with a rating of "A-" from Standard & Poor's (S&P), "A3" from Moody's and "A-" from Fitch.

At end of December 2006, the Arab Bank Group achieved a pre-tax profit of US $790 million. Total assets reached almost US $32.5 billion, while shareholders' equity base is US $5.9 billion.

The Bank's products and services fall within four major areas: Personal Banking, Corporate and Investment Banking (CIB), Wealth Management and Treasury, all of which are catered to serve the needs of individuals, corporations, government agencies and other international financial institutions.

The Arab Bank has been and continues to be a key player in facilitating Pan-Arab trade, and in creating bridges connecting the world to MENA markets.

Arab Bank
P.O. Box 950545
Amman 11195 Jordan

Web: www.arabbank.com

AQABA DEVELOPMENT CORPORATION

Introducing the Aqaba Development Corporation
The Aqaba Development Corporation (ADC) was launched in 2004 with the objective of unlocking the potential of the Aqaba Special Economic Zone by accelerating its economic growth and development.

Launched by ASEZA and the Government of Jordan at the beginning of 2004, ADC owns Aqaba's seaport, airport and strategic parcels of land as well as the development and management rights for these assets in addition to key infrastructure and utilities.

ADC's Mandate
ADC is mandated to develop ASEZ through building new or expanding existing infrastructure and the required superstructure, creating business enablers for ASEZ, and managing or operating its key facilities. This will be achieved through maximizing the attraction of private sector developers and operators. ADC also has the responsibility to implement the ASEZ Master Plan in a manner that ensures integrated development and transforms Aqaba into a leading business and leisure hub on the Red Sea.

Private Sector Approach
A private shareholding company governed by a board of directors, ADC is currently wholly owned by the Government of Jordan and ASEZA, each with a 50% stake. ADC is operated as a private sector organization and has secured a world-class multi-national private sector team to operate it, supported by a world-class consortium of multi-disciplinary firms.

Private sector participation in the development and management of ASEZ's strategic assets will be accelerated by ADC either on a stand-alone basis or through public-private partnerships or other means that optimally leverage ADC and private sector strengths.

THE UNIQUE BUSINESS PLAN THAT IS ADC
ADC's Objectives
ADC's main objective is to unlock Aqaba's economic potential by mobilizing private investment through the packaging of opportunities and prudently leveraging public resources. To do this, ADC has identified five main objectives to realize its mission:

Strategic Assets
Develop and manage ASEZ's strategic assets such as its ports and airports in accordance with sound business principles and practices to optimize private sector participation in their development and management so as to accelerate their performance and ASEZ's economic growth and development.

Business Enabling Infrastructure and Projects
Develop and manage business enabling projects and infrastructure to underpin and optimize private sector participation so as to accelerate ASEZ's economic growth and development.

Economic Development
Undertake transactions that stimulate ASEZ's economy and promote the overall economic growth and development of ASEZ and the Kingdom of Jordan

Sustainable Results and Returns
Realize its business objectives on a viable and sustainable basis that not only realizes the economic and social development of ASEZ and the Kingdom, but also generates adequate returns for ADC's shareholders and investors in the zone.

Private Sector Ownership and Operation
Enable significant private sector management of ADC and maximize private sector participation in all its deals.

The value proposition that is ASEZ
Welcome to the Aqaba Special Economic Zone (ASEZ)

The future of Aqaba is envisioned as an oasis for commerce, a premium destination for tourism, an incubator for modern technology and a regional hub for transport and logistics.

The Aqaba Special Economic Zone (ASEZ) was launched in 2001 with the objective of delivering that vision through the creation of a favourable business environment for attracting foreign and domestic investment and turning Aqaba into a world class business and leisure destination. ASEZ operates as a liberalized, low tax, duty free multi-sector economic development zone with a simplified business environment and streamlined administrative system.

From tourism & recreational services to multi-modal transport and logistics, value added industries & light manufacturing, ASEZ offers investors 375km^2 of investment opportunities with attractive incentives packages based on international best practices and aimed at increasing investors' operating efficiency and providing for all their investment needs.

ASEZ is regulated by the Aqaba Special Economic Zone Authority (ASEZA), which is responsible for managing, regulating and providing municipal services within ASEZ. ASEZA is a truly e-enabled one stop shop for all investment needs including issuing license, permits, national certificates of origin, visas and residency permits.

Competitive Advantages of ASEZ
ASEZ offers investors a wide range of competitive advantages in order to maximize private sector participation and build Aqaba into a world class business and leisure destination. The success of ASEZ to date is attributable to a host of competitive advantages, including:

- Attractive investment opportunities in tourism, services and industries.
- Projects packaged for fast-track startup and accelerated approval processes.
- Low cost of doing business and Investor friendly regulations and business environment.
- Strategic location at the convergence of the Levant bordering Egypt, Saudi Arabia and Israel.
- Full-service utility networks including power, telecommunications, natural gas and global international communications connectivity through FLAG.
- A distribution hub for the Middle East and North Africa, with free zone storage supported by a full-service seaport, an

open-skies international airport and world class air cargo facilities.

- Preferential access to global markets arising from Jordan's World Trade Organization membership and free trade agreements with the United States, the European Union and several Arab countries.
- Multi-modal transport hub whereby an investor can bring in goods & passengers by land, air or sea.
- An open skies policy at Aqaba's King Hussein International Airport.
- Serviced land/facilities for light/medium manufacturing, warehousing, residential and commercial uses.
- Access to a pool of highly-skilled Jordanian labour.
- Untapped opportunities for the development of tourism as a stand-alone Red Sea resort destination and as part of Jordan's Golden Tourism Triangle - Petra, Wadi Rum and Aqaba.

Investment Incentives - The Aqaba Equation

The Aqaba Special Economic Zone enjoys special fiscal regulations offering a favourable investment environment for investors from all over the world which include the following:

- A flat 5% tax on net profits and exemption from social services tax.
- Exemption from annual land and building taxes on utilized land.
- Exemption from taxes on distributed dividends and profits.
- No sales tax on the vast majority of goods and services.
- No foreign equity restrictions on investments
- No foreign currency restrictions
- Full repatriation of profits and capital
- Streamlined labour and immigration procedures
- 100% foreign ownership
- Up to 70% foreign labour
- Availability of land for lease or sale.
- Full guarantees on rights and ownership.

ASEZ – Setting the Standards for Jordan

The Aqaba Special Economic Zone and the model of decentralization that it represents has been recognised as a catalyst and setting a precedent for the Jordanian Government's economic, social and political reform efforts nationwide. Since its launch, ASEZ proudly includes the following as the FIRST of its kind in Jordan -

- The FIRST town to adopt a comprehensive Master Plan aimed at maximizing the potential of Aqaba.

- The FIRST to enforce a Model Environmental protection framework.

- The FIRST to establish a Central Development Company (ADC).

- The FIRST airport to operate an open skies policy.

- The FIRST to implement a truly e-enabled single point of contact for all investor's needs.

- The FIRST to implement an electronic food health certification system.

- The FIRST model of private utility companies (Aqaba Water Company and Aqaba Gas Company).

- The FIRST model of rehabilitated automated customs operations.

Aqaba Development Corporation
PO BOX 2680
Aqaba 77110
Jordan

Email: info@adc.jo
Web: www.adc.jo

Embrace natural serene beauty, follow the echoes of a past era and feel the ageless charm of the Jordanian dunes of Aqaba.

The Aqaba Special Economic Zone (ASEZ) distinctively blends the vibrant urban metropolis and the rejuvenating tranquil elegant lifestyle, in an environment that nurtures human and intellectual wealth. It stands for a strategic international business hub and stretches a multifunctional bridge of progressive policies and proactive development priorities to all industries for world-class infrastructure and services.

The ASEZ poses the perfect investment opportunity creating an aura of gentle beauty and sumptuousness in an imposing land where "Sand Turns into Gold".

Turn Sand into Gold

AQABA
SPECIAL ECONOMIC ZONE
AUTHORITY

P.O.Box 2565   Aqaba 77110 Jordan   Tel 962 3 203 5757   Fax 962 3 203 0912
E-mail i n f o @ a s e z a . j o   w w w . a q a b a z o n e . c o m

Introducing the Aqaba Special Economic Zone (ASEZ)

In year 2001, the Aqaba Special Economic Zone (ASEZ) was
inaugurated. Being a liberalized, low tax, duty free and multi-sector
development Zone, the ASEZ is part of Jordan's assertive reform
strategy to provide investors, from all over the world, with an
attractive business environment.

Strategically located on the cross roads between three continents
and four countries , ASEZ covers an area of 375 Km2 encompassing
the total Jordanian coastline (27 km), the sea-ports of Jordan, an
international airport ,operating under an Open Skies airport policy,
and the historical city of Aqaba with a current population of 90,000
people. The Aqaba Special Economic Zone Authority (ASEZA) is
financially and administratively autonomous institution responsible
for the management, regulation and development of the ASEZ.
Governed by six ministerial level commissioners, ASEZA enjoys a
vast and unprecedented set of authorities.

Turning it into Jordan's first model of de-centralization in the
Kingdom and a truly enabled one stop shop for all investors' needs

Starting and operating business in the ASEZ

ASEZA strives to create, regulate and sustain a globally competitive
investor friendly environment and optimize the efficient utilization of
entrusted resources in harmony with the Master Plan to
internationally recognized practices.

ASEZA has created a special investor's One-Stop-Shop window that
delivers all kinds of services. It has also elaborated an electronically
enabled Enterprise Registration and Permitting System (ERPS) that
holds an ISO certification for Labor, Registration, Permitting and
Investment Promotion. Complementing its service-oriented
approach, ASEZA makes sure the needed guidance is provided
thanks to the Real Estate Marketing Division and the independent

Customs Commission. ASEZA personnel are always ready to achieve the highest-quality delivery services in a business-friendly environment.

Registered Enterprises in the ASEZ enjoy the following tax benefits:

- Special 5% tax rate on the total taxable income of Registered Enterprises for activities within the ASEZ and outside Jordan
- Exemption from social services tax
- Exemption from annual land and building taxes on utilized property
- Exemption from taxes on distributed dividends and profits on activities in the ASEZ and outside Jordan

Aqaba Special Economic Zone (ASEZ)
P.O.Box 2565
Aqaba 77110
Jordan

Contact: Oula Ayyoub, Business Development and Marketing
Email: info@aseza.jo

Tel: +96232091000 ext. 2055
Fax: +96232030912

GIVE YOUR INVESTMENT THE BREAK IT DESERVES.
INVEST IN JORDAN

Sea, Jordan

TOURISM

FINANCIAL & PROFESSIONAL SERVICES

EDUCATION & TRAINING

ICT & R&D

HEALTH CARE & PHARMACEUTICALS

INFRASTRUCTURE & REAL ESTATE

INDUSTRY

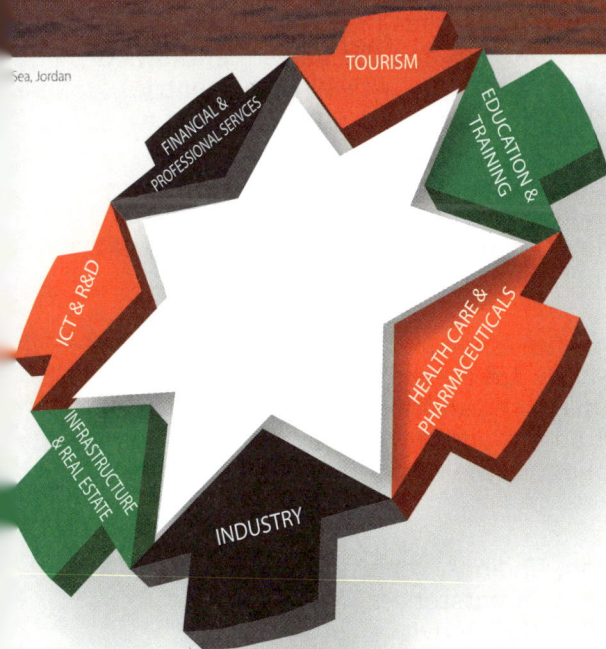

Jordan, located at the heart of a region interconnecting the three continents of the old world, naturally became a hub of world business since time immemorial. Within Jordan, lying more than 300 meters below sea level, the Dead Sea, with the miraculous healing power of its salts, became one of the world's first spas, frequented by international businessmen trekking on the spice and silk routes or residents of Rome's Decapolis and other cities.

Today, as in ancient times, more and more companies, including world leaders in their respective sectors that embrace manufacturing industries, ICT, pharmaceuticals, health services, tourism, financial and professional services, and real estate are choosing Jordan as the base for their investments and regional operations.

All these people recognized that the right place and the right time fuse in Jordan today, and they take advantage of that opportunity while enjoying the good life that Jordan offers them.

There are plenty of opportunities out there, so don't miss out. Give your enterprise the break that it deserves. **INVEST IN JORDAN**.

مؤسسة تشجيع الأستثمار
JORDAN
Investment Board

P.O. Box: 893 Amman, 11821 Jordan - Telephone : (962-6) 5608400/15 - 5531081/2/3 - Fax : (962-6) 5608416 - 5608427 - 5521084 - E-mail : info@jib.com.jo
www.jordaninvestment.com

JORDAN INVESTMENT BOARD

مؤسسة تشجيع الإستثمار
JORDAN
Investment Board

Introducing the Jordan Investment Board and Investment Opportunities in Jordan

In today's world of open markets and cross-border flows of private sector investment, countries compete to maximize their competitiveness by creating opportunities and offering incentives to local as well as international investors. In the case of Jordan, the attractions are obvious. They start with the country's strategic location bordering five countries at the heart of a region interconnecting three continents, include Jordan's agreeable weather and friendly hard working people, and do not end with the persistent efforts of the Jordanian Government to encourage private sector investment, both local and international.

Institutional Support

An important landmark in these efforts was the promulgation of the Investment Promotion Law of 1995 and the Investment laws of 2003, which today regulate investment activities in the country. These laws established the Jordan Investment Board (JIB) as a governmental body enjoying both financial and administrative independence, which works to promote Jordan as a unique destination for foreign direct investment and to sustain domestic investment, in order to achieve economic prosperity, create new job opportunities, increase national exports, and facilitate the transfer of technology.

To achieve these objectives, The JIB presents state of the art services and works to streamline registration and licensing procedures for projects that do not end with the establishment of the project, but extend throughout the business cycle. The JIB's services include:

• Disseminating information, findings, reports, surveys and studies through JIB publications, Conferences, Media Communication, and Public Relation Activities.

- Granting financial exemptions, mainly customs duties and sales and other tax exemptions and income tax reduction.
- Highlighting a wide range of business opportunities, which can include pre-feasibility studies that cover the national strategic sectors in which Jordan maintain a competitive and comparative advantage: Information Technology, Pharmaceuticals, Dead Sea & Mining, Food Sector, Tourism and Entertainment, and Biotechnology.
- Setting marketing themes for Jordan's image building.
- Policy Advocacy through surveying the private sector's issues and assisting by lobbying with government official channels.
- SME support in cooperation with other organizations

An Enabling Legislative Environment
The JIB works with investors to help them maximize their benefit from the incentives offered by the present laws, which include an exemption from fees and taxes on imported fixed assets and spare parts valued at less than 15% of fixed assets, and on fixed assets needed for expansion, plus a 25% - 75% exemption from income and social service taxes for exempted projects for 10 years. Hotels and hospitals receive an exemption from fees and taxes once every seven years for renovation purposes. These exemptions remain effective if the project changes ownership during the exemption period. In addition, an investor has the right to mortgage the fixed assets of any project as security for extended credit facilities and he has the right to manage the project in the manner he deems appropriate.

Most importantly, the laws provide the same treatment for Jordanian and non-Jordanian investors. Non-Jordanian investors may invest through ownership, partnership, or shareholding. They may own any project wholly or partially, and they are entitled to remit abroad the foreign capital transferred to Jordan for investment together with any returns and profits. Non-Jordanian employees also have the right to transfer their salaries abroad without hindrance.

Continuous Reform
The present investment laws attracted to Jordan investments in 3,121 projects to the value of JD 5.5 billion (£4.2 billion) between

the end of 1996 and May 2006. These projects created 188,000 new job opportunities of which more than 48% were of high added value. But despite the evident success of the present legislation, the Government of Jordan submitted to Parliament new draft legislation in 2006 in order to upgrade its incentives to investors.

The new legislation would focus on tax incentives, expand the definition of fixed assets, and accord to the Council of Ministers the power to grant additional exemptions. The new law would annul the Investment Promotion Committee since exemptions become automatic by law.

All projects in the exempted sectors (agri-food, pharmaceuticals, information technology, textiles and garments, cosmetics, and the automotive industry) will enjoy:

- total exemption from customs duties on fixed assets and production inputs,
- zero sales tax on all goods, services, fixed assets and production inputs, whether imported or purchased locally,
- exemption from the special sales tax on fixed assets and production inputs, and,
- exemption from income tax and social services tax in accordance with special bylaws to be issued by the Council of Ministers.

Special Zones
To further help investors, Jordan created a series of special zones (free zones, industrial estates, Qualified Industrial estates – QIZs, in addition to the Aqaba Special Industrial Zone –ASEZ) where investors receive added incentives.

Free Zones
Jordan's Free Zones were established to promote export-oriented industries; they accommodate processing industries, in addition to trading, warehousing, and other activities. Commodities and goods of various origins are deposited in the Free Zone areas for storage and manufacturing without payment of the usual excise fees and taxes. To qualify for a license to operate within a Free Zone area, an enterprise must introduce new industries utilizing modern technology, complement domestic industries, use local raw

materials or manufacturing parts, upgrade the skills of local workers, and produce goods with limited availability in the domestic market.

Jordan's Free Zones always look for ways to attract direct foreign investments with attention focused on those that generate export revenues, such as technology parks for software, assembly of electronic components, assembly of automotive products, light machinery, and other non-traditional exports. These could be complemented by service industries such as: business, financial and architecture services, back-office centers, medical diagnosis and programming, logistics and transport, as well as design, research and development, and tourism.

Industrial Estates
The Jordan Industrial Estates Corporation is a semi-governmental corporation that was established in 1984 with both public and private ownership. Its catalytic role is to contribute to the development of small and medium-sized industries (SMIs) by providing suitable home for both local and foreign investors. In 1996 the JIEC inaugurated its Centre of Excellence, which will function as an incubator for new enterprises and as a catalyst for the interaction between industry and academia.

Industrial estates offer to investors100% exemptions for two years of income and social services tax for industrial projects located within JIEC industrial estates, total exemption from buildings and land tax, exemption or reduction on most municipal fees, and 100% exemption of taxes and fees on fixed assets for the project, fixed assets needed for expansion or modernization, and on spare parts.

QIZs
Three of the operating public industrial estates also hold QIZ status, which allows exporters of goods manufactured in these zones to benefit from duty-free and quota-free access to the US market. There are also private industrial parks that enjoy QIZ designation equally.

Aqaba Special Economic Zone (ASEZ)
Considered one of the largest free zones ever created, the Aqaba

Special Economic Zone (ASEZ) was established as a low-tax, duty-free multi-sector development area with streamlined administration to attract investments and maximize private sector participation. The project seeks to attract JD 6.4 billion (£4.9 billion) in investments and create 75,000 jobs by 2020.

Businesses operating in Aqaba benefit from a duty-free trade environment. Imported goods are exempt from custom duties and taxes, with the exception of cars. There are no foreign equity restrictions on investment in tourism, industry, retail, and other commercial services, and businesses are allowed full repatriation of profits and capital. Aqaba is a regional multi-modal transportation hub with a full-service seaport and international airport, catering to Jordan and the Middle East region.

Network of Trade Agreements
And cognizant of the limited market potential offered by a population slightly over 5 million, Jordan expanded its market to 1 billion consumers through a large network of bilateral and multilateral trade agreements that include:

- Greater Arab Free Trade Area (GAFTA),
- Association agreement with the European Union,
- Free trade agreement (FTA) with the United States of America,
- Membership agreement of the World Trade Organization (WTO)
- Free trade agreement with the European Free Trade Association (EFTA),
- Free trade agreement with Singapore

In addition, Jordan concluded over 60 agreements with Arab and foreign countries that aim to protect and encourage investments and prevent double taxation. By 2004, the overall value of goods traded through trade agreements was JD 3,502 million (nearly £2.7 million), with 46.2% of that consisting of goods traded under the WTO agreement. The value of goods traded under the Qualified Industrial Zone agreement accounted for the highest growth (59%) in the years 2003-2004.

One-Stop Shop – An Investment Gateway
One of the principal facilities introduced by the investment laws is the one-stop shop, which the draft legislation develops into a veritable investment gateway. In its present form, the one-stop shop reduced the time required for registration and licensing from 98 to 14 working days, and the JIB is working to restructure and streamline procedures in order to reduce this period further to 7 working days by the end of the current year.

The new law is expected to enhance the work of the investment gateway by specifically stipulating the establishment of a single investment window located at the JIB to provide services and issue licenses to investors, which will be manned by representatives of all organizations concerned. Moreover, even if the law does not define a maximum period for registration and licensing, that period would be 7 working days, and should license not be granted within it then the license would be valid de facto, in accordance with the new law.

The JIB's work, which is summed up by its motto to investors: "Welcome to Jordan, your investment ally," has earned it the third prize in the prestigious King Abdullah II Award for Excellence in Government Services and Transparency for 2003.

But an important point that JIB staff press upon potential investors is that the benefits of investing in Jordan are not limited to systems that work and low-risk-high-returns on investment. One of the most important advantages is the Jordanian lifestyle that has earned Jordan regional and international respect for its traditions and achievements such as tolerance, hard work, and economic progress through openness to the world.

Jordan Investment Board
PO BOX 893
Amman 11821
Jordan

Email: info@jib.com.jo
Web: www.jordaninvestment.com

JORDAN GATE

Energizing Jordan and Beyond

شركة بيان القابضة
Bayan Holding Company

Gulf Finance House

kfic
لشركة الكويتية للتمويل والاستثمار
KUWAIT FINANCE & INVESTMENT COMPANY

www.jordan-gate.com

Gulf Finance House

Introducing the Gulf Finance House

Established on 16 October 1999 in the Kingdom of Bahrain as an Islamic investment bank, Gulf Finance House (GFH) has an authorized capital of US$ 300 million and a paid up capital of US$ 150 million, which was increased to US$ 212 million in March 2006. This was followed by the listing of GFH's shares on the Dubai Financial Market in May 2006, where the bank has been listed on the Bahrain and Kuwait stock exchanges since 2004. At the cutting edge of the rapidly expanding international Islamic banking industry, the Bank's commitment is to the Islamic Sharia'a philosophy of wealth management, and this shapes the structure and direction of its investment products. GFH is also one of the first Islamic investment banks in the world to receive an investment grade credit rating (BBB-) by Standard & Poor.

GFH is dedicated to providing its clients with carefully selected investment opportunities that balance risk with reward. From its inception GFH has provided Islamic investment banking services with an emphasis on regional development, capitalizing on an increasing willingness amongst Islamic investors to back local and regional opportunities. This has resulted in various investments around the region, taking advantage of the many reforms initiated by GCC governments to diversify and liberalize their economies, in addition to many international investments creating a balanced portfolio of opportunity for GFH clients.

During its seven years of operations, GFH has successfully launched projects and investments with an aggregate final value exceeding US$12 billion. This was indeed a significant feat in a short period of time that was made possible by the participation of a broad base of investors from across the GCC. GFH was one of the first GCC banks to focus on private equity investments in companies based in the GCC and other MENA countries. These companies include a pioneering aluminum extruder in the GCC, a company specializing in Islamic finance, and a fund created to invest in GCC and MENA technology companies.

GFH also introduced innovative Sharia'a-compliant structures such as "Investment Notes", "Financing Notes" and "Participating Rights" that have since found wide acceptance in the market and which have enabled GFH to consolidate its pioneering position among other Islamic and conventional banks.

In addition, GFH either directly launched or is significantly participating in several innovative infrastructure development projects that include Bahrain Financial Harbour and Al Areen Development in the Kingdom of Bahrain, Legends in Dubailand in the United Arab Emirates, Royal Metropolis in the Hashemite Kingdom of Jordan, Prince Abdul Aziz Bin Mousaed Economic City in the Kingdom of Saudi Arabia, Gateway to Morocco in the Kingdom of Morocco, Energy City Qatar in Doha and the transportation infrastructure development project in the Arab Republic of Egypt. Recently, GFH, in association with Gulf Energy, launched India's first integrated energy business district – Energy City India.

GFH aims to lead the Islamic investment banking industry in the GCC, Middle East and North African countries and has already established its pedigree. In addition to past awards and recognition, in 2006 alone the Bank has won numerous local and international awards culminating in "Bank of the Year" in 2006 by Arabian Business, "Best Investment Bank 2006" awarded by Banker Middle East, the Sheikh Mohammad Bin Rashid Al Makhtoum Award for "Global Contribution in Islamic Private Equity/Venture Capital 2006" at the International Islamic Finance Forum and the 'Excellence in Islamic Banking and Finance: Islamic Bank of the Year' award by the Accounting and Auditing Organization for Islamic Financial Institutions (AAOIFI).

Gulf Finance House has evolved into a bank capable of continued performance to the highest level. We have built a solidly profitable and strategically sound platform on which we can continue to grow for years to come.

Gulf Finance House
Al Salam Tower (6, 7, 8, 14 & 15 Floor)
Diplomatic Area
PO Box 10006
Manama, Kingdom of Bahrain

Email: info@gfhouse.com
Web: www.gfhouse.com

Tel: +973 17 538 538 (Ext. 434),
Fax: +973 17 540 006,

The Royal Metropolis in Jordan

ROYAL METROPOLIS

Introducing The Royal Metropolis in Jordan

Excellent progress has been achieved so far on the Royal Metropolis project. Unveiled in 2005, Royal Metropolis is GFH's first project in the Hashemite Kingdom of Jordan with a total investment value exceeding US$1.3 billion. The project constitutes of two main developments, which include Jordan Gate in the heart of the capital Amman,(2) Royal Village, within the outskirts of Amman.

Jordan Gate

Jordan Gate is one of the main projects of Royal Metropolis creating a futuristic and iconic development on a prime site in Amman comprising two high-rise twin towers and a quality retail shopping mall. Jordan Gate will provide prime office space for local, regional and international companies operating in Jordan and the surrounding region. It will also incorporate a five star hotel operated by Hilton International. Jordan Gate is located on the 6th Circle junction, one of the highest points in the city and will form the new landmark for the Jordanian Capital Amman. The project is being undertaken in partnership with the Municipality of Greater Amman and Kuwait Finance and Investment Company, and is scheduled for completion in May 2008.

Royal Village

Located on the main highway to the Dead Sea, Royal Village is a mixed use development

ROYAL VILLAGE

spreading over an area of approximately 470,000 square meters, comprising a gated residential community with more than 300 different types of villas and 1000 apartments, and a state of the art shopping and commercial center offering high-class living with modern amenities. The Royal Village project foundation stone was laid by his Majesty King Abdullah II in November 2005, and in September 2006 the company launched its Head Office and Sales Centre on the project site. This launch signified the start of sales, where the project achieved 30% sales within the last quarter of the year. The project is jointly promoted and developed in conjunction with Kuwait Finance and Investment Company.

Bayan Holding Company

شركة بيــان القابضة
Bayan Holding Company

The US$409 million Bayan Holding Company private placement was successfully closed in 2005. This Kuwaiti-based company will act as a vehicle to enable investors to invest in the Jordan Gate and the Royal Metropolis project in the Hashemite Kingdom of Jordan.

Part One

Background

1.1

Geography, Geology and History of Jordan

Philip Dew,
The Philip Dew Consultancy Limited

Background

The Hashemite Kingdom of Jordan officially came into existence in 1946 and is bounded to the north by Syria, the northeast by Iraq, the east and south by the Kingdom of Saudi Arabia and to the west by Palestine and Israel. Overall, the country comprises a total area 98,342 square kilometres (37,970 square miles) of which 88,802 square kilometres (34,286 square miles) is land and 540 square kilometres (208 square miles) is water.

In late 2006, the population of Jordan was approximately 6 million, a vast majority of whom, 98 per cent, are Arabs of various tribal origins. The remaining number is made up of Circassians, whose forebears arrived from north of the Caucasus in the 19th century, Chechens, Armenians and expatriates of many nationalities. The population figure quoted above does not account for more than 600,000 Iraqis now residing in the country. Although the population is overwhelmingly Muslim, mainly Sunnis (90 per cent), Jordan is officially a secular state whose constitution grants freedom of religion, race and colour as a statutory right. Arabic is the country's official language although English is widely spoken.

Physical geography

A major part of Jordan comprises a plateau lying some 700 to 1,000 metres above sea level and continuing on into the neighbouring countries of Syria, Iraq and Saudi Arabia. The borders between Jordan and these countries are artificial, being a series of straight lines connecting defined map references.

To the west of the plateau is a mountainous area rising a further 300 to 700 metres above the plateau and falling to the Jordan Valley to the west. This valley, at the northern end of the Great Rift valley, contains the Dead Sea, the lowest point on the earth's surface, whose surface is 419 metres below sea level and falls at an approximate rate of 1 metre a year, and whose maximum depth is 330 metres. The valley also contains the Jordan River, some 152 kilometres of which lies within Jordanian territory, and is the country's most fertile area.

Climate

Climatically Jordan has hot summers and fairly cold winters. A maximum temperature of 49°C has been recorded in the Jordan Valley whilst on higher ground temperatures can fall to zero with frosts and some snow.

However, average temperatures during the summers are nearly 32°C and in winters are approximately 13°C. Strong winds can also be anticipated, sometimes from the south/southeast accompanied by heavy dust storms and at other times from the north/northwest.

Of particular importance to Jordan, which is exceptionally short of water, is the annual rainfall, the occurrence of which is highly unpredictable. In the higher parts of the country 380 to 630 millimetres of rainfall occurs, mainly between November and April, sufficient to support the agriculture of the eastern Jordan Valley. Elsewhere, there is an absolute maximum of 200 millimetres of rainfall and, in some areas, none at all. The net result is that only about a quarter of the country can be cultivated and in much of the cultivable area only at a subsistence level.

Geology[1]

Jordan is located in the northwestern part of the Arabian Peninsula, about 85 per cent of Jordan's territory is underlain by sedimentary rocks, which attain a thickness of more than 12 kilometres in the Jordan Rift graben. Further to the east, in the Azraq and Risha areas, sedimentary rocks are approximately 7 kilometres thick. Most of the country is covered by 4 to 5 kilometres of sediments. The section overlying its crystalline basement consists of units ranging in the age from late Proterozoic to Holocene.

In its simplest form, the geology of Jordan consists of a sequence of mainly marine sediments that surround a small area of precambrian crystalline outcrop in the southwestern part of the country and thicken

---

[1] This information has been provided by the Natural Resources Authority

towards the north and the east. Close to the precambrian outcrop, the units are thin and separated by many unconformities. Proceeding in the basinward direction, the unconformities diminish as more of the units missing in the outcrop are encountered.

Structurally, Jordan can be divided into a series of broad, carbonate plateau arches and gently dibbing desert-covered basins. The basic tectonic features, which developed at different rates, are intersected by long, essentially linear graben and half graben, along which significant strike slip movement has occurred. The most fundamental of these linear fault zones strike northwest, parallel to the Red Sea trend. They are cut off obliquely by the Dead Sea Rift trend striking north and northeast. The Dead Sea rift is a tertiary feature with left lateral displacement of about 107 kilometres. It is technically linked to the Red Sea spread centre and the Gulf of Suez graben system, with its oil-producing horst feature. The Dead Sea Rift forms the western boundary of the Arabian Plate and transforms from spreading in the Red Sea to compression in the Taurus Zagros compressional margin. In Jordan, the Dead Sea Rift has a significant extensional component, giving rise to both the subsea depressions in the Jordan Valley and the thick late tertiary sediments that underlie the valley. Several sub-basins occur along the rift and probably reach a thickness of up to 12,000 metres. Transgressive and regressive movements within the Tethys seaways entering from the north largely controlled the tectonic trends within the late Paleozoic and Mesozoic basins.

The basalt plateau is covered by approximately 11,500 square kilometres of thin basalt over a basin that contains a thick Mesozoic section with Paleozoic elements beneath. Direct natural evidence for the existence of oil in Jordan is provided by the surface occurrence of oil and gas seepages, bituminous calcareous sediments, asphalt and tar sand. Some of these features have been known since the beginning of recorded history.

History

Jordan, as we know it today, has been home to some of the oldest civilizations in the world with archaeological remains on the West Bank of the River Jordan dating back as far back as 9000 BCE and those at Beidha, in the south of the country close to Petra, being regarded as the first ever recorded human settlement. However, the country's documented history begins around 2000 BC, when the Ammonites settled along the River Jordan in Canaan and the warring kingdoms of Edom, Gilead and Moab, mentioned many times in the Bible, prevailed on the country's East Bank and in the nearby mountains. From that time and for the succeeding 3,000 years, a succession of invaders and settlers arrived in the area including the Hittites, Egyptians, Israelites, Assyrians, Babylonians, Persians, Greeks, Romans, Arab Muslims, Christian Crusaders, Mamelukes, Ottoman Turks, who ruled the region for 400 years between 1517 and 1918, and, finally, the British.

After the end of the First World War, the League of Nations, as the mandate holder for Palestine and Transjordan, awarded the territory now comprising Israel, Jordan, the West Bank, Gaza and Jerusalem to the United Kingdom. Subsequently, in 1922, the British divided the mandate by establishing the semi-autonomous Emirate of Transjordan under the nominal rule of Abdullah bin Hussein, while continuing its direct administration of Palestine. Six years later, in 1928, Transjordan obtained a degree of independence from Great Britain but it was not until 3 days after the mandate ended on 22 May 1946 that the country became the independent Hashemite Kingdom of Transjordan.

Transjordan was one of the Arab states that assisted Palestinian nationalists who were opposed to the creation of Israel in May 1948 and took part in the ensuing war with the newly founded State of Israel. On conclusion of the hostilities, the armistice agreements of April 1949 left Jordan in control of the West Bank but provided that the demarcation lines be without prejudice to future territorial settlements or boundary lines. In 1950, Transjordan, including those areas of Palestine annexed by King Abdullah, became the Hashemite Kingdom of Jordan. Subsequently, in 1957, Jordan ended its special defence treaty relationship with the United Kingdom.

In May 1967, Jordan signed a mutual defence pact with Egypt and participated just 1 month later with that country, Syria and Iraq in hostilities against Israel. During this war, Israel gained control of the West Bank and all of Jerusalem and substantial numbers of Palestinians moved to Jordan, whose Palestinian refugee population grew to total 1 million. The power and importance of Palestinian resistance elements within the diaspora in Jordan constituted a growing threat to the sovereignty and security of the Hashemite state and open fighting erupted and subsided in June 1970.

No fighting occurred along the 1967 River Jordan ceasefire line during the October 1973 Arab–Israeli war but Jordan did send a brigade to Syria to fight Israeli units on Syrian territory. Later, in 1988, Jordan renounced all claims to the West Bank but retained an administrative role pending a final settlement. Jordan did not participate in the Gulf war against Iraq in 1991 but agreed that year, along with Syria, Lebanon and the representatives of the Palestinians, to participate in direct peace negotiations with Israel, ultimately signing a peace treaty in 1994, since when Jordan has sought to remain at peace with all its neighbours.

Political Structure and Decision-making

Sana Abdallah

Introduction

The 1952 Constitution of the Hashemite Kingdom of Jordan, one of the most modern constitutions in the region, is the source of the country's political structure and specifies the role of each branch of government. A hereditary monarchy with a parliamentary system, the political structure is divided into the executive, legislative and judicial branches, with the reigning king as the head of state, chief executive and the commander-in-chief of the armed forces.

The constitution

Comprising 6 chapters and 109 articles, the Jordanian constitution, first drawn up in 1947 and amended in 1952, is the blueprint for the country's system of government, legislation and the rights and duties of Jordanians, calling for the separation of the three branches of government. It defines the kingdom as an 'independent sovereign Arab state' with Islam as the state's religion. However, the constitution also insists that 'the state shall safeguard the free exercise of all forms of worship and religious rites'.

The constitution stipulates that all Jordanians are equal before the law, prohibits discrimination between them on the grounds of race, language or religion and guarantees personal freedom. Often used by civil and political rights advocates as the basis for protecting these rights, the document bans detention or imprisonment except in accordance with the provisions of the law, prohibits deportation of any Jordanian and protects freedom of opinion, free expression and freedom of press.

It also gives Jordanians the right to free assembly and freedom to establish political parties – regulated by law – so long as their methods are peaceful. It bans the extradition of political refugees on account of their political beliefs or for the defence of liberty.

Since most of the liberal rights guaranteed by the constitution are regulated by law, bills have been issued, whether as provisional laws by the government in the absence of parliament or endorsed by the National Assembly in session, that restrict these freedoms. However, the reigning King Abdullah II has instructed his consecutive governments to ensure greater freedoms for his subjects by drafting liberalized amended legislation that will fulfil the spirit of the constitution.

The king

Jordan's King Abdullah II became the country's fourth monarch since the inception of the kingdom in 1921 under the reign of King Abdullah Bin al-Hussein, son of Sharif Hussein of Mecca. The ruling monarchs have been: King Abdullah (1921–51) King Talal bin Abdullah (1951–52), eldest son of King Abdullah King Hussein bin Talal (1952–99), eldest son of King Talal and King Abdullah bin Al-Hussein (1999–present), eldest son of King Hussein.

The Hashemite family members are direct descendants of Prophet Mohammad through his daughter, Fatima, and her husband, Ali Bin Abi-Talib, the Prophet's paternal first cousin and the fourth Caliph of Islam. The throne of the kingdom is hereditary to the dynasty of King Abdullah Bin al-Hussein, with the royal title being passed from the king to his eldest son, and to the eldest son of that son in linear succession thereafter.

An amendment was introduced to the constitution in 1965 allowing the king to select one of his brothers as heir apparent, which King Hussein did when he named his younger brother, Hassan, as Crown Prince. The amendment came amid repeated attempts on Hussein's life and when his eldest son Abdullah was only 3 years old. Shortly before his death, however, Hussein replaced his brother with his son Abdullah, who inherited the throne from his father when he died in February 1999 after a battle with cancer.

The executive branch

King's role

As the chief executive, the reigning king, Abdullah II, appoints the prime minister who then forms a cabinet in close consultation with the palace. As head of the state, the monarch is immune from any liability and responsibility. The king's powers in the executive branch include the following:

- Appointing and dismissing of the prime minister and dismissing any cabinet minister upon the recommendation of the prime minister.
- Appointing members of the upper house of parliament.
- Ordering the holding of parliamentary elections.
- Dissolving the lower house of parliament.
- Endorsing laws before they are enacted, although this can be overruled by a two-thirds majority of the National Assembly, or both houses of parliament.
- Authorizing the appointment and dismissal of judges, regional governors and the mayor of the capital, Amman.
- Approving constitutional amendments.
- Declaring war as commander-in-chief.
- Concluding and ratifying treaties and accords, with the approval of the cabinet and the National Assembly.
- Creating, conferring and withdrawing civil and military ranks, medals and honorific titles, and delegating this authority to any other person by special law.
- Granting special pardons and commuting sentences, as well as general amnesties determined by a special law.

Prime minister and cabinet

The prime minister, who also takes the portfolio of defence minister, and cabinet members must be endorsed by the lower house of parliament in a vote of confidence after the prime minister presents his or her government's policy statement. If the lower house votes against the prime minister, he or she and the entire cabinet must resign. A single cabinet minister must also resign if he or she is voted out by the lower house.

The prime minister and cabinet are responsible for the administration of all Jordan's internal and external affairs. The cabinet usually meets twice a week to discuss matters of the state, take administrative decisions, issue regulations and draft legislation to be presented to parliament for debate and approval. Each minister is responsible for running the affairs of his or her department in line with the policy statement presented to the legislature.

The latest cabinet, comprising 23 ministers (including one woman) and headed by Prime Minister Marouf Al-Bakhit, was sworn in on 27 November 2005. King Abdullah designated Bakhit, the fifth prime minister since this monarch assumed the throne, to form a new government shortly after unprecedented suicide terrorist attacks on 9

November targeted three busy hotels in Amman, killing 60 people and injuring 100 others. Bakhit, a retired army major general who served as Jordan's ambassador to Turkey and Israel, was Director of National Security when King Abdullah asked him to form a new government.

The king asked Bakhit's government to accelerate legislation and reforms pertaining to political life, including new political parties and elections laws, as well as an anti-terrorism bill to prevent further attacks and to combat the 'culture that condones the killing of innocent civilians or persons labelled as "infidels",' by extremist Muslims. In August 2006, parliament endorsed a controversial anti-terrorism law, the first of its kind in the Arab world, giving the security services a carte blanche to take measures against those the authorities believe support terror ideas, incite attacks or express sympathy for suicide bombings. One month later, parliament approved another controversial bill bringing Muslim mosque imams and teachers under government control, requiring them to obtain prior written approval from the Ministry of Awqaf and Religious Affairs for sermons and classes. The government said this legislation was necessary to 'fight against terrorism and ideas promoting violence'.

Other laws aimed at introducing political and economic reforms, such as an anti-corruption bill, were also approved by parliament, as the government continued to work on draft legislation on elections and political parties intended to encourage greater political participation.

The legislative branch

The National Assembly

Legislative power is shared by the king and the National Assembly, or parliament. The National Assembly consists of an elected 110-member lower house of parliament, or house of deputies, and a 55-seat upper house of parliament, or Senate, whose members are appointed by the king. The normal parliamentary term is 4 years, but the king has the power to dissolve both houses of parliament and dismiss any of their members – although dismissal of a member of the lower house is subject to specific conditions.

The Senate is a component of the king's legislative powers and its appointed members normally represent the king's vision. The Senate cannot constitutionally number more than half of the elected lower house, though it enjoys the same degree of free expression when speaking in Parliament.

The house of deputies benefits from powers that the upper house does not, such as questioning the government on any public issues. It can also raise a no-confidence vote against the government or any individual cabinet minister, who must then resign if voted out by a majority.

The National Assembly can submit legislation to the government in the form of a draft law. It also initiates debates and votes on proposals submitted by the prime minister to the house of deputies, which can endorse, amend or reject them. Each proposed piece of legislation is referred to a specialized committee in the house of deputies for review and, if accepted, is conveyed back to the government for the drafting of the proposal in the form of a bill.

The government draft law is then debated by the house of deputies. If approved, it is sent to the Senate for discussion and a vote. In case the Senate rejects the draft bill, it is returned to the lower house with its proposed amendments. Should the two houses disagree, they hold a joint session in which the matter is settled by a two-thirds majority vote by both.

When the upper house approves a draft bill as accepted by the lower house, it is submitted to the king, who can endorse it, thus enacting the law, or return it unapproved to the lower house of parliament for another review and vote. If both houses insist on approving the bill in a joint session with a two-thirds majority, it becomes an 'act of parliament', overruling the king's veto.

Parliamentary elections

Jordan's first free parliamentary elections in more than 22 years were held under King Hussein's reign in 1989, in which the electorate were entitled to as many votes as the number of seats allocated for their district. A quota was placed for the country's minorities, giving six seats to the Bedouins, three to the Circassian and Chechen communities and nine for the Christian minority. These polls brought to the house of deputies, which was an 80-seat parliament at the time, a cross-section of representatives of the country's diverse socio-political and ethnic communities.

A few months before the 1993 polls, a provisional bill issued by the government amended the Elections Law according to the principle of 'one person, one vote', whereby the country was divided into 20 electoral districts, and each voter could elect only one candidate. This law remained in place when the following elections were held, prompting a boycott by the opposition parties, led by the Islamic Action Front – the political arm of the influential Muslim Brotherhood Movement.

General elections that were due to be held in 2001 were delayed for 2 years by the government, citing 'regional circumstances', in reference to the Palestinian uprising and clashes with Israeli occupation forces across Jordan's western borders, and the growing tension in the kingdom's eastern neighbour, Iraq, which eventually led to the US-led military invasion of that country in March 2003. The government did not want what it said were 'radical voices' to exploit the situation across the two borders to win seats in a parliament by appealing to a population frustrated by US policies in the region.

But an election day was finally set shortly after US forces overthrew the regime of Saddam Hussein in Iraq in April 2003. By the time the polls were held in June 2003, the elections law had been amended again, raising the number of seats from 80 to 110, including a six-seat quota for women for the first time. Although the 'one person, one vote' system remained in place, the Islamic Action Front and other opposition groups ended their boycott and fielded candidates across the country.

Despite the relatively low voter turnout of 58.8 per cent of the 2.3 million eligible voters, the 2003 parliamentary elections brought to the lower house of parliament a majority of 62 seats for pro-regime candidates, including former government officials, former legislators and tribal leaders known for their loyalty to the ruling Hashemite monarchy.

The Islamic Action Front won 17 seats, while an additional 8 independent Islamists secured membership. The remaining legislators were independent, leftists and pan-Arab nationalists.

None of the 54 women candidates managed to win seats outside the 6-seat quota, and those who obtained the highest percentage of votes for the quota were all from districts outside the capital, Amman.

After a 2-year absence of parliamentary life, the new legislature inherited 211 provisional bills, most of them economic, issued by the government that needed to be reviewed during its 4-year term.

In November 2003, King Abdullah issued a royal decree increasing the number of seats in the Senate from 40 to 55, appointing representatives from all sectors of society. Two years later, shortly after the triple hotel bombings in November 2005, the monarch dissolved the upper house of parliament and appointed new members, mostly made up of former prime ministers, former senior officials and public dignitaries, including six women.

Local councils

Women are also relatively well represented in the kingdom's municipal councils, half of whose members are elected and the other half appointed by the government. Where no woman has been elected to a council, the government has appointed at least one in every district.

Jordan is divided into 12 regional governorates headed by a governor appointed by the king through the Ministry of Interior. Each governorate is divided into smaller administrative sub-regions. The district government is responsible for executing cabinet decisions at the local level, and is directly supervised by the Ministry of Interior. The kingdom's 99 municipal councils are headed by mayors who supervise the daily affairs of towns and cities that are handled by the municipal councils.

In the July 2003 polls, only 58 per cent of the 803,000 eligible voters cast their ballots for half of the seats of the municipal councils, where candidates in 17 municipalities competed unopposed. But voter turnout in rural areas was higher than in the cities, possibly due to public apathy and low confidence in the controversial amended municipal law that allowed the government to appoint half the council members and mayors.

The judiciary

Introduction

The Jordanian Constitution specifically states that the role and functions of the judiciary must be completely independent of any influences by the executive and legislative branches. The courts are subjected to no other authority than that of the law.

Judges are appointed by the Ministry of Justice but require endorsement by a royal decree. They are normally graduates of recognized universities who have served as clerks and officers of the court. The Ministry of Justice, with approval of the king, assigns judges to serve in courts, transfers, promotes and dismisses them.

There are three types of courts: the civil, religious and special courts, made up of one or more judges, but no juries.

Civil courts

The civil judiciary is a four-level system: the 14 Magistrates' Courts, 7 Courts of First Instance, the Court of Appeal and the Court of Cassation (the supreme court of the kingdom.)

The jurisdiction of the Magistrates' Courts is to hear civil and criminal cases of issues involving small fines and a maximum prison term of 2 years.

The Courts of First Instance have general jurisdiction over all criminal and civil matters not granted to other courts' jurisdiction, and also hear appeals for judgements of the Magistrates' Courts.

The next judicial tier, the Court of Appeals, is presided over by a tribunal of three judges in Amman. It hears appeals of the decisions of the Magistrates' Courts, decides appeals from decisions of the Courts of First Instance and the Religious Courts.

The Court of Cassation, the highest judiciary, is presided by a judge appointed by the king who serves as the country's chief justice. All the court's seven judges sit in full panel when important cases are being argued, but for most appeals of verdicts made by the Court of Appeals, five judges hear and rule on the cases.

Religious courts

The religious courts are divided into the Sharia (Islamic law) Courts for the Muslims, the Tribunals of Religious Communities for non-Muslims or the Ecclesiastical Courts for the minority Christian communities.

These courts have jurisdiction over cases of personal status, such as marriage, divorce, child custody, alimony and inheritance, as well as communal endowment. Rulings of religious courts may be appealed at the Court of Appeals in Amman.

Individuals not of the same religion who do not agree to the jurisdiction of a religious court are allowed to bring their case to the specialized civil court. If there is a conflict of jurisdiction between two religious courts, or between a religious and civil court, the president of the Court of Cassation forms a three-judge tribunal to decide jurisdiction or to hear the case.

One judge sits in each Sharia Court and rules on cases according to Islamic law, and sometimes based on parts of the Civil Status Law if divorce, for example, is involved.

Each Christian court is made up of three judges, usually members of the clergy, who base their rulings on different aspects of canon law interpreted by the Greek Orthodox, Roman Catholic and Anglican traditions. However, they apply Islamic law in inheritance cases.

Special courts

Special courts mainly involve the State Security Court, which hears cases related to drug trafficking, illegal smuggling, economic crimes, but mostly security-related cases. The State Security Court, which replaced the military courts of the martial law period in Jordan between 1956 and 1990, comprises a panel of two military and one civilian judges who try both military personnel and civilians. Its verdicts are not final and may be appealed at the Court of Cassation. Dozens of terror-related cases have been heard since the beginning of the millennium, many of them involving alleged plots foiled before being carried out.

Special courts also include the Supreme Council, the Special Council and the High Court of Justice. The Supreme Council interprets the constitution at the request of the prime minister, the lower house or the upper house of parliament. The Special Council, called on by the prime minister at any time, interprets any law that has not been interpreted by the courts of law. The High Court of Justice is constituted when necessary by the Court of Cassation. Its jurisdiction includes hearing petitions, issuing injunctions involving public servants charged with wrongdoing and trying cabinet ministers charged with offences.

1.3

The Jordanian Economy in 2007: After a 3-year Boom Prospects Remain Buoyant but Vulnerable

Marwan A Kardoosh, Jordan Center for Public Policy Research & Dialogue

The first edition of *Doing Business with Jordan* was published in early 2004, a few months after the start of the US-led war in Iraq. At the time, it was unclear what impact this war would have on the Jordanian economy. The overriding concern was mostly about the loss of Iraqi oil subsidy and its ramifications. Since then, however, the Jordanian economy has once more confirmed its ability to withstand shocks and maintain momentum. The war on Iraq, which started in March 2003, had a damaging, albeit transient, impact on economic activity. Far from loosing its allure, the Jordanian economy capitalized on several factors that enabled it to shrug off the impact of the war and to grow very rapidly during 2004–05, this despite worries about high energy prices and the loss of the Iraqi oil subsidy. That economic performance has been highly correlated with resilience was also evident in late 2005, when the economy comfortably sailed through the effects of the terrorist attacks of 9 November.

In many ways, the current economic boom marks the end of an era, and the start of another, for the Jordanian economy, with capital flows from abroad and exports joining remittances-fed consumption and investment as the main drivers of economic growth.

Following the economic crisis of 1988–89, and for the better part of the 1990s, Jordanian economic performance was abysmal, except for a short episode of relatively rapid expansion during 1992–95. The slowdown in economic activity was most pronounced during the second half of the 1990s, with real GDP growth averaging 3.0 per cent between 1996 and

1999. As the same period witnessed more than 3 per cent annual population growth, real per capita GDP stagnated.

Things began to change at the turn of the millennium, and a period of relatively rapid economic growth ensued, with GDP expanding at an average annual rate of about 4.9 per cent during 1999–2003 – well above the population rate of growth for that period (2.8 per cent). The war in Iraq and its aftermath brought an even more rapid period of economic prosperity to Jordan, with GDP growth at constant 1994 basic prices accelerating to 8.5 per cent in 2004. The strong momentum from 2004 continued into 2005, when growth in real terms approached 7.2 per cent. Preliminary estimates released by the Jordan Department of Statistics put the year-on-year growth rate during the first three quarters of 2006 at 6.8 per cent (7.1 per cent, 6.3 per cent and 6.9 per cent in Q1, Q2 and Q3, respectively).

A near-mirror image of the sectoral performance in 2004–05, growth during the first 9 months of 2006 was broad-based with all major sectors of the economy expanding except for 'mining and quarrying'. The 'manufacturing' sector grew fastest, by nearly 11.4 per cent, to meet demand from the expenditure of tourists, migrating businesses and immigrants (externalities of the Iraqi situation) commodity export markets and linkages to the construction sector. The latter grew by 9.7 per cent during the first three quarters of 2006.

There were several reasons for this, including demographic developments, mainly reflecting rapid growth in new household formation, the result of Jordan's relatively young population demand for housing and real estate by Jordanians working abroad demand for buildings and housing by the swelling expatriate community, mainly Iraqi households and businesses and reform and development in the mortgage market.

Against the background of rising economic growth, living standards, as measured by GDP per capita using constant 1994 basic prices, improved markedly: from 990.4 Jordanian dinars in 2001 to 1,164.1 Jordanian dinars in 2005, an increase of 17.5 per cent. On an annual average basis, this amounts to a growth rate of 4.1 per cent. Yet, despite these improvements, real per capita GDP is still below the level that was there before the economic crisis of the late 1980s, and poverty remains extensive, though declining somewhat. Rising inflation, combined with planned subsidy cuts in 2007 on fuel, only threaten a tighter squeeze.

The Amman Stock Exchange (ASE) was to be no exception to the general upswing, with volume up 104 per cent in 2004 and market capitalization rising from 7.8 billion Jordanian dinars in 2003 to 13 billion Jordanian dinars 12 months later. In the process, the ASE index rose by 62.4 per cent, from 2,614.5 to 4,245.6 as at end-December 2004. The strong momentum from 2004 continued into 2005, with total trading volume up 345 per cent and market capitalization doubling from 13.0 billion Jordanian dinars in 2004 to 26.7 billion Jordanian dinars. The benchmark 70-share ASE index weighted by market capitalization rose by just under 93 per cent year-on-year to close at 8,192 points. The index was nevertheless down 12 per cent on its intra-year high of 9,348 points reached one day before the November 2005 terrorist attacks.

So what has caused this successful turnaround? Several things but mostly they boil down to the buoyancy of domestic effective demand, mainly in the form of consumption and investment expenditure, fuelled by remittances from Jordanian migrant workers in the Gulf the savings of expatriate Iraqi businesses and households who fled Iraq to find a safe haven in Jordan and the inflow of foreign investment income, primarily from the Gulf region and mainly due to record oil revenues.

Remittances

With rising oil prices boosting incomes in the Gulf region, including those of Jordanian workers, migrant remittances grew rapidly, from 1,404.5 million Jordanian dinars in 2003 to 1,459.6 million Jordanian dinars in 2004 and to 1,544.8 million Jordanian dinars in 2005 (equivalent to 17.1 per cent of GDP). The year-on-year growth rate for 2005, at around 5.8 per cent, was the highest since 2002.

Iraq externalities

The US invasion of Iraq in March 2003 and the subsequent sinking of that country in a quagmire of chaos resulted in a sharp increase in the number of Iraqi expatriates using Jordan as a base, be it for residential purposes or for business reasons. Jordan's 'safe haven' status has either way served it well, acting as an economic and political island of stability within a notoriously turbulent region.

Foreign investment

Also contributing to the surge in consumption and investment expenditures, and consequently, domestic effective demand, was the rise in foreign investment, much of it from the oil-flush Gulf. Official Jordanian figures show that in 2005 net foreign direct investment inflows in the capital and financial account more than doubled, from 461.6 million Jordanian dinars in 2004 to 1,086 million Jordanian dinars last year. Rising oil prices are fuelling this growth, helped by Jordan's long-standing advantages – such as low political risk, strong property rights and an investment-friendly regulatory environment – and, after 11 September 2001, a growing desire among Arab investors to keep their money in the region.

Three other factors help to explain the economy's stellar performance in 2004–05:

1.   The rapid growth in export earnings
2.   The explosive growth in equities and real estate
3.   The acceleration of reforms

Exports

After several years of stagnation, merchandise exports grew by an annual average of 19.4 per cent during 2001–05. The comparable figure for 1996–2000 is 1.5 per cent. The uptrend in exports was also evident in the area of services, with travel receipts in the balance of payments growing by an annual average of 16.3 per cent during 2001–05, compared to a mere 2.3 per cent during 1996–2000.

Much of the jump in merchandise exports is being driven by a number of extra-regional preferential trade arrangements. This is especially true of qualifying industrial zones (QIZs), introduced by the United States to the Middle East in the mid-1990s. The QIZ model essentially extends the benefits of the US–Israel Free Trade Area Implementation Act of 1985 to include exports from geographically circumscribed areas in Jordan, provided Israel is involved in the manufacturing process. From almost nothing in the late 1990s Jordanian exports to the United States, mostly in the form of wearing apparel, have surged to more than 790.2 million Jordanian dinars in 2005.

Rosy as it may seem, lots of teething problems remain in the Jordanian export sector, of which the most important is the failure to diversify the export base away from low value-added manufacturing towards high value-added industry. As a result, the kingdom still relies heavily on a small basket of goods for its merchandise export earnings.

This would typically include mineral exports, basic consumer goods and, to a lesser extent, fruits and vegetables, though more recent export figures seem to suggest that clothing items (mainly produced in QIZs) are now part of this basket. That this is a step in the right direction is not in doubt what can be questioned, however, is the sustainability of these exports. The future of QIZs is now subject to factors over which Jordan has little or no control. For starters, the 'Egyptian Threat' is now real, and some investors have indicated that they would be moving to Egypt, a country that produces many of the raw materials for garments and that generally has lower costs of production. Hence it is only normal for any industry, especially a 'footloose' one to migrate from Jordan to Egypt. In any case, even in the event that the threat from Egypt does not prove to be lethal, trade concessions in other economies near Jordan could still act to lure QIZ investors into those countries.

Another reason why the trend may now be for clothing exports to become less important is the end of the Multi Fibre Agreement. Though this did not have the 'big bang' effect people had expected, things might now be moving in a different direction. This is mainly reflected in the slowing pace of foreign direct investment in QIZs, though so far exports from these zones are holding their own.

If QIZs were to remain a valid investment proposition beyond 2006, one inevitable strategy would be to push for greater diversification, away from garments and more towards fashion-wear and higher value-added items. By moving up the value chain, Jordan can avoid competition from low-cost suppliers such as China and India, as well as increase its export revenue base.

With export product diversification becoming an issue for Jordan, a closely related challenge is to help the local companies penetrate new markets. The one sector where this continues to pose a major challenge is agriculture, with the vast majority of exports still going to neighbouring countries within the region. Though some Jordanian growers have attempted to break into the European market, poor packaging, high transport costs and limited marketing skills have undermined their effort.

Stock market and real estate

A direct result of the huge volume of foreign capital entering Jordan in 2004–05 and the explosive run-up in property prices and equity values appears to have generated a lot of wealth for Jordanian households that own such assets, pushing the consumption of these households (and perhaps others via the 'demonstration effect') to dizzying heights. Of course such a conclusion is tentative and more empirical investigation is necessary. A key question to answer is whether or not the Jordanian economy was affected by these rises at the macro level.

Reform

The other important factor contributing to the recent improvement in Jordanian economic performance has been the marked progress in economic reform efforts aimed at further liberalization of the trade regime and, to a lesser extent, of domestic markets. These coincided with measures encouraging private enterprise and foreign investment, all part of a programme that the Bretton Woods institutions and others have been urging on Jordan for years. A few quibbles aside, it is hard to find any bit of government economic policy that looks truly wrong-headed. However, there is still ample room for improvement and the process should not stop at any one point.

This is especially true of privatization, where Jordan does not seem to have a clear policy. Unlike neighbouring Egypt and Syria, Jordan did not have a large concentration of nationalized industries to privatize and, as a result, was restricted to public utilities that had been the exclusive preserve of the state. While the government of Jordan has declared its commitment to the process, there is still no conceptual framework for it. The legislation that intended to provide such a framework focuses primarily on procedural issues rather than on substance it does very little to articulate Jordan's privatization philosophy and objectives. Instead of promoting privatization as a policy instrument for securing competitive markets, privatization is narrowly interpreted as the divestiture of public assets to private (mostly foreign) interests. Practically no efforts were made to ensure the competitiveness of the large number of markets that were already in the domain of the private sector.

That Jordan has been engaged in serious economic reforms (including structural adjustment and liberalization measures) over the past few years is not in doubt what can be questioned however is whether such reform efforts are sufficient to cope with the kingdom's many difficulties, some of which are structural and the result of weaknesses in the economy, in the system of economic management, or both, while others are dynamic and specific to the current period. As a result, the immediate road ahead for the Jordanian economy still looks bumpy.

A main concern for the economy in 2007 is that oil prices, which fell in October and November 2006, could rise again beyond the US $60–70 per barrel range even without a major political or terrorist disruption, and much higher with one. A second is unemployment. A third is inflation. A fourth is the country's trade and current account deficits. A fifth relates to the budget profile, which seems to be improving, though not necessarily in the right direction, as will be briefly discussed below.

Oil prices

The single biggest challenge facing the Jordanian economy this year is energy prices, and the kingdom remains particularly vulnerable to steep rises in the price of oil. One way of quantifying this vulnerability is by using the ratio of oil imports to GDP. The ratio of oil imports to GDP, which stood at 19.0 per cent in 2005, rose to 23.8 per cent during the first quarter of 2006. It is estimated that in the year to end-March of 2006, oil imports (including petroleum products) cost the Jordanian economy 527.2 million Jordanian dinars, up 41.0 per cent from the corresponding period in 2005. On such a trajectory, the oil bill would exceed 2.3 billion Jordanian dinars by year-end.

Fortunately for Jordan, hope is in sight, and the general feeling now is that some of the kingdom's oil woes could find a solution in the next few months. Within its drive to ease pressures on the economy, and also for important political reasons, Jordan has recently opened up its trade with Iraq. Most notably, it has announced the conclusion of a new oil deal by which Baghdad would supply the kingdom with some 30 per cent of its crude oil daily needs (30,000 barrels/day) at a price US $18 less than the international level.

Unemployment

The situation in the labour market remains problematic, marred by high unemployment, rapid population growth, low female participation rates, out-migration of skills, retirement at an early age in the public sector and a severe mismatch between the labour market and the education system. Official estimates put the rate of unemployment in 2005 at 14.8 per cent: 12.8 per cent for males and 25.9 per cent for females. However, that is only the beginning of the problem. Jordan has particularly acute problems getting its young people into work. The unemployment rate for the 20- to 24-year-olds remains dreadful, estimated at almost twice the national average (28.7 per cent as opposed to an overall rate of 14.8 per cent). A high concentration of unemployment among Jordan's young can be very costly for the economy, representing a depletion of human capital. The result is the migration of bright young Jordanians for better opportunities elsewhere in the region and beyond. Much of this poor performance stems from the inability of the Jordanian productive system to develop fast enough to provide employment for young people entering the labour force every year.

For unemployment in Jordan to start falling, efforts to improve the quality of education and training need to be intensified. With bold government intervention, the 'mega' projects currently being implemented in Jordan, especially in the construction sector, could provide an unprecedented opportunity for upgrading the skills of Jordanian labourers through 'on-the-job' training.

Inflation

A third concern for the economy in 2006 is inflation, which is starting to creep up. Jordan's average rate of consumer-price inflation rose to 5.6 per cent in the year to May 2006, up from 2.4 per cent during the corresponding period in 2005 and well above the twelve-month inflation rate for the whole of last year (3.5 per cent). This compares with 3.4 per cent in 2004, 1.6 per cent in 2003 and 1.8 per cent in 2002 and 2001. The blame for this jump in inflation lies largely with higher oil prices. Jordan in 2007 may also have to grapple with 'imported inflation', the result of declining terms of trade, due in part to a weakening US dollar and, by extension, the Jordanian dinar.

Current account deficit

One aspect of Jordanian economic performance that should evoke concern among economists and policymakers is the country's large and growing external current account deficit – the measure of dependence on foreigners for borrowing and capital inflows. In 2005, that deficit stood at 1,638.7 million Jordanian dinars, or about 18.2 per cent of GDP. Corresponding to that deficit, Jordan had – to the extent that the government abstained from drawing on its foreign exchange reserves – to raise 1,638.7 million Jordanian dinars on international capital markets. The current account deficit has been on a steep upward trajectory in recent years, moving from a relatively strong surplus position of 835.7 million Jordanian dinars (11.6 per cent of GDP) in 2003 to a modest deficit of 12.7 million Jordanian dinars (0.2 per cent of GDP) in 2004 on its way to its current alarming imbalance.

The yawning current account deficit, meanwhile, has carried on into 2006, with a sharp widening in the commodity trade deficit and a worsening services balance, leading to a 148 per cent rise in the deficit, from 233.3 million Jordanian dinars in the first quarter of 2005 to 579 million Jordanian dinars during the corresponding period in 2006. The latter is equivalent to 26.1 per cent of GDP. On such a trajectory, the deficit would exceed 2,316 million Jordanian dinars by end-2006. The situation would be still worse if future increases in energy prices and the budget deficit compound such developments, as they surely could.

To put the Jordanian current account and trade deficits back on a sustainable path will require structural reforms aimed at encouraging faster growth, boosting household saving rates, balancing the budget and opening up new markets for Jordanian exports, particularly of services.

Fiscal deficit

The budget deficit (including grants) rose to 5.2 per cent of GDP in 2005, despite a 21.4 per cent reduction in capital spending and a 19.3 per cent rise in domestic revenues. Two factors contributed to the worsening fiscal deficit in 2005. First was the significant drop in foreign grants, from 811.3 million Jordanian dinars in 2004 to 500.3 million Jordanian dinars last year. The budget for 2005 had targeted foreign grants of 1,060 million Jordanian dinars. This freefall was not unexpected however, with the United States and others signalling clearly that the sharp rise in disbursements during 2003–04 was temporary. The second factor was the increase in current expenditure, from 2,377.8 million Jordanian dinars in 2004 to 2,908 million Jordanian dinars in 2005. The budget for 2005 had projected current expenditures of 2,545.0 million Jordanian dinars. There were several reasons for this, including the following:

1. Rising oil subsidy costs (to about 531 million Jordanian dinars).

2. Increased expenditure on defence and security (to 698.8 million Jordanian dinars in 2005).

3. A growing wage and salaries bill (up by 10.7 per cent, to 489.9 million Jordanian dinars).

4. An increase in interest payments (from 229 million Jordanian dinars in 2004 to 267.1 million Jordanian dinars in 2005).

The economic consequences of a worsening fiscal imbalance are indisputably negative. For Jordan, a large budget deficit reduces the country's already low savings rate. To the extent that the government borrows from the private sector to finance its deficit, it is likely to crowd out private investment and reduce long-term economic growth. Jordan is already enormously reliant on the outside world to fund its spending. As noted above, the current account deficit, the measure of annual dependence on external resources, is at a near-historic high of 26.1 per cent of GDP. A large budget deficit will aggravate these external imbalances and so raise the risk of financial volatility, even a Jordanian dinar crisis. Over the next few years, that perhaps is the biggest risk that the government's fiscal policy poses for the Jordanian economy.

For now, however, such concerns are not so pressing. In the first 6 months of 2006, total revenues and grants stood at 1,786.3 million Jordanian dinars, an improvement on the comparable 2005 figure of 1,551.1 million Jordanian dinars. This came despite a sharp drop in foreign grants, from 234.4 million Jordanian dinars in the first half of 2005 to 110.1 million Jordanian dinars during the corresponding period in 2006. Offsetting the negative impact of falling foreign grants on government revenues was the simultaneous rise in tax and non-tax receipts. The former rose by 25.5 per cent to 1,141.1 million Jordanian dinars, propelled by buoyant general sales tax (up 17.8 per cent) and income tax receipts (up 59.4 per cent), while the latter rose by 34.3 per cent to 515.5 million Jordanian dinars.

Outlook for 2007

That the Jordanian economy will continue to grow in 2007 is not in doubt. What can be questioned however is whether the economy is set to slow down dramatically in the coming months. Whatever happens, analysts at Moody's seem to have made up their mind. The international rating agency downgraded Jordan's economic outlook for 2006 from 'stable' to 'negative', citing Jordan's worsening balance of payments position as the main reason.

In another sign of weakening prospects, the past few months have witnessed a sizeable correction in the bourse, marked by volatile trading in Jordanian stocks. The benchmark 70-share ASE index weighted by market capitalization, down 36.6 per cent from its all-time peak on 8 November and 26.1 per cent in 2006, has been sinking fast of late. The reasons for this upheaval are manifold, and include the high valuations of stocks (resulting in a significant correction), the large growth in corporate earnings from investment income (rather than from core business activities), upward movements in interest rates, a significant rise in the number of IPOs (that has absorbed much of the liquidity available in the market), a drop in investor confidence, panic that has struck other bourses in the region, as well as recent changes in market regulations such as cash trading guidelines (which have led to heightened fears of a market slowdown). Equally important has been the high leverage in the market, which has increased margin calls and pushed down the market even further.

Yet, many of those charged with economic management in Jordan have tended to put forward the notion that barring a few mishaps the strong growth dynamic is set to continue. Consumption and investment demand will be fed by record levels of workers remittances from the Gulf and augmented by strong growth in the services sector. Buoyant Iraqi import demand will also have a positive impact on services earnings. Investments in power generation and telecommunications should remain firm, though as mentioned in a recent report on Jordan by the Economist Intelligence Unit, broader public investment is set to be scaled back slightly. Meanwhile, a boom in the construction and real estate sectors is being fuelled by very strong local demand and by Iraqi nationals, other Arabs and extra-regional foreign firms establishing bases in Jordan (in order to continue benefiting from Iraqi business at lower security risks). These dynamics are expected to continue in 2007. The tourism sector is also expected to show robust growth, and is likely to ride out the impact of the November 2005 blasts and the recent Israeli onslaught on Lebanon. The latter factor, complicated recently by internal Lebanese instability, may in fact prove to be a boon to tourism in Jordan, with many of the regional travellers choosing Amman over Beirut in the next few months.

The overall picture for the Jordanian economy can get murky if economic fundamentals depart from their anticipated trajectories and/or if the geopolitics of the region move against it. The wild cards for 2007 include, in addition to an Israeli-induced US attack on Iran and/or Syria, major terrorist attacks in Jordan, a further deterioration of the situation in Iraq, further rises in energy prices, big jumps in inflation, the out-migration of QIZ investors, fluctuations in private capital inflows, stock market volatility, an increase in the debt burden and a slowdown in the pace of privatization. For now, the Jordanian economy can keep steaming ahead. One day, the investment boom will cool, but not yet. Much hope lies in reform acceleration.

1.4

Jordan Facts and Figures

Highlights

- In spite of the various challenges faced in 2005, the Jordanian economy succeeded in achieving real GDP growth of around 7.2 per cent, buoyed by strong domestic consumer demand along with the 135 per cent rise in foreign direct investment. Consequently, real GDP per capita witnessed a 4.8 per cent increase to reach US $1,883 implying an advancement in overall living standards. During the first 6 months of 2006, real GDP reached US $5,174 million, a 6.4 per cent growth compared to the same period last year.
- Jordan's current account and overall budget recorded deficits of US $2,260 million and US $672 million, respectively, in 2005, affected by soaring oil prices and the sharp drop in foreign grants. This widening budget deficit prompted authorities to implement plans to reduce fuel subsidies and impose further fiscal adjustments, which led to a budget surplus of US $102 million during the first 6 months of 2006.
- Though growth in exports reached 10.8 per cent during 2005, it was outpaced by imports growth of 28.4 per cent, thus widening the trade balance deficit by 44.2 per cent to reach US $6,196 million. The first half of 2006 followed the same trend with imports exceeding exports by US $3,306 million.
- Exports to the United States, Jordan's number one export destination, represented 29.4 per cent of total exports through June 2006. In terms of products, textiles were by far the most significant export commodity contributing 28.8 per cent of total exports. On the imports front, Saudi Arabian imports constituted the largest share of total imported goods, accounting for around 26.6 per cent. As expected, crude oil's share of total imports increased to 18.0 per cent compared to 13.2 per cent and 16.3 per cent in 2004 and 2005, respectively.
- The nominal US dollar to Jordanian dinar peg (1 Jordanian dinar = US $0.709) remained stable during 2005, while the steady appreciation of the US dollar against all major currencies translated into an appreciation of the Jordanian dinar with respect to these currencies. This provided for cheaper imports and less attractive exports, in addition to lowering the country's foreign debt burden

largely denominated in euros. These effects were reversed in part during the first half of 2006 as the US dollar depreciated vis-á-vis the euro and British pound.

- The country's growing labour force led to a higher unemployment rate of around 14.8 per cent in 2005, requiring the government to direct more attention towards job creation activities. The inflation rate as measured by the growth in the consumer price index (CPI) reached 3.5 per cent in 2005. Moreover, last year's rising energy costs and strong growth dynamic have shown significant effects on consumer prices during the first half of 2006, as indicated by the further 6.2 per cent increase recorded in the CPI compared to the same period of 2005.
- The Amman Stock Exchange (ASE) performed exceptionally well during 2005, with the ASE index consistently reaching new highs throughout the year. The ASE closed the year at 8,191.5 points, a 92.9 per cent increase compared to the close of 2004. Market capitalization more than doubled to reach US $37.612 billion by year-end, an increase of 104.6 per cent. However, the ASE witnessed a sharp correction during the first half of 2006 as the index and market capitalization dropped by 26.1 per cent and 15.4 per cent, respectively.

	2005
Geography	
Surface (km²)	89,342
Coast Length (km)	26
Maximum Altitude: Um Dami Mount (m)	1,854
Lowest Point in the World: Dead Sea (in metres below sea level)	416
Average Temperature (degrees centigrade)	23.6
Demography	
Population (million)	5.473
Population Growth Rate	2.3%
Population Density (per km²)	61.26
Urban Population	82.6%
Total Number of Households	1,130,518
Average Size of Households	5.4
Life Expectancy at Birth (years)	71.5
Male (years)	70.6
Female (years)	72.4
Birth Rate (births/1,000 population)	28
Death Rate (deaths/1,000 population)	7
Age Structure	
0–14 years	37.1%
15–64 years	59.1%
65 years and over	3.8%

Unemployment

Unemployment Rate	14.8%
Male	12.8%
Female	25.9%

Education

Adult Literacy Rate	91.1%
Male	95.2%
Female	87.0%

Natural Resources

Phosphates, Potash, Shale Oil

Infrastructure

Paved Roads (km)	7,596
Railways (km)	621

Airports: Queen Alia International Airport, Amman Marka International Airport, Aqaba International Airport

Port: Aqaba Port

General

Currency: Jordanian dinar

Official language: Arabic (English is widely spoken)

Business Hours

Government: 08.00 am to 03.00 pm, Sunday through Thursday

Bank's counters: 08.30 am to 03.00 pm, Sunday through Thursday

	2004	2005	1H 2006
Macroeconomic Indicators			
Nominal GDP at Market Prices (US dollars, in million)	11,398	12,711	6,705
Real GDP Growth Rate at Market Prices	8.4%	7.2%	6.4%*
Real GDP per Capita (US dollars)	1,797	1,883	N/A
Inflation Rate (change in GDP deflator)	3.1%	4.0%	N/A
Newly Registered Companies by Economic Activity			
Agriculture	55	100	86
Industry	981	1,127	785
Construction	112	202	146
Trade	2,986	3,272	2,143
Other Services	2,398	3,005	1,834
Total	6,532	7,706	4,994
Total Capital (US dollars, in million)	563	1,199	942
Agriculture			
Agricultural Exports (US dollars, in million)	283	388	201
Agricultural Exports/Total Exports	8.71%	10.70%	10.28%
Construction			
Number of Construction Permits	27,064	25,683	12,283

Area (1,000 m²), of which	9,974	12,231	6,232
Amman (1,000 m²)	6,353	8,144	4,281
Irbid (1,000 m²)	1,092	1,062	499
Zarqa (1,000 m²)	833	947	453
Mining and Quarrying			
Potash	1,929	1,829	862
(1,000 tonnes)			
Phosphate (1,000 tonnes)	6,223	6,375	3,002
Potash and Phosphate Exports (US dollars, in million)	397	445	180
Potash and Phosphate Exports/Total Exports	12.19%	12.27%	9.20%
Manufacturing (1,000 tonnes)			
Fertilizers	779	790	419
Chemical Acids	1,651	1,614	818
Clinker	3,401	3,375	1,604
Cement	3,908	4,046	1,902
Petroleum Products	3,947	4,214	2,042
Transport			
Aqaba Port Activity:			
Number of Vessels	2,888	2,933	1,357
Number of Passengers	879,534	921,722	475,469
Merchandise (1,000 tonnes)	21,036	20,430	9,907

*Year-on-year growth for the first 6 months of 2006.

	2004	2005	1H 2006
Textiles			
Textile Exports (US dollars, in million)	1,000	1,051	562
Textile Imports (US dollars, in million)	151	197	118
Pharmaceutical			
Pharmaceutical Exports (US dollars, in million)	223	280	155
Pharmaceutical Imports (US dollars, in million)	236	264	138
Tourism			
Number of Tourists (million)	2.85	2.98	1.30
Tourist Receipts (US dollars, in million)	1,330	1,441	653
Tourist Receipts/GDP	11.67%	11.34%	9.74%
Energy			
Electricity Generated (million KWh)	8,709	9,359	4,280
Crude Oil Imports (US dollars, in million)	1,082	1,711	1,013
External Sector (US dollars, in million)			
Domestic Exports	3,253	3,625	1,952
Re-exports	630	676	364
Total Exports	3,883	4,301	2,316

Imports (including imports of non-resident agencies)	8,179	10,498	5,622
Total External Trade	11,433	14,123	7,574
Trade Balance	(4,296)	(6,196)	(3,306)
Exports to Main Trade Partners			
United States	31.31%	30.74%	29.38%
Iraq	15.69%	14.77%	13.51%
India	7.73%	9.59%	9.02%
Saudi Arabia	6.00%	6.70%	7.83%
United Arab Emirates	8.15%	8.74%	6.60%
Imports from Main Trade Partners			
Saudi Arabia	19.77%	23.62%	26.59%
China	8.44%	9.23%	9.35%
Germany	6.81%	8.02%	8.29%
United States	6.79%	5.60%	4.63%
Egypt	3.70%	3.50%	4.23%
Main Exports			
Clothes	30.74%	29.00%	28.80%
Pharmaceutical Products	6.87%	7.72%	7.95%
Vegetables	5.54%	6.17%	6.17%
Potash	7.09%	7.63%	5.09%
Fertilizers	5.37%	4.77%	4.94%
Main Imports			
Crude Oil	13.23%	16.30%	18.02%
Transport Equipment and Spare Parts	9.06%	9.57%	10.25%
Textiles, Yarn and Fabrics	7.91%	6.50%	6.52%
Telecommunication Equipment	3.64%	4.95%	4.69%
Petroleum Products	3.56%	4.28%	4.19%

	2004	2005	1H 2006
Balance of Payments (US dollars, in million)			
Current Account, of which	(2)	(2,260)	(1,533)
Trade Balance	(3,378)	(5,016)	(2,680)
Services Account	(73)	(208)	(236)
Current Transfers	3,216	2,588	1,151
Capital and Financial Account, of which	(454)	1,368	1,475
Foreign Direct Investment	651	1,532	1,976
Reserve Assets	(81)	(2)	(173)
Public Finance (US dollars, in million)			
Government Domestic Revenues, of which	3,028	3,613	2,364
Tax Revenues	2,015	2,491	1,609
Foreign Grants	1,144	706	155
Government Expenditures, of which	4,486	4,991	2,417
Interest Payments (commitment basis)	323	377	202
Budget Deficit/Surplus (commitment basis)	(313)	(672)	102
Rescheduled Interest	96	85	36

Budget Deficit/Surplus (cash basis)	(217)	(588)	138
Net Total Debt, of which	10,131	10,569	10,705
Net Internal Debt	2,587	3,437	3,403
Foreign Debt (including collateralized Brady Bonds)	7,544	7,132	7,301
Monetary Situation (US dollars, in million)			
M1 (currency in circulation + Jordanian dinar demand deposits)	4,503	5,728	6,239
M2 (M1+quasi-money)	14,910	17,439	18,703
Counterparts of M2			
Net Foreign Assets	8,289	8,526	9,160
Net Domestic Assets, of which	6,621	8,912	9,544
Claims on the Public Sector	2,574	3,233	3,247
Claims on the Private Sector	8,300	10,816	12,696
Other items – Net	(4,253)	(5,137)	(6,399)
CBJ Certificates of Deposit	3,574	3,215	3,006
Commercial Banks' Legal Reserves at the CBJ	638	798	844
Commercial Banks' Excess Reserves at the CBJ	568	665	649
Gross Official Reserves of Foreign Currencies	4,824	4,744	4,908
Prices and Wages			
CPI (2002=100)	105.0	108.7	113.5
Percentage Change	3.4%	3.5%	6.2%
Minimum Wage (US dollars)	120	134	155
US Dollar and Jordanian Dinar Exchange Rate (fixed)	0.709	0.709	0.709

	2004	2005	1H 2006
ASE: Basic Figures			
Number of Listed Companies	192	201	214
Market Capitalization (US dollars, in million)	18,383	37,612	31,815
Market Capitalization/GDP	185%	327%	247%
Value Traded (US dollars, in million)	5,350	23,795	11,259
Number of Shares Traded (million)	1,339	2,583	1,916
ASE General Weighted Price Index (points)	4,245.6	8,191.5	6,055.0
ASE General Un-weighted Price Index (points)	1,535.9	2,171.0	1,717.6
Non-Jordanian Ownership of Market Capitalization	41%	45%	44%
Net Investment of Non-Jordanians (US dollar, in million)	97	583	210
P/E ratio (times)	31.1	44.2	18.2
P/BV ratio (times)	2.7	3.2	3.2
Banking System			
Number of Licensed Banks	24	23	23

Activity Highlights (US dollars, in million)

Total Assets	25,136	29,741	32,246
Gross Direct Credit Facilities	8,729	10,923	13,047
Total Liabilities, of which	22,492	26,564	27,896
Total Deposits	16,310	18,504	19,439
Capital, Reserves and Allowances	2,644	3,177	4,350

Interest Rate Structure (per cent)

	2004	2005	1H 2006
Overnight Deposit Window Rate	2.25	4.50	5.25
Re-discount Rate	3.75	6.50	7.50
Repo Rate	4.75	7.50	8.50
Weighted Average Interest Rate on Time Deposits	2.49	3.52	4.50
Weighted Average Interest Rate on Overdrafts	8.79	9.26	8.69
Weighted Average Interest Rate on Loans and Advances	7.59	8.10	8.02
Prime Lending Rate	6.00	7.00	6.75

Top 10 Banks by Shareholders' Equity as of 30 June 2006 (US dollars, in million)

	Equity	Assets	Market Capitalization (29 June 2006)
1. Arab Bank plc	4,152.8	25,818.7	12,461.5
2. Housing Bank for Trade and Finance	1,102.9	5,423.1	2,780.7
3. Jordan National Bank	258.4	2,355.9	446.0
4. Jordan Kuwait Bank	230.5	2,164.3	607.2
5. Capital Bank of Jordan	198.2	1,249.8	326.9
6. Cairo Amman Bank	186.1	1,598.6	395.1
7. Bank of Jordan	179.1	1,822.8	390.6
8. Union Bank for Saving and Investment	142.0	1,075.8	285.5
9. Jordan Islamic Bank for Finance and Investment	111.4	1,928.6	240.5
10. Jordan Investment & Finance Bank	101.3	872.5	163.2

1.5

Government Planning

The Ministry of Planning and International Cooperation

Over the past eight years Jordan has embarked on a comprehensive political, social and economic reform agenda, with the aim of building a modern state based on economic vitality with substantial potential for growth and prosperity, political inclusion and social stability.

Jordan has come to realise its vision of becoming an active contributor to the global economy with the aim of achieving sustainable economic development, propelling export-led growth and an enabling investment environment. Accordingly, Jordan has made great strides in opening up and liberalising its economy, notably in investment and trade-related legislation, and in its privatisation programme. The country is open to foreign investment and the investment climate is favourable. To this end, the reform agenda has clearly corresponded to the evolving global trends, and success has been attained in moulding a lucrative investment climate, in which businesses can thrive by tapping into the vast world market.

Jordan has also witnessed an accelerated economic reform process through dynamic privatisation schemes and rapid integration into the global economy as evident by the country's accession to the World Trade Organization and the signing of a series of international and regional free trade arrangements such as the EU-Jordan Association Agreement, the European Free Trade Association, the US-Jordan Free Trade Agreement, the Arab Free Trade Agreement, Free Trade Agreement with Singapore and the Mediterranean Arab Free Trade Area (Aghadir Process). The main goal is to focus on export expansion through competitiveness and minimised government intervention, so allowing market forces to shape the future of Jordan, integrating the private sector into the highest policy-making framework and facilitating private sector led growth.

Moreover, new export platforms were developed such as the Aqaba Special Economic Zone, Qualifying Industrial Zones (QIZs), Industrial Estates and Free Zones that offer: world class investment infrastructure, free access to major world markets and lucrative investment incentive packages.

The commitment to attract direct investment is coupled with a comprehensive public sector reform programme, including legislative, administrative and judicial reforms to enhance the efficiency of the public sector, improve the investment environment and ensure the strict and transparent implementation of the rule of law. Legislative reforms included amending and enacting numerous laws and regulations, as well as the streamlining of investment related laws. As for monetary and fiscal reforms, efforts have been undertaken by the Government of Jordan in order to strengthen fiscal discipline, reform the tax system, maintain a stable exchange rate and sustain a high level of foreign currency reserves.

In the area of good governance and political and social inclusion, Jordan is moving ahead with a wide range of reforms aimed at increased transparency, broadening public participation in the decision making process, promoting judicial independence, promoting greater accountability of the government and combating corruption.

In this context, the Government of Jordan has adopted a number of laws and measures that were approved by Parliament, such as the Financial Disclosure Law and the Anti Corruption Commission Law. A number of laws were also ratified by Parliament concerning human rights, including the National Human Rights Centre Law that provides the Centre with full authority to promote a human rights' culture, protect and provide consultation and legal assistance and observe human rights violations. Moreover, equal opportunities and gender mainstreaming are cross-cutting issues on Jordan's reform agenda and development vision.

On another front, human resource development has always ranked high on the reform agenda, as enhancing the quality of investment in human capital will affect Jordan's ability to transform itself into a knowledge-based economy. Policy measures aimed at channelling additional qualitative investment in education and vocational training to match the output of the education and training systems and the requirements of the labour market were also undertaken. One important element of the education reform effort is institutionalising a mechanism that fosters innovation and excellence in education, which is an essential element in the realisation of Jordan's development vision.

Since the private sector is regarded as the key engine for growth and the driving force of the economy, the Government of Jordan is keen on continuous development of a partnership with the private sector, as well as with civil society, to reach a national consensus on the path that Jordan is to take to realise its developmental objectives. This has been evident in a number of initiatives, such as the first and second national economic forums held in 1999 and 2001, the establishment of the Economic Consultative Council and, more recently, the National Agenda and Kuluna Al Urdun (We are all Jordan) initiative.

Despite regional instability, favourable results at the macroeconomic level have been achieved over the past few years. GDP has been growing steadily scoring 6.4% growth in 2006, while domestic exports increased to US$4.1 billion during the same year. Official foreign currency reserves presently stand at US$6.4 billion (providing around six months of import cover). Market capitalization of locally quoted companies rose to US$29.7 billion during 2006 while private investment reached US$2.5 billion, compared to US$1.05 billion in 2005, and US$589 million in 2004. The fastest growing sectors in 2006 were the manufacturing industry (16.7%), construction (13.1%), telecommunications and transport (11.8%), electricity and water (10.7%), wholesale, retail, restaurants and hotels (9.9%), and the financial and real estate sectors (9.4%).

In spite of the encouraging macroeconomic achievements, Jordan continues to face a number of critical challenges most importantly, poverty and unemployment. However, Jordan realises the importance of maintaining the thrust of its bold reform agenda. Achieving sustained growth with enhanced competitiveness, equitable distribution of gains, as well as transforming Jordan from a lower-middle income country into a modern knowledge-based economy with increased productivity and employment continue to be at the core of Jordan's long-term development vision. This vision is emphasised in the National Agenda and Kuluna al Urdun initiative, which is a framework for Jordan's future plan for reform and development in all sectors that was developed through a private-public partnership.

In November 2005, Jordan developed a comprehensive strategy known as the "National Agenda" that supports bold reform and modernisation of the country's economic, institutional and political infrastructure. The main goal of the National Agenda is to improve the quality of life of Jordanians through the creation of income-generating opportunities, the improvement of standards of living and the guarantee of social welfare where it is most needed.

However, to ensure real ownership of the reform process, the Kuluna al Urdun initiative was launched by His Majesty King Abdullah II in July 2006, engaging over 700 Jordanians from all walks of life and from all political parties and parliamentary blocks, thereby bringing together representatives from across Jordanian society to develop consensus on the future reform agenda of the country. Kuluna al Urdun seeks to ensure that Jordanian society as a whole contributes to and supports the country's bold reform and modernisation efforts.

Moreover, from 2007 Kuluna al Urdun will encourage active participation by the Jordanian people in Jordan's development process. It will also provide an overarching framework for all reform initiatives including the National Agenda. A major addition to this process is the involvement of youth in the debate on reforms through the Youth Commission of

Kuluna al Urdun. National priorities that Jordanians seek to achieve over the coming few years include strengthening the internal front, political reforms, economic reforms, social stability, regional challenges and detailed attention to the Palestinian cause.

Within this context, priority reforms, key development projects and time-bound action plans were identified in the areas of political development and inclusion, legislation and justice, investment development, fiscal discipline and financial services, employment support and vocational training, social welfare, education, higher education, scientific research and innovation and the up-grading of the infrastructure. Accordingly, to ensure the momentum of reform continues, a 3-year Executive Program (2007-2009) for the Kuluna Al-Urdun/National Agenda Initiative has been charged with keeping the reform initiatives focused on concrete actions, with related budget allocations.

The Executive Program was conceived on a holistic basis, to better define comprehensive strategies and initiatives with a view to realising social, economic and political development. It presents a list of reforms and measures to be undertaken in different fields including the investment framework, fiscal policy, good governance, justice, employment and education policies, basic rights and freedom, as well as services and infrastructure.

Carrying out the reform agenda as in the Executive Program will be imperative in enabling Jordan to achieve real progress in socioeconomic development. The future development agenda will continue to focus on sustaining the thrust of the socioeconomic reform process in order to achieve sustainable development at the micro and macro levels. Indeed, enhancing the investment climate and preparing the legal and institutional frameworks to enable further private investment, both local and foreign, in the Jordanian economy represent a major component of this Executive Program.

The rigorous agenda for financial and administrative reforms, as well as the adoption of policies that would encourage further private sector investment and export-oriented strategies, will further facilitate the transition into an investment-driven and knowledge-based economy. Therefore, the Government of Jordan will continue to engage the private sector as a vital partner in the development process of the country in order to encourage market openness and global integration, as well as create an environment conducive to business investment.

1.6

The Growing Role of Industry – A Statistical Overview

Juma Abu-Hakmeh, Former Director General of the Amman Chamber of Industry

Introduction

Industry plays a key role in the process of modernization and economic development as it provides the framework within which national resources and factors of production are utilized, know-how acquired, technology transferred and new skills developed. It links all the economic activities of society together and interacts with all sections in meaningful ways.

Industry is one of the key contributors to economic growth and main generators of national income in Jordan. Some 25.7 per cent of Jordan's GDP in 2005 or US $2.8 billion was contributed by the relatively fast-growing industrial sector. More importantly, industry contributes about 90 per cent of the total value of national exports, a very significant and welcome phenomenon for a country keen to establish itself in world markets.

Jordanian industry has also developed a significant degree of diversity. The Amman Chamber of Industry classifies its associated range of productive activities into 10 sub-sectors. These include several traditional sectors, such as the mining of national resources (potash and phosphate), and a number of new ones, such as engineering and manufacturing industries that provide products to meet consumer needs and other requirements, both local and export. The total value of national industrial exports reached about US $3.61 billion in 2005 of which US $3.2 billion was made up of industrial products. These figures are especially significant in that they indicate an advance beyond the previous reliance

on mining industries for export earnings, diversifying into industries
that rely on know-how, technology and human skills.

The Industrial Sector: Basic Indicators (2002)

Number of Firms	28,000*
Number of Employees	180,000
Industrial Exports (US dollars, in million)	3,300
Employee Salaries and Compensation (US dollars, in million)	650
Ratio of Industrial Exports to National Exports	90%
Contribution of Manufacturing to GDP	20.6%
Contribution of Mining	2.4%
Contribution of Electricity	2.7%

*Industrial production index 1999 = 100

	2003	2004	2005
Mining and Quarrying	109.3	105.4	103.8
Manufacturing Industry	117.1	133.4	148.8
Food Products	113.2	130.8	155.1
Paints	140.5	186.3	220
Pharmaceuticals	123.1	134.7	163.2

Quantities produced by major industries

	2003 (1,000 tonnes)	2004 (1,000 tonnes)	2005 (1,000 tonnes)
Mining and Quarrying			
Phosphate	6,762	6,223	6,375
Potash	1,961	1,929	1,829
Fertilizers	634	779	790
Chemical Acids	1,499	1,651	1,614
Cement	3,515	3,908	4,046
Electricity	7,721 (million KWh)	9,109 (million KWh)	9,359 (million KWh)

Source: Amman Chamber of Industry.

Experience and access to foreign markets

Aware of the small size of Jordan's economy and endeavouring to reach new markets, Jordanian companies have developed excellent knowledge of the markets of the Middle East and North Africa, and especially of Arab countries, over the years. They exploit not only their cultural affinity in the region, but also the easy access by land, air and sea. What makes this access even more attractive is the fact that Jordan has developed, over the last two decades, a network of bilateral agreements of counter-trade with several major countries in the region. Jordan joined the Euro-Mediterranean agreement, the World Trade Organization, the Great Arab Free Trade Agreement, the EFTA Trade Agreement and the Jordan–US Free Trade Agreement, which together provide links through Jordan to other countries worldwide.

Main industrial exports

Jordan's main industrial exports include phosphates, potash, medicines, fertilizers, detergents and soap, cement, clothing, plastic products, paper and cardboard and paints. Total exports from industrial sectors in 2003, 2004 and 2005 were US $2,362 million, US $3,253 million and US $3,243 million, respectively. Overall growth over the period was 50 per cent in 2 years. The highest growth rate was seen in clothing, which alone accounted for actual growth of US $376 million or 34 per cent of the increase.

Main industrial exports (in millions of US dollars)

	2003	2004	2005
Clothing	675	1,000	1,051
Medical and Pharmacy Products	185	223	280
Potash	204	231	276
Phosphates	128	166	168
Vegetable Oils	48	145	85
Phosphoric Acid	85	90	98
Cleaning and Perfume	67	69	56
Paper and Cardboard	43	50	63
Beverages and Tobacco	63	59	68
Cement	41	30	17
Buses	10	19	23
Plastic Products	5	5	8
Industrial Exports	2,150	2,984	3,243
National Exports	2,362	3,253	3,624

Destination of exports

- 41% of all exports go to other Arab countries, of which fruit and vegetables alone account for 16%, with the remainder coming from a range of industrial products.
- 30% go to the United States, of which more than 90% is apparel from the qualifying industrial zones.
- 14% go to Southeast Asia, mainly phosphates, potash and fertilizers.
- 3% go to members of the European Union.
- 12% go to other countries.

Jordan–US Trade: Qualifying Industrial Zones and the Free Trade Agreement

Jordan benefits from many preferential agreements and programmes when exporting to the United States.

Qualified industrial zone agreement

Definition

Qualified industrial zones (QIZs) are areas designated by local authorities and approved by the US government, where the products of these zones, meeting certain requirements, can be exported duty free to the United States under the terms of the Israel Free Trade Area Agreement with the United States.

The QIZ agreement, signed between Jordan and Israel in Doha in November 1997, allows products of designated QIZ areas, after fulfilling the agreement's requirements, instant duty-free entry into the United States. This agreement has generated a huge amount of economic activity. It attracted foreign direct investments of over US $750 million from China, Hong Kong, Taiwan, Turkey, India, Pakistan, Bangladesh, Sri Lanka, UAE, the United States and the United Kingdom, as well as Jordan. Exports to the United States multiplied, attracting international buyers, including JC Penney, Levi's, Wal-Mart, Target, Liz Claiborne, Nautica, the Banana Republic and many others.

These zones' purpose includes the following:

- Encouraging peace in the region.
- Stimulating the Jordanian economy by increasing exports to US markets.
- Creating jobs for Jordanians, improving the life of thousands of workers especially those from rural areas and empowering women.

A product is eligible for duty-free entry to the United States (rules of origin requirements) under the QIZ agreement if:

1. *It is wholly the growth, product or the manufacture of the QIZ.
2. *The sum of:

a) the cost or value of the materials produced in the QIZ, the West Bank, the Gaza Strip or Israel, and
b) the direct cost of processing operations performed in the QIZ, West Bank, the Gaza Strip or Israel, which should not be less than 35 per cent of the appraised values (ex-factory FOB price).

3. *It is imported directly from the QIZ or Israel.
4. *It is substantially transformed, meaning the product is a new and different article of commerce.

Simple combination or packaging operations or mere dilution with water or another substance are not considered substantial transformation.

The requirements for the qualification of a product under the QIZ agreement are as follows:

Method 1:

1. *11.7 per cent of content must be added by the Jordanian manufacturer in the QIZ (1/3 of the 35 per cent)
2. *11.7 per cent of content must be added by the Israeli manufacturer (1/3 of the content). This requirement was reduced to 8 per cent and 7 per cent for high-tech products for a period of 5 years starting February 1999 and ending February 2004.
3. *The remainder of the 35 per cent can come from the QIZ, Israel, Gaza Strip or the United States (with a maximum of 15 per cent from the United States).

For this method, only direct costs are applied to the calculation of the content.

Method 2:

Jordanian and Israeli manufacturers must each contribute at least 20 per cent of the total cost of production of the QIZ product. For this method, both direct and indirect costs are applied to the calculation of the content.

Method 3 (mixing and matching of the above two alternatives):

One side contributes to the content as per Method 1 above and the other side contributes to the total cost of production as per Method 2.

For textiles and apparel produced under this agreement, rules of origin set out in section 334 of the Uruguay Round Agreement Act, 19 USC 3592, apply.

Types of QIZs

Currently there are 13 QIZs located throughout Jordan: 3 located in publicly run industrial estates and 10 privately owned.

Public QIZs

1. Al-Hassan Industrial Estate

The world's first QIZ was designated in March 1998 and is located near Irbid, 80 km north of Amman. Total area: 1,005,000 m². www.jiec.com, e-mail: info@jiec.com.jo.

2. Al-Hussein Bin Abdullah II Industrial Estate (Karak)

Al-Karak, the second QIZ, is located 110 km south of Amman and is linked by highway to the port of Aqaba on the Red Sea. Total area: 580,000 m². www.jiec.com, e-mail: karak@jiec.com.jo.

3. Aqaba QIZ

Located in the Aqaba Special Economic Zone.

Private QIZs

1. Al-Dulayl Industrial Park

Al-Dulayl Industrial Park is located in central Jordan. Easily accessible by highway, only 45 km northeast of Amman. Total area: 720,000 m². www.Ad-Dulayl.com, e-mail: Ad-Dulayl@nets.com.jo.

2. Al-Tajamouat Industrial Park

A privately owned industrial estate in Jordan located 20 km from downtown Amman and 26 km from Queen Alia International Airport. Total area: 300,000 m². www.altajamouat.com, e-mail: info@altajamouat.com.

3. Gateway Park

Gateway Park is located within a free zone in northern Jordan, 8 km south of Sheikh Hussein Bridge and 90 km from Amman. Total area: 50,000 m². www.jordan-gateway.com, e-mail: gateway@go.com.jo.

4. Cyber City Park

An information technology and light industrial park with QIZ and special export free zone status. The 4 km^2 is located near Irbid. www.cybercity.com.jo, e-mail: info@cybercity.com.jo.

5. Hashemite University

An industrial park located near Zarqa. Total area: 1,500,000 m^2. www.hillwood.com, e-mail: sahar.aloul@hillwood.com.jo.

6. Al-Qastal Industrial Park

A privately owned industrial park located 3 km from Queen Alia International Airport and 22 km south of Amman. Total area: 4,000 km^2. E-mail: info@utg.com.jo.

7. Al-Mushata Qualified Industrial Complex

Al-Mushata QIZ is located in Quneitra, east of Queen Alia International Airport. Total area: 4,000 km^2. E-mail: uai@nets.com.jo.

8. Hillwood Hashemite University

Hillwood Hashemite University is located at al-Zarka Hashemite University. E-mail: huniv@hu.edu.jo.

9. Al-Hallabat Industrial Park

Al-Hallabat Industrial Park is located in Ad-Dulayl. E-mail: invest@hallabat.com.

10. Al-Mawarid

Al-Mawarid, the Resources Company for Development & Investment, is located in Mawaqar. E-mail: mail@madaen.com.

The FTA agreement

The main and most important agreement between Jordan and the United States is the Jordan–US Free Trade Area Agreement (JUSFTA) that was signed on 24 October 2000 and came into effect on 17 December 2001. Jordan is the fourth country to have signed a free trade agreement with the United States after Israel (1985), Canada (1989) and NAFTA (the North American Free Trade Agreement with Canada and Mexico, 1994). The United States has since signed many free trade area agreements with other countries and regions, including Chile, Singapore, Bahrain, Morocco, Australia, CAFTA (the Central America Free Trade Area) and many more.

Overview of the articles covered by the FTA agreement

- Trade in goods: Reciprocal tariff reductions over 10 years
- Trade in services: Services covered include business, communication, construction, engineering services, education, environmental, health and social services, tourism, transport services
- Bilateral e-commerce: Encouragement and facilitation of e-commerce
- Relations on intellectual property rights:
  - c) Trademarks
  - d) Copyrights
  - e) Patents
- Relations on environment and labour: Standards will not be lowered to facilitate trade
- Visa commitments
- Safeguards and countervailing measures: Against serious injury, conformity within the World Trade Organization (WTO), recognizing infant industries
- Topics related to the administration of JUSFTA relations in accordance with the provisions of the agreement
- Economic cooperation and technical assistance

JUSFTA aims at the elimination of custom duties over a period of 10 years, reaching mutual duty-free status in 2010. Further, it was agreed to consider the period from 17 December 2001 till December 2001 as a full year, thus as of 1 January 2006, custom duties have reached their sixth year of elimination.

The FTA staging categories (Scenarios for custom duties elimination) is as follows:

Category	Tariff Base Rate	Tariff Reduction Scenario
A	<5%	50% reduction per year
		Duty free since 1 January 2002
B	5–10%	25% reduction per year
		Duty free since 1 January 2004
C	10–20%	20% reduction per year
		Duty free since 1 January 2005
D	>20%	10% reduction per year
		Duty free on 1 January 2010
E		WTO duty elimination commitments for
		Jordan and the United States

Comparison between QIZ and FTA agreements

Criteria	QIZ	JUFTA
Type of Agreement	Unilateral – granted for Jordanian exports of goods	Bilateral – covers trade in goods and services
Legal Framework	Israeli–US FTA of 1985, Presidential Proclamation 6955, November 1996 (based on the US–Israeli FTA)	JUFTA, in effect since 17 December 2001
Preferential Tariff Provision	Immediate tariff-free access for manufactured goods qualified for compliance with the RO	Gradual phase out of tariffs over a period of 10 years (2001–10)
Activities Covered	Only manufacturing	Manufacturing and services
Designated Areas	Defined areas within the country, approved by USTR as QIZs	Entire country
Eligibility Criteria for Trade in Goods	1. Wholly the growth, product or the manufacture of a QIZ, or substantially transformed. The sum of the cost or value of the materials produced in the QIZ, the West Bank, the Gaza Strip or Israel, plus the direct cost of processing operations performed in the QIZ, the West Bank, the Gaza Strip or Israel, is not less than 35%* of the appraised value. *Minimum 11.7% Jordanian, minimum 11.7% Israeli the remainder of the 35% can originate from the QIZ, Israel, Gaza Strip, the West Bank or the United States, with a maximum of 15% from the United States. Direct shipment from Jordan or Israel to the United States.	1. Wholly the growth, product or manufacture of one party, or substantially transformed. 2. The sum of the cost or value of the materials produced in one party, plus the direct cost of processing operations performed in that party is not less than 35% of the appraised value of the article. The cost or value of materials that are used in the production of an article in one party and that are products of the other party may be counted in an amount up to 15% of the appraised value of the article. 3. Direct shipment from one party to the other party.
Special Provisions	None	E-commerce, intellectual property rights, environment, labour, dispute settlement, safeguarding measures

Exports under both FTA and QIZ benefit from preferential custom duties rates of up to 32 per cent, depending on the product, when exported to the United States.

Some US special staging categories applied to Jordanian products:

Category	Products Affected (examples)	Tariff Reduction Scenario
F	Certain apparel items that were produced in the QIZs	No change in tariff until 1 January 2010, at which point all custom duties will be reduced to zero
G	GSP-eligible products	Duty free since the effective date of the agreement (17 December 2001) due to inclusion in the United States (GSP)

Many Jordanian products are also allowed duty-free access into the United States under the Generalized System of Preferences (GSP), which allows products from developing countries duty-free access to the markets of many developed countries.

Jordan, being a member of the WTO, allows its exports to benefit from custom duties preferences available to fellow members of the WTO and referred to as most favoured nation (MFN), or normal trade relations (NTR).

Jordanian products are exported under all the preferential programmes and agreements to the United States, with the highest dependence on the QIZ since it provides products with the highest custom duties an instant duty-free status (the highest custom duties in the US tariff is for garments, textiles and footwear). Since Jordan is not restricted by quotas on its exports to the United States, all the exports from the QIZ are garment products. Below is a table showing the Jordanian exports (in thousands of US dollars) to the United States as per agreement:

The above table shows the shift of Jordanian exports from the QIZ to the FTA. Now that it is in the fifth year of customs elimination, 98 per cent of Jordanian products can be exported duty free to the United States under the FTA. The fact that GSP-eligible items can also be exported duty free under the FTA has led to a shift to the latter category, since the FTA is more reliable than the GSP system. The GSP undergoes an annual product and country-eligibility review, under which countries can be eliminated from the list of eligible countries and products can be removed from the list of eligible products, thanks to ceilings imposed on GSP benefits for each product and country. The chart given below shows the Jordanian exports to the United States during 2001–05:

The United States is the largest export market for Jordan, amounting to 30 per cent of its domestic exports. The trade balance is in favour of Jordan, as shown below (in US dollars):

Comparison between QIZ and FTA agreements

Import Programme	2001	2002	2003	2004	2005	(1–7) 2005	(1–7) 2006	Per Cent Change (1–7) 2005 to (1–7) 2006
QIZ	180,787	369,455	563,928	927,330	945,018	526,913	572,287	8.60
FTA	0	12,601	27,910	20,695	246,462	107,700	169,271	57.20
NTR	38,850	24,050	46,397	54,755	63,922	40,661	37,682	−7.30
GSP	9,473	5,977	35,011	89,767	11,664	6,983	8,376	19.90
Total	229,110	412,084	673,290	1,092,575	1,267,068	682,257	787,618	15.44

Comparison between QIZ and FTA agreements

Year	2000	2001	2002	2003	2004	2005	(1–7) 2006
Imports from the United States	305,596,827	339,129,451	396,616,744	479,310,070	531,415,446	607,308,367	363,964,675
Exports to the United States	72,841,570	229,110,002	412,083,889	673,289,981	1,092,574,743	1,267,068	787,618,000
Trade Balance	−232,755,257	−110,019,449	15,467,145	193,979,911	561,159,297	660,215,792	423,653,325

Part 2

Sector Overviews

2.1

Electricity Sector in Jordan

Dr Hiyasat, National Electric Power Company

Introduction

Jordan is almost entirely dependent on imported oil to meet its commercial energy needs, importing about 7.028 million tonnes of oil equivalent (TOE) in 2005, up 8.3 per cent on the year before. The country's modest energy resources consist of small amounts of proven oil and natural gas reserves near the eastern border with Iraq and oil shale deposits (about 40 billion tonnes of proven reserves) mainly in the central part of the country. As a result of this situation, substantial efforts have been made to promote solar and wind energy.

The year in which the electricity industry in Jordan began is 1947. That year the first electric power company was established by private investors to generate and distribute electricity in the Amman area. This company is known as the Jordan Electrical Power Company (JEPCO). In 1961, another privately owned electric power company was established to serve the northern area of the country, called the Irbid District Electricity Company (IDECO). However, it was not until the 1960s that real development of national electrification began. It required huge investments outside the capabilities of the two private shareholding companies JEPCO and IDECO. Therefore, the government established the Jordan Electricity Authority (JEA) in 1967 as an independent government utility to take care of electricity generation and transmission all over Jordan, and to complete the electrification of the country outside the concession areas of JEPCO and IDECO, including the rural areas.

In 1984, the Ministry of Energy and Mineral Resources (MEMR) was established in order to formulate a coherent set of national policies to achieve energy security through improving efficiency, diversifying supply sources and ensuring the efficient and reliable operation of the entire energy system. In September 1996, JEA became a shareholding company owned completely by the government. The new company was named the National Electric Power Company (NEPCO), and was later to split into three companies.

In 2004 Samra Electric Power Generation Company (SEPGCO) was established as a private shareholding generation company, which started the production of electrical energy in the beginning of September 2005.

Jordan now has a modern electricity system including many power stations and a national network extending over almost all of the country, with the remaining areas likely to be covered in the very near future.

The following table shows the significant figures for the electricity sector in Jordan in 2004/2005.

Significant figures for electricity sector in Jordan

	2004	2005	Growth (per cent)
Peak Load of Jordan (MW)	1,555	1,751	12.6
Available Capacity (MW)	1,789	2,019	12.9
Generated Energy (GWh)	8,967	9,654	7.7
Steam Units	7,590	7,969	5.0
Diesel Units	75	73	—2.7
Gas Turbines/Diesel	464	341	—26.5
Gas Turbines/Natural Gas	776	648	—16.5
Hydro Units	53	57	7.5
Wind Energy	3	3	–
Biogas	6	5	—16.7
Combined Cycle*	–	558	–
Consumed Energy (GWh)	8,089	8,712	7.7
Energy Exported (GWh)	3.1	3.8	22.6
Energy Imported from Egypt (GWh)	788	741	—6.0
Energy Imported from Syria (GWh)	38	241	534.2
Loss Percentage	17.37	18.10	–
Average (kWh) Consumed per Capita	1,830	1,939	6.0
Electricity Fuel Consumption (thousands of tonnes)**	2,329	2,475	6.3
Heavy Fuel	936	809	—13.6
Natural Gas	1,234	1,428	15.7
Diesel	159	238	49.7
National Grid Transmission Lines			
132 kV and Above (km-circuit)	3,346	3,400	1.6
Substations Installed Capacities			
132/33 kV (MVA)	3,413	3,429	0.5
Number Of Consumers (thousands)	1,067	1,129	5.8
Population under Supply (thousands)	5,345	5,480	2.5
Percentage of Population under Supply			
All Jordan.	99.9	99.9	–
Rural	99.8	99.8	–
Number of Employees	6,992	7,200	3.0

*Rehab SS.
**Equivalent Heavy Fuel Oil.

The national electrical grid in Jordan

Privatization and restructuring programmes of the electricity sector

Background

The government of Jordan has encouraged private sector participation and ownership in several public sector institutions, in accordance with the Economic and Social Development Plan (1993–97). The plan was based on a range of basic principles, which determine the future course of the national economy. Some of these principles are related to the role of the private sector, namely:

- Reducing the government's role in direct production and enhancing the role of the private sector by improving incentives for domestic and foreign investment
- Activating the role of the private sector in the areas of infrastructure and basic services and increasing private sector participation in the management and ownership of public sector institutions on an equitable and well-considered basis

In conformance with this prevailing trend towards privatization and restructuring, the government has taken certain steps in reforming, restructuring and privatizing several sectors. Electricity was among the first major sectors appointed for privatization.

Policies of the privatization and restructuring programmes

The main policies of the privatization and restructuring programmes for the power sector in the areas of technical, administrative and financial activities are as follows:

- Utilizing of local energy sources including available natural gas as well as the imported energy resources for electricity generation on a commercial basis
- Encouraging of electrical interconnection links and power exchange with neighbouring countries
- Implementing load research and load management programmes to define the consumption patterns of consumer categories to reduce long-run investment in generation projects and to improve the system's performance

Objectives of the privatization and restructuring programmes

The major objectives of the privatization and restructuring programmes for the electricity sector in Jordan can be summarized as follows:

- To develop and maintain a supply of electricity to meet the needs of the people of Jordan on a continuous basis, at the lowest possible cost, giving attention to energy rationalization and environmental protection
- To develop, operate and maintain power plants and transmission and distribution networks to meet customers needs with high reliability and safety
- To develop, operate and maintain transmission and distribution networks to meet customers' needs with high reliability and safety
- To implement safety instructions, programmes and procedures to improve safety and security of all personnel and equipment and to have qualified, trained, motivated and productive manpower of the appropriate size and skills
- To achieve the planned financial targets agreed from time to time, and to acquire the financial requirements necessary to fulfil the operational and development plans for the sector's utilities on the best terms and conditions

Implementation mechanism of the privatization and restructuring programmes

In 1994, the Cabinet of Ministers decided to restructure JEA as a first step towards privatization of the electricity sector in Jordan. In September 1996 a new Electricity Law no. (10) was issued and, in accordance with this law, JEA was converted into a public shareholding company fully owned by the government and renamed the National Electric Power Company (NEPCO).

In 1997, the cabinet decided to proceed with the restructuring of NEPCO and the unbundling of its activities into three different functions: generation, transmission and distribution. Also, the cabinet decided that the construction of any new power station should be executed by the private sector (independent power producer (IPP)) through the (build, own, operate (BOO)) model.

The modified General Electricity Law no. (13) was issued in 1999 in order to ensure a suitably competitive environment encouraging the private sector to invest in developing electricity projects. To accomplish this in line with the new Electricity Law, NEPCO was restructured by dividing it into three companies, as follows:

- National Electric Power Company (NEPCO): responsible for transmission and control activities, besides responsibility for interconnection with neighbouring countries
- Central Electricity Generating Company (CEGCO): responsible for electricity production from the available power stations
- Electricity Distribution Company (EDCO): responsible for the distribution of electricity in the areas outside the concession of the two existing private distribution companies, mainly in southern and eastern areas and the Jordan Valley

NEPCO's assets were re-evaluated and divided between the three companies, each according to its activities and some of NEPCO's employees were transferred to CEGCO and EDCO. Since the beginning of 1999, the three companies have been working successfully as separate entities.

In February 2000, the MEMR appointed a consultancy firm to study and make recommendations on the tariffs to be applied between the different electricity companies, in identifying the technical boundaries between the three companies and the allocation of the loans payable by NEPCO to the three companies that resulted from its restructuring.

In 2001, and in accordance with the new General Electricity Law no. (13), a regulatory commission for the power sector was established. In December 2001, the MEMR appointed another consultancy firm to advise the government of Jordan on developing and implementing the strategy for the privatization of the government assets in CEGCO, EDCO and IDECO.

Strategy of the privatization and restructuring programmes

The privatization and restructuring programmes are being implemented to a defined strategy in two stages:

Stage I

- All viable privatization options of the above-mentioned companies will be analysed and evaluated
- The groupings of generation plant and distribution entities will be arranged so as to ensure successful privatization
- The legal and regulatory framework for the industry to support the efficient development and operation of the electricity sector will be put into place

Stage II

- All generation and distribution will be majority-owned and managed by private sector companies
- All new generation will be provided by the private sector
- The legal and regulatory framework for the industry will be designed to promote efficient development and operation of the sector whilst in private sector ownership
- The transmission activity performed by NEPCO will remain in government ownership

The General Electricity Law of 2003

The General Electricity Law was reviewed and amended by consultants and a new version of the law was issued in 2003, the main features of which are as follows:

- Electricity sector structure: According to the new electricity law, the following structure for the electricity sector in Jordan will be implemented:
  - Separate generation, transmission and distribution utilities. (Implemented)
  - Independent Electricity Sector Regulatory Commission (ERC). (Established)
  - MEMR with policy role and responsibility for IPPs.
  - Single buyer model, transition to bilateral contract.
  - Cost-reflective tariffs, by distribution companies.
- The role of MEMR: According to the new electricity law, the ministry shall assume the following mandate and powers:
  - To set and prepare the general policies of the sector and submit them to the council of ministers for approval in accordance with the needs of economic and social development in the kingdom, and to follow up the development of these policies.
  - To cooperate with other countries for the purpose of electrical interconnection and trading of electric power, as well as to conclude agreements necessary to that effect with the consent of the council of ministers, and to follow up performance of the contractual obligations with those countries.
  - To promote the interests of the kingdom with other countries and regional and international organizations on issues relating to electric power, and to represent the kingdom before such organizations.
  - To adopt the necessary measures for the provision of supplemental sources of generation of electric power in case of prolonged shortfalls if no alternative means to overcome the shortfall are available.

- ◆ To request the bulk supply licensee, if necessary, to provide fuel for electricity companies set for privatization and licensed for generation, whether before or after their privatization, and for independent power producers.
- ◆ To promote the use of renewable energy for generation.
- ◆ To recommend to the council of ministers to switch to a competitive electricity market pursuant to this law.
- The role of ERC: According to the new electricity law, the Electricity Sector Regulatory Commission will assume the following mandate and powers:
  - ◆ To license persons engaged in generation, transmission, supply, distribution and system operation.
  - ◆ To regulate persons engaged in generation, transmission, supply, distribution and system operation in the kingdom so as to provide reliable electricity services to consumers in an efficient and economic manner that accords with the developments in electricity technology, taking into account the provisions of this law.
  - ◆ To determine the electric tariff, subscription fees, services fees, disbursements, royalties and the connection charges to the transmission system and distribution system.
  - ◆ To participate in determining the technical standards relating to the electric appliances and electrical installations, by way of consulting with other concerned parties in order to have such standards issued by the Standards and Metrology Corporation.
  - ◆ To participate in determining the necessary requirements for the implementation of the environmental standards to which electrical installations ought to conform by way of consulting with other concerned parties and to have them issued according to the legislation in force.
  - ◆ To render expert advice and opinion on any issue that is related to the sector in a way that fulfils the commission's purposes and objectives.
  - ◆ To make recommendations to the ministry to switch from the single buyer model to a competitive electricity market structure in accordance with this law.
  - ◆ Any other activity or mandate pertaining to the functions of the commission pursuant to the provisions of this law.
- The licences: According to this new law a separate licence will be given to each activity as follows:
  - a) No person is allowed to construct, own or operate an undertaking or in any way engage in the business of generation, transmission, system operation, supply or distribution, except in accordance with a licence issued pursuant to this law or in accordance with a permission granted by the council of ministers in accordance with this law.

b) Notwithstanding paragraph (a) of this article, a person may without holding a licence:
  - Construct, own or operate an undertaking for generating electric power not exceeding 1 MW in aggregate at the same site.
  - Construct, own or operate an undertaking for distribution of electric power to serve a peak demand not exceeding 100 kW in aggregate at the same site.
  - Construct, own or operate an undertaking for auto-generation.
c) The Commission may, by a directive, grant exemption to a class of persons from the requirement of:
  - Having a generation licence for a power station with an installed capacity not exceeding 5 MW in aggregate at the same site, subject to compliance with such conditions as may be specified by the council for that purpose.
  - Having a supply licence, subject to compliance with such conditions as may be specified by the council for that purpose, provided that the council shall not grant any exemption in any area falling within the area of supply of a licensee except with the consent of that licensee.

The first private generation project

In 2006 MEMR in cooperation with NEPCO awarded the tender of the Amman East Power Generation Project to an American–Japanese consortium, to build a combined cycle power plant burning natural gas as the main fuel.

The generating capacity of the plant is 372 MW: two gas turbines at 124 MW each plus one steam turbine at 124 MW. The simple cycle of the project is to be completed by the summer of 2008, while the combined cycle (steam) will be done by the summer of 2009.

The project is based on BOO model, and a tolling power purchase agreement, among other agreements, will be signed between the consortium on the one side and NEPCO and other governmental institutions on the other side, after the financial closing of the project, which is expected in February 2007.

2.2

Agriculture and Agro-industry in Jordan

Dr Abdullah Arar, Land and Water Development Consultant

Background

People living and working in the rural environment form an important part of Jordanian society. They contribute to the national economy and rural development, play a role in enhancing social and economic stability and help to achieve food security and conserve natural resources and the environment. Agriculture constitutes the backbone of the rural economy and needs to receive the appropriate attention and support in order to sustain the rural population and their role. Therefore, the Ministry of Agriculture of Jordan has initiated an agricultural sector development programme for the period 2001–10 aimed at addressing the needs of rural people and contributing to balanced development in Jordan. In this chapter the relevant data available from this agricultural development programme have been used extensively.

The agricultural sector

The agricultural sector is of vital socio-economic importance for the rural population and at the same time is strongly interlinked with the natural environment.

Geography and climate

The total area of Jordan including the Dead Sea is about 90,000 square kilometres. The country can be divided into the following three main geographic and climatic zones:

1.The rift valley

The Jordan rift valley can be divided into the Jordan Valley, the Dead Sea and Wadi Araba. The Jordan Valley is the most fertile region in the kingdom. It is several degrees warmer than the rest of the country in winter, which permits year-round agricultural production. Fertile soil and extensive irrigation during the dry summer months along with irrigation that is supplementary to the rainfall in winter, which varies from 100 millimetres in the south to 300 millimetres in the north, have made the Jordan Valley the breadbasket of the country.

The Jordan Valley is divided into north and south Ghors, with the former extending from the northern border of Jordan down to the Dead Sea with altitudes ranging from 220 metres below sea level in the north to 407 metres below sea level at the Dead Sea. The area that has been developed in the valley has reached 360,000 dunums (1 dunum = 0.1 hectare) out of a total of 427,000 dunums and is mostly fully irrigated. The south Ghors are situated to the east and southeast of the Dead Sea and has about 64,000 dunums under irrigation.

2. The highlands

The highlands extend from the north to the south throughout the western part of Jordan and thus separate the Jordan rift valley from the eastern desert. Elevation in the highlands varies from 600 metres to about 1,500 metres above sea level. This area receives the highest rainfall in Jordan and is the most vegetated region in the country. However, due to the steep slopes and shallow soil over most parts of the region, the area with good agricultural soils is limited. About 90 per cent of Jordan's population lives in this region, which in agricultural terms has developed rapidly in the last 20 years as hundreds of thousands of olive trees and tens of thousands of fruit trees were planted. Afforestation programmes by the government have succeeded in increasing forest areas to 77,000 dunums (about 1 per cent of the country).

3. The eastern desert

The eastern desert comprises around 88 per cent of Jordan's total area with elevations varying between 600 and 900 metres above sea level. Rainfall is extremely low throughout the year ranging from 200 millimetres to zero precipitation, with an average of less than 50 millimetres annually.

The climate is generally arid, with more than 90 per cent of Jordan's total area receiving less than 200 millimetres of rainfall per year, with more than 70 per cent of that area receiving less than 100 millimetres a year. Only around 2 per cent of the total area, located in the northwestern highlands, receives rain in excess of 300 millimetres, although in the northern highlands it can reach up to 600 millimetres. Around 5.5 per cent of Jordan is considered dry land with annual rainfall ranging from 200 to 300 millimetres. The pattern of rainfall is characterized by uneven distributions over the various regions and strong fluctuations from year to year in terms of quantity and timing, thus Jordan is one of the poorest countries in the world in terms of water resources.

Table 2.2.1 Distribution of precipitation in Jordan

Climatic Zone	Average Annual Rainfall (millimetre per square metre)	Area (in square kilometres)	Area (in per cent of total)
Desert (Badia)	<200	80,800	90.5
Arid	200–300	4,900	5.5
Semi-arid	300–400	1,700	1.9
Semi-humid	>400	1,900	2.1
Total		89,300	100.0

Source: Agricultural Sector Development Programme, 2001–10.

Land resources

- The total available land in 1999 was around 9 million dunums, with a cultivated area in the 1990–99 period of about 3 million dunums, representing 3.4 per cent of the total Jordanian area and less than 1 dunum per capita.
- Range land extends over wide parts of the eastern desert and comprises approximately 81 million dunums, which constitutes about 90 per cent of the land. As mentioned before, rainfall is low, irregular and uneven in distribution. These lands are in a general state of degradation due to harsh environmental conditions, misuse from overgrazing and the cultivation of marginal areas.
- Forestland comprised about 1.3 million dunums in 1999, mainly in elevated regions, of which about 770,000 dunums were covered with natural and man-made forests.
- The total irrigated area was 284,000 dunums in 1967 and has constantly increased to reach almost 538,000 dunums in 1990 and over 1 million dunums in 1998.

Table 2.2.2 Irrigated area in Jordan (crop area, 1000 dunums)

	1990	1992	1994	1996	1998
Jordan Valley	227.5	304.8	291.2	293.3	323.8
Other Areas	310.4	507.7	492.5	552.5	705.7
Total	537.9	812.5	783.7	845.8	1,029.5

Source: Agricultural Sector Development Programme, 2001–10.

Due to the variation in rainfall, the increase in the irrigated area, the move to cultivating more profitable crops and major changes in the traditional markets for Jordanian agricultural products, the irrigation pattern has changed as follows:

- The area of field crops declined from 14 per cent of the total irrigated area in 1990 to 8.1 per cent in 1998.
- Due to the shrinking of export markets and declining comparative profitability the area under vegetables decreased from 45.5 per cent of the irrigated area in 1990 to reach 39.7 per cent in 1998.
- Fruit production increased dramatically reaching 40.5 per cent of the irrigated area in 1990 and 52.2 per cent in 1998.

Water resources

The average renewable freshwater resource is about 680 million cubic metres per year or approximately 135 cubic metres per capita for all uses. The current rate of water use already exceeds the available renewable supplies and Jordan covers the increasing deficit through overdrafting of highland aquifers and exploitation of non-renewable groundwater. The annual average for overdrafting of groundwater resources during the period 1990–96 reached more than 230 million cubic metres.

Total water consumption increased from 755 million cubic metres during 1985–90 to 859 million cubic metres during 1994–96. The water for municipal uses showed the highest increase from 153 million cubic metres to 216 million cubic metres (from 20 per cent to 25 per cent of the total water used) and in regard to irrigation its share dropped from 75 per cent to 70 per cent of the total water used during these two periods. However, in quantitative terms it increased from 560 million cubic metres in 1985–90 to 600 million cubic metres between 1991 and 1996. Industrial water use is about 33 million cubic metres, which is around 4 per cent of the total water consumption.

The share of agriculture in water resource consumption is about 70 per cent and the present government policy is to reduce this share in order to minimize the overexploitation of the groundwater and to meet the increasing demand for fresh water for municipal uses. To minimize the negative impact of this on agricultural production, efforts are being made to increase the water resources available by using treated wastewater for irrigation purposes , by increasing water use efficiency through improved irrigation methods and by maximizing the production per unit of water used for irrigation. The projected water resources of Jordan for 2005–20 in terms of water supply and demand and the allocation of water for agricultural uses are summarized in Tables 1–3 of 'Water Resources and Projects'.

Table 2.2.3 Conventional and treated wastewater use for irrigation

	Year	1998	2005	2010	2015	2020
1	Conventional Water	486	656	597	519	461
2	Treated Wastewater	69	93	156	197	220
3	Total	555	745	753	716	681
4	Per Cent Of Treated To the Total	12.4	12.4	20.6	27.3	32.3

Source: Ministry of Water and Irrigation, 2001.

Table 2.2.3 shows that the water allocation for agriculture will be reduced from 2010 and the contribution of treated wastewater will increase from 12 per cent of the total allocated water for irrigation at present to reach 32.3 per cent of the total in 2020.

Economic situation

- Population – The population of Jordan increased from about 4.3 million in 1995 to reach about 5.5 million in 2002, with a growth rate of about 3.3 per cent in 1999. In the latter year the average annual income per capita was US $1,524 and unemployment was estimated at about 17 per cent.
- Agricultural production – The agricultural sector achieved a high growth rate due to the increase in the farm areas under irrigation. The introduction of modern production technologies, the provision of a favourable environment for investments in the sector, especially the planting of fruit trees, the establishment of commercial-scale livestock projects and the absence of major obstacles for Jordanian exports to traditional and foreign markets all played a major role in increasing agricultural production. By the end of the 1980s and the early 1990s, the growth rate of the sector declined due to the economic crisis in Jordan, the regional and international political developments and the Gulf crisis with the ensuing closure of most of the traditional markets for Jordanian agricultural exports.

Development of crops and livestock

The following paragraphs give an overview on the development of crop and livestock products during the 1990s.

Crop production:

From Table 2.2.4 it can be noted that the total cultivated area fluctuated due to high variations in precipitation, with the area under field crops declining because it is dependent on the amount of rainfall. Vegetable production, which depends on irrigation and is concentrated mainly in

Table 2.2.4 Agricultural crop production in Jordan

	1990 Area (thousands of dunums)	Production (thousands of tonnes)	Area (thousands of dunums)	Production (thousands of tonnes)	Area (thousands of dunums)	Production (thousands of tonnes)
Field	1,196	137	1,448	100	173	25*
Crops	338	978	405	1,119	396	1,214
Vegetables	311	240	366	360	449	440
Fruit Trees	623	73	793	97	1,056	43*
Olives						
Total	2,468	1,428	3,012	1,676	2,074	1,722

*The figures mirror the effect of a serious drought in the 1998/99 season.
Source: Agricultural Sector Development Programme, 2001–10.

the Jordan Valley, has stabilized in around 400,000 dunums. Fruits and olives have increased steadily in terms of area and production, which reflects the growing awareness about limited water resources. Although the total area has declined, the total production output has stabilized at around 1.7 million tonnes.

Livestock production:

From Table 2.2.5 the following can be noted:

- The total number of sheep, goats and cattle have increased in the mid-1990s by about 50 per cent and decreased again towards the end of the 1990s by about 30 per cent due to the prolonged drought.
- Total meat and milk production has increased mainly because of a sharp increase in cattle productivity resulting from improved cattle breeding and good management.
- The number of head of poultry increased between 1990 and 1999 by about 170 per cent. Poultry meat production has more than doubled and egg production has increased by about 44 per cent, indicating that broiler keeping is considered of higher priority than layer raising.

To sum up, water is the main limiting factor for the increase of crop and livestock productivity. However, there is a consensus between institutions working in rural areas that the most suitable, feasible and practicable agricultural activity for the rural population in the dry areas is sheep, goat and cattle breeding.

Agricultural contribution to GDP

The contribution of agriculture to GDP decreased from 213.5 million Jordanian dinars in 1991 to 147.5 million Jordanian dinars in 1997 and

Table 2.2.5 Livestock production in Jordan

	1990 Heads (thousands)	Meat (tonnes)	Milk (tonnes)	Heads (thousands)	Meat (tonnes)	Milk (tonnes)	Heads (thousands)	Meat (tonnes)	Milk (tonnes)
Sheep	1,556	6,300	25,200	2,211	9,000	35,800	1,581	13,395	20,491
Goats	479	1,800	12,100	814	2,900	19,700	631	3,425	11,962
Cattle	42	1,700	59,100	61	3,900	95,900	65	3,913	140,617
Total	2,077	9,800	96,400	3,086	15,800	151,400	2,277	20,733	173,070
	Heads (thousands)	Meat (tonnes)	Eggs (thousands)	Heads (thousands)	Meat (tonnes)	Eggs (thousands)	Heads (thousands)	Meat (tonnes)	Eggs (thousands)
Poultry	17,500	50,000	530,000	26,000	90,700	871,000	29,400	110,700	762,000

Source: Agricultural Sector Development Programme, 2001–10.

Table 2.2.6 GDP of Jordan and the agricultural sector

| Year | GDP at Current Prices | | |
	Jordan (in millions of Jordanian dinars)	Agriculture (in millions of Jordanian dinars)	Share of Agriculture (in per cent)
1990	2,324.5	187.8	8.1
1991	2,505.6	213.5	8.5
1992	2,960.9	246.9	8.3
1993	3,204.9	193.3	6.0
1994	3,332.0	193.2	5.8
1995	3,879.7	171.8	4.4
1996	4,019.7	160.7	4.0
1997	4,226.2	147.5	3.5
1998	4,134.3	144.7	3.5
1999	3,870.0	116.1	3.0
2000	3,015.8	114.6	3.8
2001	4,972.0	124.3	2.5
2002	6,630.5	134.6	2.03

Source: Agricultural Sector Development Programme, 2001–10.

to 134.6 million Jordanian dinars in 2002 and the agricultural share of total GDP was only 8.5 per cent in 1991 and decreased to 3.5 per cent in 1997 and to 2.03 per cent in 2002. This declining share of agriculture is a direct result of structural changes in the Jordanian economy. However, if agriculture-related activities (upstream and downstream linkage like agribusiness services, inputs and agro-industry) are included, the share in GDP would increase to about 29 per cent.

Contribution of agriculture to employment

On average, agriculture employed almost 50,000 Jordanian nationals or around 7.5 per cent of the total Jordanian workforce in the period 1975–97. Agriculture currently employs 5.7 per cent of the national workforce, which provides an important income source for about 15 per cent of the population. Women constitute 6.6 per cent of the labour force in the sector and about 4 per cent of the total number of the workforce in all sectors. In addition, registered foreign labour in the sector amounts to about 62,000.

Exports, imports and home consumption

Table 2.2.8 shows that agricultural exports increased from 57.3 million Jordanian dinars (about 9.4 per cent of total exports) in 1990 to 181.3 million Jordanian dinars (about 17 per cent of total exports) in 1997. In

Table 2.2.7 Employment in Jordan and in the agricultural sector

Year	Number of Employed Persons		
	Jordan (in thousands)	Agriculture (in thousands)	Share of Agriculture (in per cent)
1975	343.1	47.0	13.7
1979	407.1	46.0	11.3
1988	522.4	39.7	7.6
1989	523.6	37.7	7.2
1990	523.9	38.3	7.3
1991	629.6	40.8	6.5
1992	705.9	44.4	6.3
1993	752.4	55.0	7.3
1994	1,140.7	60.0	5.3
1995	1,076.7	61.8	5.7
1996	1,092.7	62.5	5.7
1997	1,132.4	65.0	5.7

Source: Agricultural Sector Development Programme, 2001–10.

the same period agricultural imports increased from 403.9 million Jordanian dinars (23.4 per cent of total imports) to 539.5 million Jordanian dinars (18.6 per cent of the total). This table clearly shows Jordan's increased dependency on imports to meet its consumption requirements for agricultural commodities and a slightly aggravated deficit of the agricultural commodity balance.

Future plans

The national strategy for agricultural development for the period 2002–10 has identified priorities and action plans for the development of Jordanian agriculture on a sustainable basis. Some of the plans that may be of interest to investors include the following:

1. The formation of agricultural production and marketing co-operatives or associations of farmers of specific important crops, such as citrus, dates, grapes and vegetables. Such organizations are to be capable of supporting expensive facilities for post-harvest activities as well as for marketing services locally and abroad.
2. The need for strong private companies for the production, processing and export of fresh fruits and vegetables. The private sector is to play a major role in this activity.
3. The establishment of centres for grading, packing, cooling and fumigation, if needed, for farmers' produce of fresh vegetables and fruits and the provision of assistance in their marketing.
4. The development of agricultural processing, such as:

Table 2.2.8 Exports and imports of Jordan and the agricultural sector

Year	All Sectors (in millions of Jordanian dinars)		Exports	Imports	Re-exports	Deficit	Exports	Imports
	Exports	Imports						
1990	612.3	1,725.8	57.3	403.9	5.0	−341.6	9.4	23.4
1991	598.6	1,710.5	81.3	417.7	28.0	−308.4	13.6	24.4
1992	633.7	2,214.0	92.0	416.0	19.0	−305.0	14.5	18.8
1993	691.3	2,453.6	140.0	435.1	7.6	−287.5	20.3	17.7
1994	793.9	2,362.6	91.2	409.7	10.2	−308.3	11.5	17.3
1995	1,004.5	2,590.2	99.5	419.2	11.3	−308.4	9.9	16.2
1996	1,039.8	3,043.6	160.1	685.9	9.6	−516.2	15.4	22.5
1997	1,067.1	2,908.1	181.3	539.5	10.3	−347.9	17.0	18.6

Source: Agricultural Sector Development Programme, 2001–10.

a) Tomatoes – paste and juices
b) Potatoes – chips and puree
c) Dates – fruits and by-products
d) Asparagus – drying and canning
e) Canning of different vegetables: strawberries, peas, beans and the like
5. Introduction of high-value crops, such as medical and aromatic plants as well as fruit trees.
6. Encouragement of organic farming for the production of vegetables, medical and aromatic plants and olive trees and the processing and marketing of the resulting produce.
7. Processing and marketing of olive oil.
8. The expansion of flower and ornamental plant production for local and overseas markets.
9. Encouragement of the expansion of protected horticulture (greenhouses).
10. Promotion of the increased use of localized irrigation systems in irrigated areas to increase water-use efficiency.
11. Production of animal feed from the farms' by-products.
12. Utilization of the by-product of date palms in the manufacture of containers, floor mats and the like.

Recent developments

Sine the adoption of the National Agriculture Strategy for 2002–10, the implementation of the above-mentioned 'Future Plans' has received top priority. The following discussion is a summary of what have been accomplished from these plans.

Introduction

The agriculture strategy having been blessed by King Abdullah and approved by the government, it was possible to prepare a very clear investment programme for all the proposed projects, for 2002–10.Furthermore, in order to achieve the planned agricultural development, it was necessary to improve and develop supporting institutions, whether by updating the existing legislation or by issuing new legislation to deal with weak points and create a favourable environment for the execution of the proposed projects within defined time frames.

The document that addresses the above-mentioned objectives consists of two main parts. Part one deals with the investment programme for the projects identified by the National Agriculture Development Strategy and part two deals with the issues related to the development of the supporting institutions.

Part One
The Investment Programme

1. General Background

Although the relative importance of the agriculture sector was expected to decline because of increased growth of other sectors, the sector has seen not only a precipitous relative decline, but also a real decline in its production. The contribution of the agricultural sector declined from 14.4 per cent in 1971 to 7.12 per cent in 1980 to 3.8 per cent in 2000 and to 2.04 per cent in 2002, and from 213 million Jordanian dinars in 1991 to 171.8 million Jordanian dinars in 1995 and to 134.6 million Jordanian dinars in 2002.

This poor performance could be attributed to several factors, namely the following:

- The government lifted subsidies to agriculture in the early 1990s as part of their entry into the WTO.
- Customs protection for local products has been cancelled through the reduction of custom fees on imported agricultural commodities.
- Rains have been scarce for several years during this period.
- Government policies have failed to encourage the private sector to participate in the development of agriculture.
- The private sector has failed to establish sizable economical agricultural projects with the required administrative and technical know-how. It has also failed to establish professional associations to strengthen its participation in development activities and in the formation of policies that lead to success.
- Public and private organizations have failed to support the development of agriculture due to the failure of co-operatives and the Farmers Union in organizing farmers and also the failure of the universities and other organizations concerned with research and technology transfer in carrying out their duties.

2. Objectives of the Investment Programme

The programme aims to overcome the negative effects of the limiting factors mentioned above and to provide a suitable environment to improve the performance of national agriculture. Its approach includes the following:

- Improving the income of the concerned people and their living conditions and creating job opportunities.
- Increasing the income of the water unit.
- Improving the quantity and quality of produce.

- Developing export-oriented crops.
- Increasing investment in the agricultural sector.
- Establishing solid foundations for sustainable economic development.
- Improving the economic situation of local communities.
- Improving the level of nutrition and health of rural families.
- Reducing the migration of rural people to the urban centres.
- Enabling the people to participate in the planning and execution of development.
- Upgrading the role of rural women in the participation in production and the development of the society.
- Reducing pollution and maintaining a healthy environment.
- Protecting the natural resources of land and water.
- Maintaining an environmental balance.
- Protecting the country's flora and fauna and maintaining soil productivity.
- Increasing vegetation cover and halting the expansion of desertification.
- Protecting the water behind dams from pollution and reducing the flow of sediment into reservoirs.

3. Summary of the Investment Programme for the Development of Agriculture, 2004–14

A. Projects for food security.

B. Projects for the development of the agricultural resources.

C. Marketing projects.

D. Technical support projects (research and technology transfer).

E. Forests, range lands and environment.

F. Projects for increasing the efficiency of agriculture production.

A: Projects for Food Security

Food security encompassed 15 projects spread all over the country with a total value of 26.0 million Jordanian dinars and the time span of about 5 years. These small projects include the introduction of crops suitable for small farms that have a high return, including honey, fish, rabbits, turkey and dairy products. The aim of these projects is to create jobs and to involve women in agricultural development, through upgrading their skills in taking care of small animals and garden crops and dairy activities. The projects also worked to help beneficiaries market their produce. This is expected to increase their income, which will improve their life, and hence to discourage the rural population from migrating to the cities.

B: Projects for the Development of Agricultural Resources (2004–10)

This category included 16 projects with a total cost of 210 million Jordanian dinars to be executed over 5 years, except for one project dealing with the reclamation of stony areas, which has a 7-year timeframe. The estimated cost of the latter project is 123.5 million Jordanian dinars, or 59 per cent of the total allocation. The remaining 15 projects cover nearly all the water catchments in the country. Their objectives are to develop these areas through the following activities:

1. Developing agricultural land through soil and water conservation, water harvesting structures and the adoption of the optimum utilization of agriculture resources in the catchments.
2. Improvement of agricultural services in the project area.
3. Construction and improvement of roads in the catchments.
4. Development of springs and their protection from pollution.
5. Enhancing the participation of women in agricultural activities and increasing the family income.
6. Providing opportunities for more jobs.
7. Strengthening the awareness regarding the importance of sustainable agriculture for the protection of the environment of the local people.

The execution of these projects started in September 2004. By the end of 2005, nine of the projects had achieved good progress. About 14,000 dunums were reclaimed and 10,500 farmers benefited from these projects during the first year of operation.

C: Marketing Projects

Marketing covered eight projects, namely:

1. Improving the infrastructure for the export of horticultural crops. This includes the construction of four centres for the grading, packing and storage of horticultural produce. This work is to be completed in 3 years starting 2003 and with an estimated cost of 4.65 million Jordanian dinars.

2. Forming a private company to market horticultural produce.
   The feasibility study for the establishment of this company was completed and was presented and discussed at the Agricultural Market-

ing conference held on 15 November 2006 in the Le Meridien Hotel, Amman.

The estimated capital required was 5 million Jordanian dinars. The Arab Agency for Investment is interested in participating and in providing about 50 per cent of the capital needed. The preparation of the by-laws of the company is in progress and will be discussed and finalized by the end of 2006. It is expected that the government of Jordan to grant the company about 1 million Jordanian dinars during the stages of its formation.

3. Improving the wholesale fruits and vegetables markets in Amman, Irbid and Zarqa.

- Improving the operation of existing markets.
- Studying the feasibility of establishing a new wholesale market in Irbid.
- Studying the facilities needed to improve the function of these markets.
- Legislation to facilitate and improve the functions of these markets.
- The cost of this evaluation is estimated at 1 million Jordanian dinars and will be completed in 3 years.

4. A project to promote the export of horticultural produce.

The components of this project are as follows:

- Providing information on local and foreign markets, establishing agricultural fairs and arranging visits to the export markets and fairs.
- Strengthening the administrative and technical skills of farmers participating in the project.
- Studying external export markets.
- Identifying potential markets for the import of new produce.
- Mobilizing the marketing extension.
- Strengthening the capacity of the laboratory for plant protection and heavy metals.

This project is to be executed in 3 years with a total cost of 6.6 million Jordanian dinars.

5. Other marketing-oriented projects:

- Establishing a regional centre for marketing services. Time of execution is 3 years and the estimated cost is 3.470 million Jordanian dinars.

- Upgrading the wholesale markets for livestock (sheep and cows). Time of execution is 3 years and total cost is 1.510 million Jordanian dinars.
- Marketing-extension for leaders in marketing. Time of execution is 3 years and total cost is 1.889 million Jordanian dinars.

D: Technical Support Projects

These include the following:

1. Establishing producers' associations to promote a single commodity. Examples include date associations, citrus associations, grape associations and so on.

Total cost of the project is 1.29 million Jordanian dinars, to be executed in 18 months.

2. Improving the agriculture quarantine service.

Establishing medical laboratories and other needed facilities, including the required equipment and trained staff. Total cost is 2.338 million Jordanian dinars over 4 years.

3. Establishment of an Agriculture Development Fund. This will provide a source of funds to help farmers finance their activities in case of emergencies, such as frost, drought, floods, high winds and extreme temperatures. Total cost is 80,000 Jordanian dinars over 3 years.

4. Surveys and database.

Surveys are being carried out to provide the following information:

- Climate database.
- Soil and water database.
- Plant cover database.
- Agriculture production database.
- Desertification database.

Total cost is 3.144 million Jordanian dinars over 3 years.

5. Range, forests and environment projects:
   These include the following:

- Improving El-Shomary National Natural Reserve.
- Creating a network for the protection of wild animals.
- Creating a network to support the national nature reserves.
- Monitoring soil pollution.
- Introducing of water harvesting technology in the range lands.

- Using treated wastewater for supplementary irrigation.
- Improving nurseries for the production of forest seedlings.

6. Projects to upgrade agricultural production for export.

- Financing agricultural projects for the purpose of exports.
- Introducing advanced methods in agriculture.
- Flower production.
- Control of the residues of pesticides.
- The safe use of pesticides.
- Integrated pest control project (IPM)

Part Two
Action Plan for the Development of Supporting Institutions

The national strategy for agricultural development recommended several actions to be carried out to improve the organization and structures and legal framework of the concerned institutions so as to better guide, support and supervise the implementation of the National Agriculture Strategy. The following actions have been initiated:

1. Reviewing the structure of the Ministry of Agriculture, taking into consideration

f)   The ability of the ministry staff to implement the new agriculture law.
g)   The ability of the ministry to implement the national strategy for agriculture development.
h)   The establishment of new units such as:
   ◆ International and financing unit.
   ◆ An investment unit to follow up with the private sector on participation in agricultural development.
   ◆ A unit to monitor the effect of the projects on the environment.

2. Proposing possible changes in the structure of the Jordan Valley Authority.

3. Establishing a national agency to issue certificates of competence similar to the Eurogap for agricultural exports.

4. Formulating a new agricultural law giving the Ministry of Agriculture more of a role in development, taking into consideration the following:

a) Preventing agricultural land from being put to any other use without ministry approval.
b) Establishing the responsibilities of the Ministry of Agriculture in relation to the use of irrigation water at the farm level.
c) Granting the ministry the authority to establish private associations that are not co-operatives.
d) Including the ministry in drawing guidelines for the use of treated wastewater and brackish water for irrigation.

5. Increasing the participation of the private sector in the management of the Agriculture Credit Agency, the National Centre for Agriculture Research and Technology Transfer and the National Agency for the Promotion of Exports.

6. Reviewing the structure of the National Centre for Agriculture and Technology Transfer and establishing in its place a National Agency for Research and Technology Transfer.

7. Reviewing the structure of the High Agriculture Council to make it more effective.

8. Changing the Agriculture Credit Agency to a bank for rural development.

9. Establishing the role of both the Ministry of Agriculture and the Ministry of Water and Irrigation in managing irrigation water.

10. Establishing a Jordan Chamber of Agriculture.

11. Establishing a fund for agriculture development.

12. Encouraging the formation of agricultural unions.

13. Amending the law governing farmers' general unions so as to allow:

The formation of work-specific unions.
    Financial support for unions.

14. Amending the municipalities' law so as to permit the private sector to establish wholesale markets within the boundaries of municipalities.

15. Developing education curricula with practical training in the Colleges of Agriculture in the universities.

16. Preparing land use maps in order to indicate the boundaries of agriculture land units and the methods of their utilization.

17. Providing a suitable environment for the private sector to participate in a more active role in the development of agriculture.

18. Establishing guidelines for the use of brackish water for irrigation.

19. Protecting the environment and wildlife using funds provided by donors for the protection of the environment and the control of desertification.

Conclusion

The National Agriculture Strategy for 2002–10 has generated serious planning followed by actions for the development of agriculture. Actions have been implemented with emphasis on:

- Active participation of the private sector and the involvement of women.
- Better utilization of natural resources.
- Upgrading skills of those involved in the production and marketing of produce.
- Emphasizing the production of high-quality and high-value produce oriented for export.
- Encouragement of small projects to ensure food security and create jobs for the rural population, including women, and thus to discourage migration to the cities.
- Emphasizing the improvement of marketing through several different projects, including:

- Improving of the infrastructure for the export of horticultural crops.
- Forming of a strong national private companies for the production, processing and marketing of fruits and vegetables.
- Improving the wholesale markets in the country.
- Promoting the export of horticultural produce through the continuation of activities initiated by ongoing projects, financed by a loan from the World Bank.

Finally, the restructuring of the supporting public institutions together with legislation to provide the legal framework. This is very important to enable these institutions to carry out their duties efficiently.

2.3

Tourism in Jordan – Investment Opportunities

Omar Alfanek, Economic Researcher, Jordan Tourism Board

Introduction

Tourism plays a major role in the Jordanian economy. As the country has minimal natural resources, the services sector leads the kingdom's economy and fuels socio-economic development. Tourism is positioned at the top of the services sector in terms of receipts, employment and investments.

Jordan is a destination that offers the best variety of attractions within a relatively small area. In addition to the moderate climate and the safe and secure atmosphere, visitors to Jordan enjoy a spectacular experience visiting the different natural, cultural and historical attractions around the kingdom. To enable further enjoyment of Jordan's many attractions, increasing investment is being sought in tourism-related projects.

Though the tourism industry has witnessed substantial development over the past few years, it is recognized that there is always potential for improvement, more opportunities and more growth. Under the leadership of His Majesty the King and by the implementation of his government's policies, the private sector has a great opportunity to invest, participate and gain from a dynamic and growing market.

Tourism-related authorities

The main tourism-related authorities in the country are the Ministry of Tourism and Antiquities and the Jordan Tourism Board (JTB).

Ministry of Tourism and Antiquities

The ministry works towards developing tourism through a comprehensive and integrated approach to express the nation's legacy, culture, history, heritage, inheritance, successive civilizations and economic prosperity as well as enhancing the noble human values based on peace and mutual respect among nations. In fulfilment of these aims the ministry seeks to:

- Develop an advanced tourism industry capable of utilizing its comparative and competitive advantages through highly developed infrastructure facilities and superstructure services.
- Develop archaeological and tourism sites and resources to enhance the tourism products, extend tourist length of stay so as to achieve higher tourism revenues and create new job opportunities.
- Expand the role of the private sector in tourism investment and capital attraction within a framework of mutual cooperation between the public and private sectors.
- Upgrade the quality of tourism services to the highest international standards.
- Develop tourism awareness of the kingdom's culture, heritage, civilizations and archaeological resources within the framework of sustainable tourism development in harmony with local communities and non-governmental organizations.
- Strengthen the institutional set-up of the tourism sector by upgrading legislation, laws, by-laws, regulations and human resources development.
- Establish and lead marketing and promotion campaigns in international and regional markets, strengthen international cooperation and promote domestic tourism.

Jordan Tourism Board

The JTB was officially launched in March 1998 as an independent public–private sector partnership committed to utilizing marketing strategies to brand, position and promote the Jordan tourism product internationally as the destination of choice.

JTB's main tasks can be summarized as follows:

- Setting plans to promote Jordan internationally.
- Endorsing domestic and international tourism.
- Recommending product and site developments.
- Cooperating in financing local events.
- Participating in international tourism events.
- Undertaking market research.

To achieve its objectives the JTB employs different marketing tools. The first of these foresees the opening of offices in defined markets for market-based representatives (MBRs). These MBRs are located in the United States, the United Kingdom, France, Germany, Spain, Italy, Switzerland, Russia, Austria, Scandinavia, the Netherlands, Belgium and the GCC.

Besides the offices abroad, the JTB participates in international exhibitions and trade fairs, organizes press and FAM trips and implements direct marketing and promotional campaigns through the media.

The National Tourism Strategy (2004–10)

The National Tourism Strategy (NTS) provides the basis for development of the tourism sector over the period to 2010. The strategy provides a scientific analysis of the sector to year-end 2003, sets targets to be attained by 2010 and defines what needs to be done to achieve these targets.

The strategy seeks to attain the following results by 2010:

1.   Double tourism receipts compared to those achieved in 2003.
2.   Create 51,000 new jobs in the sector.
3.   Achieve taxation yields to the government of more than US $637 million.

The strategy document includes a comprehensive action plan and monitoring system to guide implementation of the strategy and includes four pillars on which to build. These are:

Pillar one: Strengthen tourism marketing objectives

- Enhance Jordan's image.
- Brand Jordan as a boutique destination.
- Increase arrivals of high-yield tourists.
- Maintain position in current markets.
- Enhance market intelligence.

Pillar two: Support product development and competitiveness objectives

- Increase visitor yield
- Enhance competitive advantage
- Diversify tourism products

Pillar three: Develop human resource objectives

- Improve tourist services.
- Increase availability of human capital.
- Expand employment opportunities.

Pillar four: Provide an effective institutional and regulatory framework

- Enhance institutional capacity and legal support for tourism's strategic objectives.

According to the NTS, priority tourism segments for Jordan are:

1. Cultural heritage
2. Religious tourism
3. Eco-tourism
4. Health and wellness
5. Cruising
6. Meetings, incentives, conferences and events (MICE)
7. Adventure
8. Scientific, academic, volunteer and educational tourism (SAVE)

Additionally a number of tourism segments deemed of good potential were also defined, these being:

1. Sports
2. Filming and photography
3. Festivals and cultural events
4. Summer and family holidays

Who comes to Jordan – The demand side

In 2005, Jordan received 5.8 million visitors, achieving a growth rate of 4.1 per cent over the previous year. According to international standards, international arrivals are divided into 'overnight tourists' and 'same day visitors (transits)'. Both are important for the Jordanian economy and the tourism industry. From the 5.8 million arrivals, about 3 million are tourists and 2.8 million are transits.

Year	2002	2003	2004	2005
Total Arrivals	4,677,018	4,599,243	5,586,659	5,817,370
Growth Rate	–	—1.6%	21.5%	4.1%

Source: Ministry of Tourism and Antiquities.

Overnight tourists are the real fuel for the tourism industry in Jordan. The GCC states that Europe and North America are the main markets for incoming tourism to Jordan. These markets, in particular, have been targeted by the JTB, in accordance with the main objectives of the NTS.

Year	2002	2003	2004	2005
Overnight Tourists	2,384,474	2,353,088	2,852,809	2,986,586
Growth Rate	–	—1.3%	21.2%	4.7%

Source: Ministry of Tourism and Antiquities.

Jordan's current capacity limits the ability of operating on the mass level. The current number of accommodation units (eg hotels, apartments and the like), ports, airports and other inputs forced the tourism authorities, the JTB in particular, to operate on the niche level by offering specific tourism products to well-defined categories of tourists. In practice, Jordan is promoted as a boutique, luxurious destination for high-yield tourists. According to the NTS, targeting high-yield tourists and increasing their average length of stay are the best ways to overcome the 'relatively' limited capacity of the supply side. That's why North America, Europe and the GCC are the main markets for the tourism sector in Jordan. Beside these markets, the JTB is always targeting new potential markets such as South Africa, the Far East and South America.

The following table shows the numbers of overnight tourists visiting Jordan from the main markets in which the JTB has market-based representation.

	2002	2003	2004	2005
Nationality		**Overnight Tourists**		
Total Arab Gulf	430,099	390,452	437,588	526,777
United States	41,398	52,046	76,055	92,245
Canada	8,030	9,049	12,513	13,234
United Kingdom	24,384	25,292	38,369	40,276
Germany	16,517	14,675	19,839	21,179
Spain	4,975	5,912	10,940	20,465
Italy	7,326	7,268	11,605	13,933
France	15,784	12,984	16,359	20,458
Russia	4,001	6,925	9,624	12,858
Scandinavia	8,269	9,649	9,989	10,762
Netherlands	4,543	5,808	6,505	7,573
Switzerland	2,926	2,874	3,889	3,832
Austria	2,513	2,056	3,361	3,783
Belgium	2,310	2,009	2,729	2,935
Total	573,075	546,999	659,366	790,312

Source: Ministry of Tourism and Antiquities.

Jordan's location at the heart of many countries makes it of major importance to transit visitors, especially those travelling by land. Jordan connects the GCC with North Africa, Syria, Lebanon, Turkey, Iraq and many other countries in and around the Middle East. Land transit travellers play a major role in the tourism industry as they spend large amounts of money on restaurants, transportation, stores and many other services during their stay in Jordan. Additionally, air transit travellers have the advantage of being able to obtain short-term visas at the airport to enable them to visit Amman, Madaba and other tourist attractions close to the airport instead of wasting time in the airport waiting for their flights.

Year	2002	2003	2004	2005
Transits	2,292,544	2,246,155	2,733,850	2,830,784
Growth Rate	–	—2%	21.7%	3.5%

Source: Ministry of Tourism and Antiquities.

As to domestic tourism, there are no official measurements of its size, features or expenditure. However, it is widely agreed that domestic tourism also plays an important role as Jordanians share interests in the existing tourism products, especially festivals and archaeological, eco- and beach tourism. Summertime, June to September, is considered the high season for domestic tourism.

The tourism authorities in Jordan rely greatly on research and scientific analysis when initiating promotional campaigns. Tourist feedback and survey findings are considered prime sources on which marketing plans are set. Furthermore, such data sources are very important to product development issues, as tourism authorities in Jordan believe that its unique tourism product is the key factor that assures offering the best experience to the tourists, especially when niche markets are being targeted.

The current tourism statistical system is very advanced. Politicians and policymakers in Jordan are getting more and more supportive and willing to allocate resources to promote the statistical system in general and for tourism in particular. In this regard, Jordan will shortly become one of the few countries to have adopted the modern Tourism Satellite Accounting system.

Tourism Receipts to GDP (2002–05)

Item	2002	2003	2004	2005
Tourism Receipts (Jordanian dollars, in million)	743.2	752.6	943	1,021.6
GDP (market prices) (Jordanian dollars, in million)	6,778.5	7,203.6	8,164.1	9,118.1
Per Cent of Tourism Receipts to GDP	11.0	10.4	11.6	11.2%

Source: Central Bank of Jordan.

Who is involved in Jordan – The supply side

By the end of 2005, there were 468 accommodation entities in the tourism sector in Jordan, of which 198 were classified hotels, 122 classified apartments and suites, 137 unclassified hotels and 11 motels and camps.

Accommodation Entity	Total Number
Five Stars	21
Four Stars	22
Three Stars	43
Two Stars	49
One Stars	63
Total Classified	198
Apartments B	16
Apartments C	83
Suites A	2
Suites B	11
Suites C	10
Total Apartment Suites	122
Unclassified Hotels	137
Hostel	2
Motel	1
Camping	8
Grand Total	468

Source: Ministry of Tourism and Antiquities.

All of the five- and four-star hotels are located in Amman, the Dead Sea, Petra and Aqaba. Most of the international chains are operating in Jordan and each year more and more projects are being established. The continuously growing demand, the secure atmosphere and government incentives are the main factors that encourage domestic and international investors and firms to invest in the hotel industry. Apartments and suites are the favourite options for Arab tourists especially from the Arabian Gulf. Tourists from this market usually arrive in family groups and their average length of stay is much longer than that of visitors from other markets. They prefer to rent apartments rather than stay in hotels for reasons of cost.

Besides the accommodation units there are 525 tourist restaurants, 431 tour operators and travel agents, 254 rent a car companies and 5 tourist transportation companies. All are key players in the sector and all have an association or a union through which they cooperate with other tourism authorities.

The following tables demonstrate the development of the tourism industry in Jordan over the years 2002–05. The growth seen can be credited largely to increasing demand for Jordan increasingly varied range of tourism products.

2005	2004	2003	2002	Item
468	463	458	461	Accommodation Entities
431	466	426	403	Travel Agents
525	448	374	376	Tourists Restaurants
254	241	232	259	Rent a car Companies
672	601	547	570	Tourist Guides
20,827	19,945	19,698	19,389	Number of Rooms
40,480	38,658	37,859	37,289	Number of Beds

Source: Ministry of Tourism and Antiquities.

Number of employees in tourism activities, 2002–05

Activity	2002	2003	2004	2005	Per Cent Change 2005/2004
Hotels	10,324	10,499	10,708	12,884	20.3
Travel Agencies	2,511	2,621	2,826	2,774	-1.8
Tourism Restaurants	5,674	6,367	6,719	9,950	48.1
Rent a Car Offices	1,036	928	1,287	1,357	5.4
Tourist Shops	347	296	310	385	24.2
Tourist Guides	570	547	601	672	11.8
Horses Guides	286	353	493	613	24.3
Tourist Transportation Companies	445	499	483	620	28.4
Diving Centres	–	–	28	32	14.3
Water Sports	–	–	89	97	9.0
Total	21,293	22,110	23,544	29,384	24.8

Source: Ministry of Tourism and Antiquities.

2005	2004	2003	2002	Nights Spent in Classified Hotels
1,636,820	1,406,229	986,641	877,307	Five Stars
1,026,401	935,723	786,256	517,006	Four Stars
839,758	810,944	501,872	465,044	Three Stars
412,046	396,462	351,730	298,010	Two Stars
225,179	210,154	171,280	208,314	One Stars

Source: Ministry of Tourism and Antiquities.

Investing in tourism in Jordan

It is suggested that the undoubted potential of Jordan as a destination for tourism investment is based on the following premises:

1. A safe and secure environment with political stability, with Jordan a major participant in seeking regional peace and security.

2. A stable monetary policy that minimizes currency risks. The Central Bank of Jordan has adopted a fixed exchange rate policy by pegging the Jordanian dinar to the US dollar at a fixed rate since 1995.

3. Continuously growing demand for tourism products. Effective promotional campaigns, the pursuit of visitors from new markets and the implementation of new product development projects are positive factors supporting this trend.

4. Jordan will apply a new, open-sky policy by 2010. This will permit increased aircraft movements and therefore increase accessibility to the kingdom and raise the demand for tourist products.

5. Amman, Petra, the Dead Sea and Aqaba are areas of huge tourist movements that still offer great opportunities for investors to participate and gain.

6. Beside the areas mentioned above, there are many other locations all over the kingdom that are attractive to investors seeking to establish new projects. The government has developed many cities, sites and regions that are considered a potential tourist-investment attraction because of the various factors that make investment in such places feasible. Jerash, Madaba, Dana, Wadi Rum, Umm Qais, Ajlun, Kerak and Shobak are just a small sample of beautiful areas with great potential.

7. A well-developed infrastructure in almost all the main cities and tourist locations in Jordan.

8. As mentioned, Jordan offers different types of tourism products, which results in different options for an investor in terms of location, size, investment and targeted customers.

9. Jordan offers a high-quality, highly trained labour force at a relatively low cost.

10. The political support and government incentives granted to foreign investors, including facilitating official procedures.

Investors have a wide range of options to establish their projects. This includes hotels, apartments and motels, restaurants, shops, entertainment centres, spas, sports facilities, camps, equipment and automobile rental (eg diving equipment, cars and motorcycles), hospitals and theatres. The opportunities are considerable and by no means confined to those mentioned – indeed, new ideas are welcomed.

2.4

Water: Resources and Projects

Dr Abdullah Arar, Land and Water Development Consultant

Introduction

Economic and social development in Jordan depends in large part on the ready availability of good-quality water. Lying as the country does in an arid to semi-arid zone with low and unpredictable rainfall, Jordan has an exceptionally low per capita water supply of less than 200 cubic metres per person per year, one of the lowest worldwide.

This situation is exacerbated by an increasing demand for water resulting from a rapid growth in population, due in part to the arrival of refugees and displaced persons, increased urbanization, improved standards of living and the continuing demands of irrigation. The net result is a serious water supply–demand imbalance that is further aggravated by increased water pollution and inefficiencies in the use of available resources. As a result, water prospects for Jordan in the coming decades are of major concern as shortages will inevitably impact adversely on the country's ability to grow and develop.

In the light of this situation, the Ministry of Water and Irrigation (MWI) has drawn up a comprehensive investment programme covering 2002–11 that seeks to provide solutions to both immediate and longer-term concerns.

Jordan's water resources

The projected water resources of Jordan, for 2005–20, in terms of the total quantities, water supplies and demands and the allocation of water for agricultural uses are summarized in the Tables 1–3, respectively.

Table 1 Expected available water during 2005–20 in million cubic metres

Source of Water	2005	2010	2015	2020
1. Surface Water*	478	487	487	487
2. Renewable Groundwater	370	338	307	275
3. Peace Water	60	90	90	90
4. Desalination of Brackish and Sea Water for Municipal Use	43	54	75	88
5. Desalination of Sea Water	5	5	17	17
6. Fossil Groundwater	62	83	93	119
Total of Fresh Water	1,018	1,057	1,069	1,076
Total Treated Wastewater	112	177	219	246
Grand Total	1,130	1,234	1,288	1,322
Percentage of Treated Wastewater to Total	10.0	14.0	17.0	18.6

*The surface water includes 185 million cubic metres, which will become available from El-Wehda, El Walah, El-Moujib and El-Tannor dams.

From Table 1 the following can be noted:

1. The total available fresh water in 2005 was about 1,018 million cubic metres per year in addition to about 112 million cubic metres of total treated wastewater, making a total of 1,130 million cubic metres per year. This total was projected to reach 1,322 million cubic metres by 2020. Out of this, about 246 million cubic metres will be treated wastewater, equivalent to 18.6 per cent of the total resources. This projection is based on the government's strategy to maximize the collection of the municipal and industrial wastewater, through the expansion of the sewage network, and the treatment and reuse of all the collected wastewater, mainly for irrigation purposes. About 200 million cubic metres of treated wastewater is to be used for irrigation, and the balance of 46 million cubic metres for industrial and other uses.
2. It could also be pointed out that in 2020 about 105 million cubic metres of desalinized brackish and sea water and about 120 million cubic metres of non-renewable (fossil) water are included in the total water resources mentioned (1,322 million cubic metres). These two components amount to 225 million cubic metres, the equivalent of about 17 per cent of the total resources.
    These sources together with the treated wastewater are called non-conventional water resources. They amount to 35.6 per cent of the total resources. This reflects the scarcity of the conventional water resources and the effort of the government to supplement this resource by adopting strategies to provide non-conventional sources

of water, which in most cases are costly but are needed to meet the increasing demand.

3. The amount of extraction from renewable groundwater in 2005 was about 370 million cubic metres but it is declining with time and is expected to become 275 million cubic metres in 2020. The safe yield, as estimated by the MWI, is about 270 million cubic metres and hence the strategy of the government is to reduce the extraction from groundwater, which has resulted in declining groundwater levels together with the increase in its salt content in most cases, until the extraction will come as close as possible to the safe yield.

Table 2 summarizes the projected water demand and supply for 2005–20.

From Table 2 it can be noted that the total water supply is less than the total water demand by about 336 million cubic metres in 2005 and will increase to 434 million cubic metres by 2020. At the same time the per capita demand per year in 2005 is about 296 cubic metres and will decline to 143 cubic metres in 2020. These are the lowest on record worldwide.

To minimize the negative impact of this shortage of water, the strategy of the country is to maximize the efficient use of water in agriculture and also in municipal supplies. In the field of agriculture, the plan is to reduce the supply of water gradually from 68 per cent of the total water supply in 2005 to 50 per cent in 2020 without affecting the total

Table 2. Projected water demand and water supplies and total water deficiency

Details	2005	2010	2015	2020
1. Population in millions	5.98	6.97	8.04	9.18
2. Water Demand				
2.1. Municipal Demand	382	435	520	615
2.2. Industrial Demand	80	102	134	168
2.3. Agricultural Demand	981	1,001	991	963
Total	1,443	1,538	1,645	1,746
3. Water Supply				
3.1 Municipal Demand	281	380	463	517
3.2 Industrial Demand	76	93	112	130
3.3 Agricultural Demand	750	746	704	665
Total	1,107	1,219	1,279	1,312
4. Total Water Deficiency	336	319	366	434
5. Per Capita per Year in cubic metres	296	175	159	143

Source: MWI working paper dated October 2001.

Table 3 Water allocation for agriculture

Details	2005	2010	2015	2020
1. Conventional Water Sources	657	590	522	464
2. Treated Wastewater	93	156	182	202
3. Total Water Allocation	750	746	704	666
4. Per Cent of Treated Water of the Total	12.4	21.0	26	30
5. Total Area to be Irrigated by Treated Wastewater in donums	93,000	156,000	182,000	202,000

Source: MWI working paper dated October 2001.

production. This is to be achieved through high water use efficiencies, high-yielding crops and good management.

Table 3 summarizes the planned water supply to agriculture use. This table shows that the total amount of water for agricultural use was 750 million cubic metres in 2005 and is to be reduced to about 666 million cubic metres in 2020. At the same time, most of the treated wastewater will be used for irrigation. This will amount to about 93 million cubic metres in 2005 (12.4 per cent of the total supply) and will increase to about 202 million cubic metres in 2020 (30 per cent of the total supply).

It is the country's strategy to increase the collection of wastewater through the provision of wastewater collection facilities and sewage systems all over the country and to treat this water to be used mainly for agricultural purposes.

Water authorities in Jordan

The Ministry of Water and Irrigation

The MWI is the official body responsible for the overall monitoring of the water sector, water supply and wastewater system and related projects, planning and management, the formulation of national water strategies and policies, research and development, information systems and the procurement of financial resources. Its role also includes the provision of centralized water-related data and the standardization and consolidation of these data.

The MWI was established in 1992 in response to Jordan's recognition of the need for a more integrated approach to national water management. Since its establishment, MWI has been supported by several donor organization projects that have assisted in the development of water policy and water master planning as well as the restructuring the water sector.

The ministry encompasses the two most important entities dealing with water in Jordan:

1. The Water Authority of Jordan (WAJ) is in charge of water and sewage systems.
2. The Jordan Valley Authority (JVA)is responsible for the socio-economic development of the Jordan Rift Valley, including water development and distribution of irrigation.

The Water Authority of Jordan

Under the terms of the Water Authority Law No. 18 of 1988, the WAJ was established as an autonomous corporate body with financial and administrative independence linked with the Minister of Water and Irrigation. WAJ carries full responsibility for the public water supply, wastewater services and related projects as well as for the overall water resources planning and monitoring, construction, operations and maintenance. The responsibilities of WAJ are to:

• Survey the different water resources, conserve them, determine ways, means and priorities for their implementation and use.
• Develop potential water resources in the kingdom, increase their capacity and improve their quality, protect them from pollution, supervise them and administer their affairs and put forth programmes and plans to meet future water needs by providing additional water resources from inside or outside the kingdom and through the use of water treatment and desalination.
• Regulate, and advise on, the construction of public and private wells, investigate groundwater resources, drill exploratory, reconnaissance and production wells and license well-drilling rigs and drillers.
• Study, design, construct, operate, maintain and administer water and public sewerage projects including collecting, purifying, treating, disposing and the use of any other methods dealing with water.
• Draw terms, specifications and special requirements in relation to the preservation of water and water basins, protect them from pollution and ascertain the safety of water and sewerage structures, public and private distribution and disposal networks and take the necessary action to ensure technical control and supervision, including all necessary tests.
• Carry out theoretical and applied research and studies regarding water and public sewerage to achieve the authority's objectives including the preparation of approved water quality standards for different uses and technical specifications concerning materials and construction in order to apply the findings to the authority's projects in coordination with other concerned departments, and to publish the final findings and standards so as to generalize their application by all means available to the authority.

- Issue permits to engineers and licensed professionals to perform public water and sewerage works and participate in organizing special training courses to qualify them in order to improve the standard of such works and to reduce water loss and pollution.
- Regulate the use of water, prevent its waste and limit its consumption.

The Jordan Valley Authority

Originally established in 1973 as the Jordan Valley Commission, it was renamed JVA in 1977, after the passage of Jordan Valley Development Law No. 18 of 1977. This law was subsequently modified by the Jordan Valley Development Law No. 19 of 1988 and its amendment in 2001. The area of JVA responsibility extends from the Yarmouk River in the north to the Red Sea in the south. The eastern extension of the area is limited by the 300-metre above mean sea level (amsl) contour line north of the Dead Sea and 500-metre amsl contour line south of the Dead Sea. The JVA service area comprises JV North, JV South, Southern Ghors and Wadi Araba.

The JVA is a governmental organization responsible for the social and economic development of the Jordan Rift Valley, including the development, utilization, protection and conservation of water resources. The King Abdullah 1 Canal represents the backbone of the JVA water distribution system north of the Dead Sea (JVA areas).

The JVA is responsible for the development and utilization of water resources in the Jordan Valley for irrigated farming, municipal, industrial and tourist purposes, generation of hydroelectric power and other beneficial uses. Its responsibilities include water resource protection and conservation.

In order to achieve its responsibilities the JVA:

1. *Carries out the studies required for the evaluation of water resources including hydro-geological and geological studies, drilling of exploratory wells and the establishment of observational stations.
2. *Plans, designs, constructs, operates and maintains irrigation projects and related structures including dams, hydropower stations, water delivery and distribution networks in addition to surface and subsurface drainage works, flood protection works, roads and buildings needed for operation and maintenance.
3. Undertakes soil surveys and classification and reclamation of land suitable for irrigated farming.
4. Settles disputes arising from the use of water resources.
5. Organizes and directs the construction of private and public wells.
6. Develops and improves the environment in the valley.
7. *Plans, designs, constructs and maintains the farm roads network.

8. Develops tourism in the valley and the construction of tourist and recreational facilities.

The National Agriculture Strategy for 2002–10 recommended the reorganization of the structure of the JVA. In this respect the following actions have to be carried out:

• To carry out a study to evaluate the present situation and to indicate the strong and weak points of the current system.
• To indicate the needs of a new system in order to solve the gaps in the present system.
• To discuss the proposals of this study with the responsible officials of JVA.
• To pass the proposal to the prime minister legislative and advisory office.
• To get final approval of the new structure.

It is reported that in July 2005, the MWI, which was made responsible for this task, passed a new law for the development of the Jordan Valley to the parliament for adoption.

Privatization of the water sector in Jordan

In 1997, the Government of Jordan embarked on a privatization programme, with the goal of orienting Jordan's economy more towards private sector participation and for presenting Jordan before the international financial community in a better manner. The specific objective of the programme included improving and consolidating the efficiency of the public sector, attracting private investment into the economy and moving towards a market economy.

After detailed study it was concluded that the granting of management contracts (MCs) was the preferred option for Jordan's water sector since it gives comprehensive solutions with immediate short-term effects as well as sustainable long-term benefits.

This approach was considered to be a good first step towards greater private sector participation. MCs for specific operations and management of facilities in Jordan's water sector require no significant change in the existing regulatory or legal structure and therefore could be implemented quickly at relatively low cost and with a minimum of effort.

Privatization projects in the water sector

Northern Governorates – Irbid, Jerash, Ajloun and Mafraq

MWI widened private sector participation in Jordan through a MC for the Northern Governorates. The proposed term of the MC is 6 years, which may be extended by another 2 years to allow sufficient time for the benefits of having a private operator to be fully realized.

Aqaba Governmental Company

MWI was delegated the authority to privatize the water and wastewater sector. In the Aqaba region, it decided to run the water and wastewater facilities as a governmental company completely owned during the first stage by the WAJ and subsequently, as a second stage, to be sold to private shareholders.

As-Samra wastewater treatment plant

MWI awarded a build–operate–transfer (BOT) contract for the As-Samra wastewater treatment plant (WWTP), the largest WWTP in Jordan. The contract was a partnership between the public and private sectors for the purpose of raising finance from the private sector and in order to share all risks, whilst ensuring technology and know-how transfer. Further details of this project are given below.

Major projects

Red Sea–Dead Sea Canal Project – The Peace Conduit

Background

The Dead Sea is the lowest point on earth, about 400 feet (1 foot =0.3 metre) below sea level. In 1935, the inflow to the Dead Sea was 1,300 million cubic metres a year, a figure that had dropped to 300 million cubic metres by 2000. As a result, the level of the Dead Sea has declined at a rate of about 1 metre per year, a situation that has caused huge environmental damage to the sea and to the surrounding groundwater resources.

Several studies have been conducted to assess the environmental damage, the most important of which was the Jordan Rift Valley study of the Trilateral Economic Committee (Jordan, Israel and the United

States) together with the World Bank and the Trilateral Government (after 1994). The study concluded there was a marked need to seek to replenish this lost water and that the construction of a canal from the Red Sea to Dead Sea, to be known as the Peace Conduit, was the most viable.

This project consists of a water conduit (a combination of tunnel and canal sections) that will convey almost 1.8 billion cubic metres per year of sea water some 180 kilometres from the Red Sea near Aqaba to the vicinity of the Dead Sea. Implementation of the project would reverse the decline in the Dead Sea, gradually resulting in an increase in the water level to historic levels, at a cost of about US $800 million, which will necessitate and promote international cooperation.

Implementation of the Peace Conduit is expected to save the Dead Sea from environmental disaster and allow the economic benefits of a restored Dead Sea to flourish, whilst enabling the self-sustaining development of very large quantities of renewable power and fresh water. The 1.8 billion metres per year of seawater that would be brought in from the Red Sea would utilize the 400-metre elevation difference between the Red Sea and the Dead Sea to generate a renewable source of power. This power will be used to operate reverse osmosis units to transform sea water to fresh water. A portion of this water (1.05 billion cubic metres per year) will be directed to the Dead Sea to reverse its decline at an ecologically prudent rate and the remaining fresh water (850 million cubic metres per year) will be directed to satisfy the fresh water demands in Jordan, Israel and Palestine, a quantity sufficient to meet the region's needs for fresh water for the foreseeable future.

The costs and financing of the project

The cost of the project will be significant and will be dependent on the final configurations. However, current estimates indicate the construction costs at US $0.8 billion for the Peace Conduit and US $3 billion for the desalination project and conveyance-to-demand centres. International financing is being sought for the Peace Conduit itself but it is believed that the desalination projects can be financed from within the region or through commercially self-sustaining ventures.

An international conference was held at the Dead Sea during the first week of December 2006. This conference was attended by representatives from donor countries as well as from other countries that are interested to know more about the project. The conference was preceded by an agreement between the donor countries, which will contribute to the feasibility study, and the World Bank who will supervise the study. The cost of the feasibility study is about US $15 million and is to be completed in 2 years. Already US $8.0 million has been committed by five countries. It is planned that all agreements will be finalized before the end of 2006 and that the study will commence early in 2007 for completion in 2 years.

Disi Amman Water Conveyor (BOT)

Objective

The main objective of the Disi-Mudawwara to Amman Water Conveyance System project is to supply additional sustainable potable water to the greater Amman area to satisfy water demands. Although its capacity might eventually be increased, the project will initially produce and transport to Amman, on average, 100 million cubic metres of high-quality water per year, with a minimum flow of 80 million cubic metres per year during the winter months and a maximum flow of 120 million cubic metres per year in the summer.

Project status

A full feasibility study on all technical, economic, financial and environmental aspects of the project was completed in mid-1996. Additionally, a preliminary design study and tender documents, including geotechnical investigation, were completed in mid-1997 and subsequently updated.

Pre-qualification has been completed and the tender documents have been delivered to the pre-qualified consortia. The technical and financial offers were received and opened on 20 August 2003.

The evaluation by the ministry revealed that the cost of water was rather high. The ministry requested that the companies that participated in the tender reconsider their terms. At present the government has extended the time of submission for their offers to April 2007. The selection of the company will be announced and the work will start in May 2007.

The estimated base capital costs of the project are US $600 million and a tentative timetable for the competition of the project is 5 years. The World Bank is ready to support the project financially through a partial risk guarantee.

Al-Wehda Dam

Construction of this dam on the Yarmouk River, which forms part of the northern boundaries of Jordan with Syria, about 120 kilometres from Amman, commenced on 26 May 2003 and continued until late 2006.

The dam will capture flood water and available base flow in the Yarmouk basin and will provide about 30 million cubic metres of water each year to irrigate 31,000 dunums of cultivated land supply Amman and its vicinity with about 50 million cubic metres of potable water each year and generate about 18,800 megawatt-hours of electricity yearly on completion.

The project cost of about 89 million Jordanian dinars is being financed by the Arab Fund for Economic and Social Development (80 per cent),

Abu Dhabi Fund for Development (10 per cent) and the government of Jordan.

Most of the work has been completed and trial storage of flood water is to be carried out in the coming flood season of 2006–07. However, Jordan is concerned about the amount of water that will be available at the dam site. For this reason an agreement was reached in the summer of 2006 between Jordan and Syria to establish a technical committee to study the effect of the construction of 37 dams and 300 wells in Syria on the water flow to the dam site. At present the summer base flow of the river has declined from 7.0 cubic metres per second to 1.2 cubic metres per second.

As-Samra Wastewater Treatment Plant Project (BOT)

Background

Construction of the first sanitary sewers in Amman began in 1964 when the population was about half a million. The first WWTP in Amman, and in Jordan, was an activated sludge facility at Ain Ghazal in the northeast of Amman that was constructed in 1968.

The plant became overloaded very quickly, and the 1982 Master Plan for Wastewater Disposal recommended the expansion of the existing activated sludge plant at Ain Ghazal (AGTP) and the construction of new plants at Upper Wadi Abdoun and Zarqa. The As-Samra Waste Stabilization Ponds (WSP) plant, with a 40-kilometre inverted siphon from Ain Ghazal to As-Samra was conceived as temporary, for use while the then-overloaded Ain Ghazal treatment plant was expanded. After such expansion, As-Samra would be used to treat peak wet weather flows. However, the occurrence of water-borne diseases in Zarqa and Russeifa, contamination of wells used for municipal supply and objectionable odours attributed to the Ain Ghazal plant led to permanent closure of its treatment facilities when the As-Samra WSP began operation in 1985. The As-Samra WSP became the sole municipal treatment facility in the Amman–Zarqa basin. Its original design was to treat 68,000 cubic metres per day, less than half the present inflow of 170,000 cubic metres per day.

The decisions to abandon the Ain Ghazal plant and to connect Zarqa and Russeifa instead of building the proposed West Zarqa plant lead quickly to an overloaded plant with frequent complaints of noxious odours and an effluent quality that does not meet Jordanian water quality effluent standards.

The WSP system is now hydraulically and organically overloaded with an estimated average daily flow to the WSP between 1998 and 2000 of about 167,000 cubic metres per day. As a result of this overload, the quality of effluent from the WSP system has degraded.

A second wastewater master plan financed by USAID for the period 2000–25 has been prepared for Amman–Zarqa basin. It has identified and evaluated sites for new and expanded treatment plants and the need for supporting conveyance lines. The Zarqa River (Seil Zarqa) basin includes most of the Greater Amman Municipality, all the sewered areas and most of the towns in Zarqa Governorate. The second master plan recommended the construction of a treatment plant at As-Samra site with a capacity of 267,000 cubic metres per day as the first stage that would be capable of treating the wastewater from the area until 2010, by when another plant is recommended to be constructed below Zarqa to take the loads from Zarqa, Russeifa and parts of Amman until 2020–25, while the As-Samra plant would be expanded in 2015 to treat the wastewater from the Amman area until 2027.

Project development

In 1999, MWI after studying different financial scenarios started the preparation of the tender documents on the selected (BOT). The project reached financial closing on 10 December 2003 after the facility and security documents were negotiated with lenders from the local banks led by the Arab Bank. Construction was to be completed by the end of 2006.

The As-Samra WWTP BOT Project

The project includes the design, construction, procurement, commissioning, operation, maintenance and financing of the new WWTP, Phase 1, at As Samra. The WWTP is to be built on the site of the existing stabilization ponds, to be taken over by the selected project company and potentially used in the project and will have a capacity of 267,000 cubic metres per day.

The project also includes the expansion and upgradation of the pre-treatment plant at Ain Ghazal, the minor refurbishment of the pumping station (PS) at West Zarqa as well as the operation and maintenance of the main conveyor lines from the pre-treatment facilities at Ain Ghazal to the WWTP and of the PSs at Hashimiyya and West Zarqa.

The construction of As Samra WWTP is divided into two stages. In the current project, Stage 1, the capacity for 2015 is to be attained, with expansion for 2025 to be included in the plans. Although it is a requirement of Stage 1 to design the layout of the plant to facilitate expansion to Stage 2, such expansion is not part of this project.

Wadi Ma'in Zara Springs Water Treatment and Conveyance Project

Background

Based on a request from the Government of Jordan, the Government of the United States of America agreed to provide technical assistance for engineering services for this project through the United States Agency for International Development (USAID) to include the following:

1. Preparing the feasibility study.
2. Studying the environmental impact assessment.
3. Preparing the minimum civil, mechanical and electrical technical requirements for the plant, pipeline and PSs including PS reservoirs
4. Preparing the minimum requirements for treatment.
5. Preparing tender documents on designing and building the project, including operation for 2 years that can be extended for a further 5-year period upon the discretion of the employer.
6. Preparing pre-qualification documents for choosing the consortia that are specialized in the related fields.

The primary objectives of this project are to supply the Greater Amman Area with 38 million cubic metres of desalinated drinkable water each year, thereby improving the water quality and decreasing the water deficit whilst reducing the salinity of the water at the As-Samra WWTP and of the water stored at the Talal reservoir for subsequent use in the irrigation of the mid-Ghor area of the Jordan Valley.

Project financing

The project is partially funded by a grant from the US government, with the balance plus land acquisition and about 8 million Jordanian dinars for electricity supply to operate the system being covered by the Government of Jordan. The USAID share is US $104 million, covering 85 per cent of the project cost and 100 per cent of the engineering supervision services.

However, due to the need for more water to Amman area, the capacity of the project was increased to 65 million cubic metres per year. Water for this project comes from a pipeline collecting water from Mujib-Walah dams and running north, drawing water from several sources along its way, mainly brackish water from wells in Wadi Hisban and from Zara–Zarqa main springs and surface flow. This brackish water will be delivered to a desalination plant with a capacity of 65 million cubic metres per year. Out of this, 10 million cubic metres will go to touristic developments on the northeast coast of the Dead Sea and about 55 million cubic metres will be pumped to Amman. The project is to be completed in 2006.

Conclusion

Much has been done to address the shortage of water in Jordan, but clearly much more remains to be implemented if the country is not to suffer serious economic and social problems in the years to come. The primary focus at this time is on the Peace Conduit, as implementation of that project alone would provide water to all of Jordan, Palestine and Israel and also could have a long-lasting impact on the peaceful coexistence of all the people of the region well into the future.

2.5

The Regeneration of Downtown Amman – From Urban Regeneration to Community Development

Jamal Itani, Chief Executive Officer, Abdali Investment and Development PSC

Urban regeneration continues to evolve as successes and failures are examined and new models of development and redevelopment are tested and implemented. Overall, it has played an undeniably important role in cities throughout the United States, England and many other nations, particularly during the 1950s, 1960s and 1970s, and has now reached the Middle East and in particular the city of Amman.

Many cities link the revitalization of the central business district and gentrification of residential neighbourhoods to earlier urban renewal programmes. Over time, urban renewal evolved into a policy based less on destruction and more on renovation and investment, and today is an integral activity of many local governments, often combined with incentives for small and big businesses.

Amman's new downtown is a case in point. The project began as a cooperative effort between the public and private sectors encompassing 350,000 square metres of military land in the centre of Amman. The military bases were relocated to the outskirts of the city, allowing for the regeneration project to add a modern downtown. When it is finished (around 2009), the result will be a new downtown with world-class facilities.

Background

Real estate in the region has been growing steadily for the past two decades. Investors, local and foreign, are waking up to the possibilities of the region, and Jordan is one of the countries marked for growth in the coming years. Several factors have led up to this. Since 11 September 2001, capital from the Arab oil economies was diverted in large part from the Western countries, and the income surged into Jordan and neighbouring countries. Instead of investing in the usual US and European niches, Arab investors have become more wary and turned closer to home. Another important contributing factor was and remains the Free Trade Agreement signed between Jordan and the United States in December 2001, which relaxed barriers between the two economies and significantly encouraged investment in Jordan. This promoted investment both ways: exports from Jordan into the United States increased, and Jordan itself gained from added investment.

Internally, the government's economic liberalization has been moving ahead on the strength of one of the region's most successful privatization programmes. Since acceding to the throne, HM King Abdullah II pushed for less bureaucracy and more incentives to attract foreign investment and launched new strategies aimed at realizing sustainable socio-economic development. These included reducing constraints that ob-structed a free business environment, organizing an annual gathering of national business leaders with the king, and articulating a well-defined policy for the near future through the design of the Social and Economic Development Plan for 2004–06. As a result, foreign investment has increased real estate's role in all this is reflected in an annual turnover of US \$4.24 billion in 2005, an increase of 80 per cent.

The capital of Jordan, Amman, with more than 1.6 million inhabitants (2000), was growing fast and receiving more attention and more visitors. With globalization taking on an increasing relevance in the country, the capital was in need of a major revival that would help it adapt to the fast-changing world, and it was felt that a modern downtown would address the issue. Previously, the only thing that Amman had close to a downtown was the old 'balad'. This was a traditional souq, which, though charming in its local appeal, lacked the grandeur and modernity that Jordan was seeking to impress on visitors and was not representative of a growing city. Hence, no city centre had been really defined until the plans for Abdali reached the table. The thinking was that the creation of a visible presence in the centre of Amman would tangibly represent the city's drive towards modernization and would further its strategy to become an important regional hub.

Vision

Historically, Amman as a city was built in a vertical structure with urban growth stretching across a line of well-defined centres. Building activity usually clustered around such centres with growth spreading in a recurring vertical pattern of central focal points. Over the years, the building activity grew horizontally and gradually encroached on the once-isolated military sites that had bordered the city. As a result, the military perimeter became prime real estate in the centre of Jordan, taking up a significant part of the city. The military sites had long bordered Amman, and the Jordanian army had traditionally maintained a visible presence within the premises of the capital because of the important role they had played in the country's history. Barracks, training centres and headquarters formerly on the rim were now near the city centre. Given the fast-paced city growth, pressure grew to use these lands more productively and efficiently. In a pioneering initiative, King Abdullah II instructed the government to establish centres that would attract international and regional companies to Jordan and buoy the economy. The strategic urban military sites were to be transformed into real estate developments to help jump-start the fledgling knowledge economy by providing electronic infrastructure facilities within such developments.

The relocation of military sites to the outskirts of Amman would pave the way for modern complexes. The Jordanian government wanted a carefully studied system to manage this transition from public real estate to viable commercial project. In the end, a public–private partnership model was chosen. Thus, the government could provide the land resources and the backing while a private company brought the much-needed know-how. The aim was for a cooperative effort between public and private, a synergy that would capitalize on the assets of each.

Mawared, or National Resources Investment and Development Corporation, a monolithic company with activities all over Jordan was the public arm of the venture. The company was one created by King Abdullah II precisely for the purpose of nurturing investment in the country, especially in real estate. In the process, it took on the role of public benefactor, creating jobs and stimulating the economy, and, in addition to handling Abdali, it also pursues other major development projects elsewhere in Jordan.

Saudi Oger, the private side of the partnership, completed the picture. The Saudi-based international conglomerate had a long history of successful projects, such as the Solidere district in Beirut, which no doubt influenced the decision. Owned by the Hariri family, it has completed projects across the Middle East and employs a huge staff of executives, professional managers and high-calibre skilled staff and has extensive experience in the sector including construction, operations and maintenance, power and telecommunications.

Mawared provided the land for the project, the largest single owned plot of land in the city centre, consisting of the former army locations. Together, the two companies formed Abdali PSC, or in its full name, Abdali Investment and Development PSC, and agreed on a 50/50 partnership as a basis. The size of the land, some 350,000 square metres, ensured that the project was far from an average development, and, with an investment worth an estimated US $1.5 billion, the project could credibly aim to create a new downtown for the capital. A strategic partner arrived in 2005, United Real Estate Company, a member of Kuwait Projects Company (Holding) – KIPCO – bringing a wealth of experience as one of the premier investment companies in the Middle East and North Africa region with substantial interests in real estate and management advisory services.

Size and ambition are the two main criteria that distinguish Abdali from the rest of the real estate developments going on in Jordan. There may be massive residential complexes, or no shortage of exceptional towers adorning the cityscape, but they fall short of the sheer transformative aspirations that Abdali carries with it. The Abdali project, once finished, is expected to bring revolutionary growth to Amman on many different levels. It represents, in the much-publicized phrase, a 'smart urban lifestyle', with a multifaceted mix of residential and commercial property. Instead of being limited to a single development category, such as residential or commercial, the project's aim is to integrate all aspects of urban life. As such, it brings together business, residential and commercial properties in an integrated approach.

The developers' vision is to give Jordan a capital to be proud of and erect a centre of world-class standards that is on a par with other great cities like Paris and New York. Riding the wave of Jordan's potential growth, Abdali would become a major tourist attraction with real potential to become a regional centre. To that end, Abdali seeks to raise the standards of living by welcoming a more urban and cosmopolitan population. This means cutting-edge technology in every home and office, modern design and a thorough blueprint with all solutions thought out in advance by experienced urban planners.

The total built-up area of the Abdali site is more than 1,000,000 square metres, consisting of 150,000 square metres for residential apartments, 480,000 square metres for office space, 200,000 square metres for commercial and retail outlets. Additionally, the project will have 10 towers once finished. Neighbouring the Shmeisani district, it is bordered by the existing parliament from the east, and the Queen Noor Boulevard from the west. To its north lies King Hussein Street with Nabulsi Street to its south.

The building of mid-rise structures is expected to finish around 2008, to be followed by the completion of the high-rise area by 2009. The master plan of the site was drawn up to a high standard by all parties involved. Great care was taken to get the infrastructure tightly in place with the complex branch of networks. Unlike other urban projects springing up everywhere in Amman, the development is in no haste to quickly complete the building or compromise on any aspect. Rather, as local media have noticed, the plan brings with it a marked professionalism and has drawn attention for its scope, design, and attention to detail, as well as the technology behind it all, distinguishing it from all other counterparts.

Abdali Downtown will have high quality construction, uniform height and street alignment. The infrastructure, completed in 2006, makes sophisticated use of fibre optics. Then, there are the traffic solutions. Besides the fact that there are parking facilities able to accommodate no less than 16,000 vehicles, the inroads were especially designed by experts to calibrate offsite traffic flow and check overall congestion. Experts put these solutions into place not only in anticipation of the huge flow of traffic that will stem from Abdali once it is erected, but also to alleviate Amman's existing traffic woes.

Other elements that have truly differentiated the project are the environmentally friendly measures taken and the ubiquitous presence of technology underlying the infrastructure. The breadth of this technology is astonishing, offering the latest in all-access innovations. The company has relied heavily on promoting the smart-city concept with high-speed Internet leading a host of other smart technologies previously missing from urban projects and unprecedented in Jordan and the Levant. These include high-quality VOIP, video-on-demand and enhanced video communication services within a network spread across the entire zone. Another novelty is district heating throughout the site. For that, the Abdali firm partnered with another leading Arab firm, Tabreed Holding, and in August signed a contract for a new private shareholding company in Jordan: Jordan District Energy PSC. The deal provides district energy solutions, while saving in energy expenditures and giving environmentally friendly energy with reduced costs for investors and the future residents of the site.

The impetus for technology lies in the project's ethos and is well-aligned to the overall vision. It aims to cater to all facets of urban lifestyle. For business in this modern day and age, high-speed connectivity, video conferencing and the rest are of paramount importance in attracting multinational business clientele and assuring designed-for-purpose headquarters in Amman. The project has built well-defined business sectors to receive the headquarters of local and international offices and made the prospects of relocating as attractive as possible.

Among the most innovative areas of the project are environmentally friendly measures such as the bioclimatic designs for one of the major towers. Designed by internationally acclaimed architects Foster and Partners, the tallest of the signature towers measures 220 metres, and the towers' integrated building management systems alongside the latest bioclimatic designs offer an ideal working environment. The ingenious cylindrical design has been carefully calculated to protect offices and lobbies from the fierce summer sun, while taking advantage of the solar gain in the months of winter. A natural gas pipeline runs through the city centre and provides clean, safe energy.

Tourism is an integral part of the Jordanian economy, and Abdali is no exception, catering to the broadest category possible. The streets will be replete with retail outlets, cinemas and European-style café-trottoirs. Designers have included a plethora of activities including social settings, gyms, piazzas and urban getaways with gardens and pools on the rooftops, with the aim of attracting Gulf nationals and the international crowd. The aim is to make the downtown the cultural heart of the city, with ongoing events and festivals. Commercially, thousands of retailers and enterprises are expected to open their doors once Abdali is inaugurated in order to profit from the massive influx of visitors.

All of which goes to show the huge leap forward that the project represents in terms of thinking and reflects an obvious change in business methods of only a few years ago. Abdali aims for a broader audience and expects the future of Amman to be a cosmopolitan city with multinationals enjoying the same standards of living as anywhere else in the world. It is a full urban integration plan featuring business, educational and cultural landmarks.

Outlook

The long-term rewards that Amman stands to gain from Abdali are numerous. The building of Abdali brings with it many important advantages for the Jordanian economy. By the time it is finished, it will have brought in over US $1.5 billion of direct investment. During the actual development, the jobs created will reach a formidable 3,000. Over and above that figure, over 10,000 jobs are expected to be created upon the project's completion. In addition to employing thousands of Jordanians from the labour pool, the project will sell parcelled land according to its comprehensive urban design and specific architectural guidelines. After the construction phase, there will remain the huge real estate property to manage. But there are other indirect benefits that Abdali brings to Amman. Abdali's prominence yields added aesthetic value and the sheer scale and ambition are gradually expected to burnish the image of Amman. The project will no doubt change the perception of the city in the minds of foreign investors, tourists and all who visit Amman. Translated in material terms, this means greater investor confidence and a greater chance that major companies will seriously consider a business foray into an untested market. Another benefit will be the added credence to Amman's prospects as a financial centre, with businesses choosing it as a base for their activities in the region. If Abdali proves to be successful, other real estate developers will be encouraged to enter the Jordanian market. By bringing Amman to the fore, Abdali will also have a chance to expose the much-touted technology it has on offer and establish the city as a serious global destination.

Abdali at its best will change the business climate of Jordan deeply it should also have a stirring communal effect on the whole city of Amman, giving residents a centre to gravitate towards and a vital source of which they can be proud. The most crucial aim that Abdali has set is to raise the profile of Jordan. Amman needs a drive to carry it into the 21st century as a global city with much to offer and immense potential all hopes are on Abdali to lead the way.

Part Three
Establishing a Business

3.1

Forming a Business Venture in Jordan

Yousef S Khalilieh, Member; Noor A Jundi, Associate; and Shereen S Said, Associate Rajai K W Dajani & Associates, Advocates and Legal Consultants, Amman

Introduction

Business ventures in Jordan are regulated and governed by several laws and regulations including the Commercial Law No. 12 of 1966 (the 'code'), the Companies Law No. 22 of 1997 and amendments thereto (the 'Companies Law'), the Investment Promotion Law No. 16 of 1995 (the 'Promotion Law') and the Non-Jordanian Investment Promotion Regulation No. 54 of 2000 issued pursuant to the Promotion Law (the 'Regulations').

In general, the Companies Law governs all registered companies undertaking commercial activities in the Hashemite Kingdom of Jordan (the kingdom) and organizes the foundation, administration, activities and liquidation of companies.

Should the Companies Law be silent on any matter relating to corporate entities, then the code applies, regulating matters such as, inter alia, merchants' status, the keeping of commercial books and the corporate register and details of commercial stores and their names.

If neither of these addresses the subject, then reference is made to the Civil Law, which regulates partnership contracts, some types of partnership, such as the joint venture partnership, and their prerequisites, management, consequences, dissolution, winding up and division. Furthermore, the provisions of commercial practice, the guidance of judicial authorities, jurisprudent interpretations and the principles of equity also apply.

Types of companies that can be registered at the Ministry of Industry and Trade

The Companies Law confines those companies that can be registered at the Ministry of Industry and Trade (the ministry) in the kingdom and supervised by the Controller of Companies (the controller) to a number of forms in order to fulfil and meet the requirements and needs of each investor, whether he or she be an individual or an entity, Jordanian or non-Jordanian, as follows:

1. General partnership company

A general partnership company may be formed by not less than 2 and not more than 20 partners, unless such an excess results from inheritance. Each partner shall not be less than 18 years old and shall therefore have acquired the capacity of a merchant.

2. Limited partnership company

A limited partnership company consists of two types of partners, whose names must be listed in the partnership agreement, as follows:

General partners, who manage the partnership and its activities and who are jointly and severally liable for all debts and liabilities of the partnership to the full extent of their private property or assets.

Limited partners, who contribute to the capital of the partnership without having the right to manage or operate the business and whose liability is limited to the amount of their individual shareholding in the partnership. However, if they do participate in the management of the business, then they will be liable to the same extent as a general partner.

3. Limited liability company

The limited liability company has become a preferred form of corporate structure in the kingdom due to the limited and independent liability of its shareholders, as it is only the company's assets and property that can be used to settle any debts or obligations.

A limited liability company must usually consist of at least two partners, although the Controller of Companies may approve such a company with just one partner.

4. Limited partnership in shares company

A limited partnership comprises two types of partner:

General partners, who must number not be less than two and who are liable for the company's debts and obligations to the full extent of their personal property.

Limited partners, who may not number less than three and who are liable for the company's debts and obligations in proportion to their respective shares in the business.

5. Private shareholding company

This type of company was introduced to the Companies Law by Temporary Law No. 4 of 2002, which was published in the *Official Gazette* on 17 February 2002, and consists of two or more shareholders, each of whom is liable for the company's debts and obligations to the extent of his or her shareholding. As of November 2003 more than 100 private shareholding companies had been registered at the ministry. The Companies Law granted the shareholders of the private shareholding company flexibility in setting its articles and memorandum of association, such as the matter of issuance of shares with different types and with certain privileges.

6. Public shareholding company

The public shareholding company consists of two or more shareholders who subscribe to shares at the stock exchange, which shares may be negotiated and transferred pursuant to the Companies Law or any other applicable legislation, with each shareholder being liable for the company's debts and obligations up to the value of his or her shareholding.

Furthermore, the public shareholding company may operate as a holding company that has financial and administrative control over one or more companies and also may operate as a joint investment company (mutual fund company) that invests its own and third parties' funds in different types of securities pursuant to the applicable securities law.

7. Companies operating at the free zones

Such companies are registered at the free zone corporations in Jordan pursuant to their relevant laws and regulations and with the controller at the ministry who maintains a special register of such companies. The said companies enjoy exemptions under the relevant laws and regulations.

8. Non-profit company

The non-profit company is registered in a special registrar at the ministry and may be of any of the above-mentioned types.

9. Civil companies

Civil companies are registered in a special register at the ministry by specialized and professional partners and are subject to the Jordanian Civil Law and to their articles and memoranda of association.

10. Exempt companies

The exempt company may be either a public or a private shareholding company, a limited partnership in shares or a limited liability company and must be registered as a Jordanian company carrying out its operations outside the kingdom. The company's name must be followed by the word 'exempt'.

11. Implied trust company

The implied trust company is a commercial understanding between two or more persons whose operations are carried out by an apparent partner and that is not subject to any registration procedures or licensing as it does not have a corporate identity.

12. Foreign companies

Foreign companies, which are registered outside Jordan, may be registered in Jordan as explained below. Foreign companies shall be registered in a special registrar and all shall be considered non-Jordanian.

Registration procedures

Articles and the memorandum of association of most of the above-defined companies, except for the private shareholding and public shareholding companies, should be prepared on the application form provided by the ministry for this purpose and with the articles stating the following information:

a) The suggested name of the company (which should be in Arabic and not previously registered or similar to any other company's name), its objectives and its headquarters
b) The name, nationality, shares and address of each shareholder
c) The share capital and value of each share
d) The management of the company (directed by a general manager or a board of directors)
e) The duration of the company
f) The method of distribution of profit
g) The fiscal year
h) Special provisions and any additional information that the shareholder may submit

Upon completion of the application, it should be submitted to the ministry and be signed before the Controller of Companies or a notary public or a licensed lawyer in Jordan and should be accompanied by a copy of the national identity card of each Jordanian shareholder or of the passport of each non-Jordanian shareholder. The shareholders of companies with a share capital exceeding 5,000 Jordanian dinars are obliged to execute the articles and the memorandum of association before a licensed lawyer in Jordan.

The controller has the right to reject any registration where the application violates applicable laws and regulations. However, the applicant may seek to remove the violation within the period prescribed by the controller.

Furthermore, pursuant to the objectives of each company, the controller, prior to approving the registration of any company, may request pre-approvals on the said registration from other official entities, such as the Central Bank of Jordan, the Ministry of Press and Publication, the Ministry of Interior and the Ministry of Labour.

Once a company has acquired pre-approval and the approval of the controller, a certificate of registration of the company will be issued stating the company's registration number, share capital and registration date. Following the registration of the company (whether limited liability, private shareholding or the public shareholding) the shareholders shall hold a first general assembly meeting for the declaration of the registration of the company, the appointment of the auditors and the management of the company. The minutes of the said meeting should be filed with the ministry within 15 days of the date of the meeting.

Applicable fees

Fees for registering companies at the ministry vary from one type to another. For instance, the fees incurred for registering a limited liability company amount to 5 per thousand of the registered capital (3 per thousand as registration fees and 2 per thousand as stamp duty) plus other minor fees such as publication fees and the costs incurred in issuing all documentation relating to the company's registration.

Non-Jordanian investors

In general, a non-Jordanian investor may own any project or economic activity in the kingdom, either in full, such as industrial activities, or in part, such as commercial activities like wholesale trade and retailing and other activities such as construction, engineering, advertising, maritime, air, rail and road transport services. However, the said ownership is regulated by the regulations.

It is worth pointing out that in general (with certain exclusions applying) and pursuant to the regulations, the non-Jordanian investor is prohibited from owning or participating in the following sectors:

a) Passenger and freight road transportation services including taxi, bus and trucks services
b) Quarries for natural sand, dimension stones, aggregates and construction stones used for construction purposes
c) Security and investigation services
d) Sports clubs including the organization of sports events services, excluding health fitness clubs services
e) Clearance services

Except in relation to the purchase of shares in a public shareholding company the investment of a non-Jordanian investor must not be less than 50,000 Jordanian dinars.

Furthermore, non-Jordanian investors may register an operating foreign company, which is a company registered outside the kingdom but which nevertheless operates within the country either on the basis of a tender awarded to the company by an official authority for a limited period of time or permanently through a licence granted to the company by the competent official authorities in the kingdom.

A non-Jordanian investor may also register a non-operating foreign company, which must be an extension of a foreign company and not an independent entity. Hence, the non-operating foreign company is registered in the name of the foreign company and is permitted to manage business for and to coordinate with its headquarters, but is prohibited from carrying out any other business or commercial activity inside the kingdom. Such a company is exempted from payment of any fees.

All documents submitted to the ministry in a language other than the Arabic language must be notarized and legalized by all judicial and diplomatic authorities in the country of the company's head office, including the Jordanian Consulate, and must then be translated into Arabic and subsequently notarized by a notary public in Jordan.

A note on names

The main concern for a foreign investor is that except for operating and non-operating foreign companies, the ministry only registers companies with Arabic names, which may constitute an obstacle to companies wishing to expand and operate outside the kingdom.

3.2

The Law of Commercial Agents and Intermediaries

Yousef S Khalilieh, Member; Noor A Jundi, Associate; and Shereen S Said, Associate Rajai K W Dajani & Associates, Advocates and Legal Consultants, Amman

Introduction

Commercial agents, intermediaries and all the various activities under-taken by any person in Jordan on the behalf of a principal are governed and regulated by the Law of Commercial Agents and Intermediaries No. 28 of 2001 (the law), which was published in the *Official Gazette* on 7 June 2001, and Regulation No. 31 of 2002.

Practice

Article 2 of the law defines the 'principal' as a producer or a manufacturer or the distributor adopted by either of them, or an exporter who supplies commercial services. The principal's seat is located outside Jordan and he or she appoints a commercial agent to represent him or her.

Article 2 of the law defines the 'commercial agent' as the person adopted by the principal to be his or her agent or representative in Jordan; or distributor of his or her products in the country whether as a commission agent or by any other consideration; or working for his or her own account by selling what he or she imports from the products of the principal.

Article 2 of the law defines a 'commercial agency' as the commercial contract concluded between a principal and the agent according to which that agent undertakes to import products of the principal, to distribute same, to sell same or to expose them or to provide commercial services within Jordan or for his or her own account on behalf of the principal.

Based on the above definitions, the law applies on all various types of activities taken by any person in Jordan on behalf of a principal.

Registration of commercial agents at the ministry

Pursuant to Article 17 of the Law any commercial agent, commercial intermediary or commercial agency registered under the law is considered registered according to its provisions and must provide the registrar with the information required.

Furthermore, Article 3 of the law provides that the commercial agent must be a Jordanian, if he or she is a natural person, or a Jordanian company registered in accordance with the local applicable law.

Article 5 of the law provides that no person shall be entitled to practice the activity of commercial agency in Jordan unless registered in the Registry of Commercial Agents at the Ministry of Trade and Industry (the ministry).

Based on the above, a commercial agent or intermediary must submit, within 60 days of appointment, an application for registration to the registry of commercial agents at the ministry accompanied by the following documents:

1. The agency contract duly notarized and legalized by all judicial and diplomatic authorities in the country of the principal, including by the Jordanian Consulate. Subsequently, the notarized document must be translated into Arabic and then notarized by a notary public in Jordan.
2. The certificate of registration of the principal.
3. A certificate issued by the ministry confirming the principal's authorized signatory.
4. A certificate of affiliation with the Chamber of Commerce.
5. A vocational licence.

The completed application must be signed by an authorized signatory of the commercial agent in the presence of the registrar.

The registrar has the right to either approve or reject a registration, the latter only where the application violates applicable laws and regulations. Any such decision must be issued within 14 days.

Once the commercial agent has received approval and paid the prescribed fees, a certificate of registration will be issued stating the number and date of registration. Pursuant to Article 7/b of the law such number must be quoted in all commercial correspondence and when the company is performing its activities or undertaking transactions.

If a commercial agent fails to register in accordance with the provisions of the law, a penalty will be payable for non-registration equal to double the registration fee, if the default period does not exceed 3 months, and five times the fee, if the default exceeds that period.

Under Article 8 of the law, a commercial agent or intermediary who discontinues his or her business or whose agency contract expires must request the registrar within a period not exceeding 30 days from the date of discontinuance or expiry of the agency agreement to strike out his or her registration or the registration of his or her agency.

The registrar retains the right to cancel the registration of a commercial agency in the following instances:

1. If it is proved that the commercial agent's or intermediary's registration is based on an application that contains false information.
2. If it has become evident to the registrar that the registration of the agency was based on false information.
3. If it is cancelled for any other reason.

Furthermore, third parties have the right to obtain information related to the name and number of a commercial agent, intermediary or agency, an agency's registration number, the name of the principal and the date of the registration of the agency or its cancellation.

Applicable fees

Regulation No. 31 of 2002 stipulated the fees pertaining to the registration of the commercial agent and the commercial agency at the ministry as follows:

1. A hundred Jordanian dinars for the registration of a commercial agent.
2. Fifty Jordanian dinars for the registration of a commercial agency.
3. Fifty Jordanian dinars for the registration of a commercial intermediary.
4. Fifteen Jordanian dinars to register any amendment in connection with commercial agencies.

Importing and selling weapons

Pursuant to Article 12 of the law and to any other legislation in force, neither a Jordanian nor a non-Jordanian is permitted to practise the profession of a commercial agent or an intermediary for the importation or selling of arms, their spare parts, parts completing or developing them or for ammunition for supply to the Jordanian Armed Forces and Security Forces, including the maintenance of such weapons, their parts or their insurance.

The council of ministers may, on an ad hoc basis and upon the recommendation of a related party, prohibit the practice of a commercial agency or a commercial intermediary or the intervention of the commercial agents or commercial intermediaries in any contracts related to the supply of instruments, equipment, machinery or their spare parts to the Jordanian Armed Forces and Security Forces. This restriction may include the maintenance of the said materials or their insurance and/or services related thereto.

Any person acting in contravention of the above article will be subject either to a punishment of not less than 6 months and not exceeding 1 year of imprisonment or to a fine of not less than 10,000 Jordanian dinars and not exceeding 25,000 Jordanian dinars or both payment of a fine and imprisonment. In addition, a fine will be imposed equal to the commissions received or profits made as a result of any such transaction, where these are known or, where this information is not known, the assessment of the court.

Nevertheless, in order to avoid impracticality with respect to sales of other products to the Jordanian Armed Forces, which could result in adverse repercussions on their tenders, in a letter from the Prime Ministry addressed to the Ministry of Industry and Trade it was stated that any limitation imposed by this law should not be 'broadly construed'.

As to the supply of goods mentioned in Article 12 without intermediation, the council of ministers has not yet specified either the supplies or the services that may be purchased directly from manufacturers, producers or suppliers.

Furthermore, the Higher Authority for Purchases Regulations No. 50 of 1994 has not yet been activated, which means that the Authority's Council has not yet been formed.

Pursuant to Article 13 of the law, no foreign company or institution registered to work in the Hashemite kingdom of Jordan can act as a commercial agent or represent foreign companies established abroad, which restriction shall not include the commercial agencies registered in its name before the promulgation of the law.

Penalties

Without any prejudice to any higher penalty provided for in any other law, Article 18 stipulates that a person shall be subject to a penalty of not less than 500 Jordanian dinars and not exceeding 2,000 Jordanian dinars if the commercial agent:

1. submits to the registrar or any official body, with a bad intention, false statements relating to the registration of the commercial agency, its amendments or substitution;
2. claims in any correspondence or printed materials related to his or her commercial business or in any manner announces that he or she is a commercial agent or intermediary without being registered;
3. contravenes the provisions of Articles 8 and 13 of the law and does not remove the contravention. In such an instance the penalty will be doubled every 3 months until removal of the cause of the breach.

Termination of an agency

Article 14 of the law provides that should a principal cancel or terminate a commercial agency before its expiry without any fault or breach on the part of the commercial agent, or without lawful cause, the agent has a right to compensation equal to the resulting damages and his or her loss of profit.

However, the level of damages awarded by the Jordanian courts in such cases is not clear because the law has not laid down the basis for calculating the amount of compensation due for unlawful termination and there are no precedents to help in defining the sums due.

Nevertheless, the Jordanian courts will take into consideration the following factors as well as the facts and particular circumstances of each case:

1. The existence of a commercial agency.
2. The duration of the agreement.
3. The annual volume of trading and the net profits realized by the commercial agent arising out of the agency.
4. The particular terms and conditions of the commercial agency.
5. The initial and subsequent promotional activities, storage facilities and efforts of the agent as well as the expenses incurred towards those ends.
6. The particular type of business.
7. The standard of performance and the achievement of the targets, if any are agreed between the parties.

8. The true reasons for termination.
9. The period and manner of the termination notice.
10. The remaining stocks, if any, and the manner of their handling upon termination.

If any compensation is to be granted by the court, the actual damages and loss of profit must be strictly proved by the claimant in accordance with the proper rules of evidence.

Usually, calculation of the amount of compensation resulting from unlawful termination is referred to a court-appointed expert involved in a business similar to that of the agreement. Naturally this expert will have to support his or her figures and assessment before the court and under cross examination, if necessary.

Pursuant to Article 15 of the Law, the principal and any newly appointed commercial agent will be jointly and severally liable for purchasing the goods covered by the commercial agency at their cost price or at the local market price, whichever is lower, and to perform all the obligations arising from the commercial agency to third parties to which the previous commercial agent was committed.

Jurisdiction

Article 16 of the law provides that the Jordanian courts will have the jurisdiction to adjudicate in any dispute or differences arising from a commercial agency or the application of the interrelated law.

Furthermore, Article 16 of the law provides that a court action in any commercial agency dispute will not be heard after the lapse of 3 years from the expiry of the contract or the date of its termination.

Concerns

The primary concern in regard to such disputes is that the law as it stands does not lay down the basis for calculation of the level of compensation payable for unlawful termination and so any final decision is subject to the discretion of experts.

3.3

Jordan Investment Board and Investment Opportunities

Dr Maen F Nsour, Chief Executive Officer, Jordan Investment Board

In today's world of open markets and cross-border flows of private sector investment, countries compete to maximize their competitiveness by creating opportunities and offering incentives to local as well as international investors. In the case of Jordan, the attractions are obvious. They start with the country's strategic location, bordering five countries at the heart of a region interconnecting three continents, include Jordan's agreeable weather and friendly hard-working people and do not end with the persistent efforts of the Jordanian Government to encourage private sector investment, both local and international.

Institutional support

An important landmark in these efforts was the promulgation of the Investment Promotion Law of 1995 and the Investment laws of 2003, which today regulate investment activities in the country. These laws established the Jordan Investment Board (JIB) as a governmental body enjoying both financial and administrative independence, which works to promote Jordan as a unique destination for foreign direct investment and to sustain domestic investment in order to achieve economic prosperity, create new job opportunities, increase national exports and facilitate the transfer of technology.

To achieve these objectives, the JIB offers state-of-the-art services and works to streamline registration and licensing procedures for projects. This commitment to streamlining and service does not end with the establishment of the project, but extends throughout the business cycle. The JIB's services include the following:

- Disseminating information, findings, reports, surveys and studies through JIB publications, conferences, media communication and public relations activities.
- Granting financial exemptions, mainly customs duties and sales and other tax exemptions and income tax reduction.
- Highlighting a wide range of business opportunities, which can include pre-feasibility studies that cover the national strategic sectors in which Jordan maintains a competitive and comparative advantage: information technology, pharmaceuticals, Dead Sea & mining, the food sector, tourism and entertainment, and biotechnology.
- Setting marketing themes to build Jordan's image.
- Advocating policy improvements through surveying the private sector's issues and assisting in lobbying through government and official channels.
- Supporting small and medium enterprises (SMEs) in cooperation with other organizations

An enabling legislative environment

The JIB works with investors to help them maximize their benefit from the incentives offered by the present laws, which include an exemption from fees and taxes on imported fixed assets and spare parts valued at less than 15 per cent of fixed assets, and on fixed assets needed for expansion, plus a 25 per cent to 75 per cent exemption from income and social service taxes for exempted projects for 10 years. Hotels and hospitals receive an exemption from fees and taxes once every 7 years for renovation purposes. These exemptions remain in effect if the project changes ownership during the exemption period. In addition, an investor has the right to mortgage the fixed assets of any project as security for extended credit facilities as well as the right to manage the project in the manner he or she deems appropriate.

Most importantly, the laws provide the same treatment for Jordanian and non-Jordanian investors. Non-Jordanian investors may invest through ownership, partnership or shareholding. They may own any project wholly or partially, and they are entitled to remit abroad the foreign capital transferred to Jordan for investment together with any returns and profits. Non-Jordanian employees also have the right to transfer their salaries abroad without hindrance.

Continuous reform

The present investment laws attracted to Jordan investments in 3,121 projects with a total value of 5.5 billion Jordanian dinars (£4.2 billion) between the end of 1996 and May 2006. These projects created 188,000 new job opportunities of which more than 48 per cent were of high added value. But, not content with the evident success of the present legislation, the Government of Jordan submitted to parliament a new draft legislation in 2006 in order to upgrade its incentives to investors.

The new legislation will focus on tax incentives, expand the definition of fixed assets and accord to the council of ministers the power to grant additional exemptions. The new law will annul the Investment Promotion Committee since exemptions become automatic by law.

All projects in the exempted sectors (agri-food, pharmaceuticals, information technology, textiles and garments, cosmetics, and the automotive industry) will enjoy the following:

- Total exemption from customs duties on fixed assets and production inputs
- Zero sales tax on all goods, services, fixed assets and production inputs, whether imported or purchased locally
- Exemption from the special sales tax on fixed assets and production inputs
- Exemption from income tax and social services tax in accordance with special by-laws to be issued by the council of ministers

Special zones

To further help investors, Jordan created a series of special zones (free zones, industrial estates, qualified industrial zones (QIZs), the Aqaba Special Economic Zone (ASEZ)) where investors receive added incentives.

Free zones

Jordan's free zones were established to promote export-oriented industries; they accommodate processing industries, in addition to trading, warehousing and other activities. Commodities and goods of various origins are deposited in the free zone areas for storage and manufacturing without payment of the usual excise fees and taxes. To qualify for a licence to operate within a free zone area, an enterprise must introduce new industries utilizing modern technology, complement domestic industries, use local raw materials or manufacturing parts, upgrade the skills of local workers and produce goods with limited availability in the domestic market.

Jordan's free zones always look for ways to attract direct foreign investments with attention focused on those that generate export revenues, such as technology parks for software, assembly of electronic components, assembly of automotive products, light machinery and other non-traditional exports. These could be complemented by service industries such as business, financial and architecture services, back-office centres, medical diagnosis and programming, logistics and transport, as well as design, research and development and tourism.

Industrial estates

The Jordan Industrial Estates Corporation (JIEC) is a semi-governmental corporation that was established in 1984 with both public and private ownership. Its catalytic role is to contribute to the development of small and medium-sized industries (SMIs) by providing a suitable home for both local and foreign investors. In 1996 the JIEC inaugurated its Centre of Excellence, which will function as an incubator for new enterprises and as a catalyst for the interaction between industry and academia.

Industrial estates offer investors 100 per cent exemptions for 2 years of income and social services tax for industrial projects located within JIEC industrial estates, a total exemption from buildings and land tax, exemption or reduction on most municipal fees and a 100 per cent exemption of taxes and fees on fixed assets for the project, on fixed assets needed for expansion or modernization and on spare parts.

Qualified industrial zones

Three of the operating public industrial estates also hold QIZ status, which allows exporters of goods manufactured in these zones to benefit from duty-free and quota-free access to the US market. There are also private industrial parks that equally enjoy QIZ designation.

Aqaba Special Economic Zone

Considered one of the largest free zones ever created, the ASEZ was established as a low-tax, duty-free multi-sector development area with streamlined administration to attract investments and maximize private sector participation. The project seeks to attract 6.4 billion Jordanian dinars (£4.9 billion) in investments and create 75,000 jobs by 2020.

Businesses operating in Aqaba benefit from a duty-free trade environment. Imported goods are exempt from custom duties and taxes, with the exception of cars. There are no foreign equity restrictions on investment in tourism, industry, retail and other commercial services, and businesses are allowed full repatriation of profits and capital. Aqaba is a regional multi-modal transportation hub with a full-service seaport and international airport, catering to Jordan and the Middle East region.

Network of trade agreements

Cognizant of the limited market potential offered by a population of slightly over 5 million, Jordan expanded its market to 1 billion consumers through a large network of bilateral and multilateral trade agreements that include the following:

- The Greater Arab Free Trade Area (GAFTA)
- An association agreement with the European Union
- A free trade agreement (FTA) with the United States
- A membership agreement in the World Trade Organization (WTO)
- A FTA with the European Free Trade Association (EFTA)
- A FTA with Singapore

In addition, Jordan concluded over 60 agreements with Arab and foreign countries that aim to protect and encourage investments and prevent double taxation. By 2004, the overall value of goods traded through trade agreements was 3,502 million Jordanian dinars (nearly £2.7 million), with 46.2 per cent of that consisting of goods traded under the WTO agreement. The value of goods traded under the QIZ agreement accounted for the highest growth (59 per cent) in 2003–04.

One-stop shop – An investment gateway

One of the principal facilities introduced by the investment laws is the one-stop shop, which the draft legislation develops into a gateway for investment. In its present form, the one-stop shop reduces the time required for registration and licensing from 98 to 14 working days, and the JIB is working to restructure and streamline procedures in order to reduce this period further to 7 working days by the end of 2006.

The new law is expected to enhance the work of the investment gateway by specifically stipulating the establishment of a single investment window located at the JIB to provide services and issue licences to investors. This window will be manned by representatives of all organizations concerned. Moreover, even if the existing law for a given regulatory branch does not define a maximum period for registration and licensing, that period would be 7 working days, and should a licence not be granted within that period of time then the licence would be valid de facto, in accordance with the new law.

The JIB's work, which is summed up by its motto to investors: 'Welcome to Jordan, your investment ally,' has earned it the third prize in the prestigious King Abdullah II Award for Excellence in Government Services and Transparency for 2003.

But the benefits of investing in Jordan are not limited to systems that work and low risk and high returns on investment. One of the most important advantages is the Jordanian lifestyle that has earned Jordan regional and international respect for its traditions and achievements such as tolerance, hard work and economic progress through openness to the world.

3.4

Jordan Free Zones

Mahmoud Qutaishat, Director General, Jordan Free Zones Corporation

Introduction

Jordan stands unique in the region with its democracy, political stability and free economy. These factors make the kingdom an ideal place for investors, while its strategic location at the crossroads of three continents and its comprehensive and ever-expanding infrastructure qualify the country to play a major role as a financial and trade centre. Jordan has also adopted several liberalization measures to serve as incentives for foreign investment in the various economic and development programmes and projects.

The Free Zones Corporation was established to carry out the following tasks:

- To establish free zones and cancel them.
- To establish warehouses, stores and any other establishments necessary for managing and developing the free zones in a manner that ensures their growth and expansion, including joint venture free zones.
- To manage, invest and develop free zones and design them to serve the national economy and to promote international trade exchange, transit trade and export-oriented industries.
- To implement the conditions and provisions relating to customs and foreign exchange control and to set up any establishments necessary for this purpose.
- To register establishments and companies at any free zone.
- To issue licences and approvals related to economic activities at the free zones in accordance with the provisions of the law, regulations and instructions.
- To protect and preserve the environment in the free zones and to ensure continuous development in accordance with standards and foundations to be determined pursuant to a regulation to be issued for

this purpose, provided that the level of such standards and foundations are no less than that applicable elsewhere in the kingdom. For this purpose the corporation shall exercise the power of the Ministry of Environment in accordance with the Protection of the Environment Law that is in force.

Exemption provided by the Free Zones Corporation

1. Exempting projects' profits from income taxes for goods exported outside the kingdom, as well as transit trade, in addition to profits accruing from selling or transferring of goods inside the borders of the free zones. Profits accruing from goods when delivered to the domestic market shall be excluded from such exemption.
2. Exempting salaries and allowances of non-Jordanian employees, who work in projects established in the free zones, from income and social service taxes.
3. Exempting goods imported into the free zones or exported therefrom, for parties other than the local market, from import fees, customs duties and all other taxes and fees payable thereon, except services charges and rents.
4. Exempting buildings and real estate constructions, which are erected in the free zones, from licensing fees and buildings and land taxes.
5. Exempting transfer of the capital invested in the free zones and the profits arising therefrom abroad from fees or charges, according to the valid laws.
6. Exempting products of industrial projects in the free zones, upon placing them for consumption in the local market, from customs duties within the extent of the cost of local materials and expenses included in their manufacturing, provided that such value be estimated by a committee chaired by the Director General or his or her deputy and representatives from the Ministry of Trade and Industry and the Ministry of Finance/Customs, to be appointed by the competent minister.

Services and facilities

1. Providing the free zones with necessary facilities, services and infrastructure such as electricity, water and modern telecommunication networks, in addition to modern networks of internal roads.
2. Constructing areas and necessary warehouses to meet the investors' requirements.

3. Opening branches of some banks inside the free zones in order to facilitate necessary banking services for investors. Also, seeing that branches of insurance and clearance companies are opened.
4. Registering companies inside the free zones instead of at the Ministry of Industry and Trade, in order to save investors' time and effort.
5. Issuing certificates of origin (free zones) for industrial products produced inside the free zones, which have local inputs of less than 40 per cent.
6. Applying one-window service for investment applications to facilitate decision-making.
7. Providing a portal site to enable customers to accomplish and follow up their transactions in addition to getting all the necessary information therefrom.

National goals of the Free Zones Corporation

The corporation seeks to achieve the national goals through the following:

1. Attracting local and foreign capital in the form of investments in different economic activities.
2. Providing work opportunities for Jordanians and enhancing their technical skills and experience.
3. Introducing advanced technology and technical skills into the kingdom.
4. Enhancing the leading role of the private sector in setting up private and joint free zones that use local raw materials in production inputs.
5. Developing new areas in the kingdom through setting up investment enterprises therein.

Public free zones

The following zones have been established and are supervised by the Free Zones Corporation:

1. Zarqa Free Zone

Established in 1983 on an international network, linking Jordan with neighbouring countries. About 5,200 dunums were allocated for this zone, and about 4,000 dunums were developed to meet the investment applications in the commercial, industrial and services fields.

2. Sahab Free Zone

Opened in 1997 on an area of 66 dunums located at King Abdullah II Industrial Estate/Sahab to serve the investors therein, whether in storage of primary raw materials or products of industries operating in the industrial estate.

3. Queen Alia International Airport Free Zone

Opened in 1998 at Queen Alia International Airport on a piece of land of 20 dunums and expanded to 35 dunums for the purpose of storing goods passing through the airport. This zone also organizes and controls the activities of the private free zones at civil airports.

4. Al-Karak Free Zone

Established in 2001 at Al-Hussein Bin Abdullah II Industrial Estate at Al-Karak, with an area of 143 dunums; this zone started business in the fourth quarter of 2003. It organizes and controls the activities of the private free zones located in the southern region.

5. Al-Karama Free Zone

The first stage of Al-Karama Free Zone, located at the Jordanian–Iraqi border, was inaugurated at the end of 2004 with an area of 500 dunums. The total area reaches 15,000 dunums, counting public and private free zones. Meanwhile, the corporation prepared a comprehensive plan to develop this zone between 2005 and 2010 to become a land port for all economic activities along with the new customs centre at the Iraqi–Jordanian border.

Private free zones

The idea of the private free zones was inspired by the government's directives to activate the role of the local and foreign private sectors, which contributes to development, absorbs a portion of national manpower and exploits local natural resources.

Many private free zones have been licensed, covering the following different economic activities:

1. The Jordan-Indo Chemicals Company: A joint venture between an Indian company (SPIC), the Jordan Phosphate Co and the Arab Company for Investment (Saudi Arabia).
2. Jordan Bromine Company: A joint venture between the Jordan Dead Sea Production Company and the American Albemarle Holding Group for the purpose of producing bromine and its derivatives.
3. Jordan Magnesia Company: A Jordanian joint company with Arab Potash Company.

4. Development of Information Technology Industrial Parks Company: A joint venture between the University of Science & Technology and Jordan QIZ Investment Ltd owned by Boscan Middle East Investment Ltd and located in the campus of the aforementioned university.
5. International Diamonds Investment Company: An industrial private free zone located at South Shuna.
6. King Abdullah II for Design and Development Centre: Located in Al-Dulail–Zarqa.
7. Hejazi & Gousheh Company for Sheep: A company specialized in the field of livestock and sheep, located in Al-Qweirah/Aqaba.
8. Trans-Jordan Livestock Company: A company specialized in the field of livestock and sheep, located in Al-Qweirah/Aqaba.
9. The Private Free Zones at the Jordanian Airports: The duty-free shops of the Jordanian Airports Company.
   a) Jordan Plane Engine Repair Company
   b) Jordan Plane Maintenance Company
   c) Jordan Flight Catering Company Ltd
   d) Jordan Flight Training and Simulation Company
   e) Jordan Plane Manufacturing & Development Company
   f) Jordan Aeronautical System Company
   g) Jordan International Air Cargo Company
   h) Sea Bird Plane Manufacturing Company

10. Jordan Duty Free Shops Company: This company operates at all seaports and land crossing points.
11. Jordan Gateway for the Multi-projects Company: A joint venture between Middle East Gateway Projects and Middle East Gateway Projects Co, located at North Gour Shuna.
12. Jordan Media City Company: Located near the Radio TV & Broadcasting Corporation Studios, it was set up as a core for the Free Media Zone Project to be established between the government and Dallah Information Production Company.
13. International Committee of the Red Cross: Operates in the field of storage and located at Al.Qastal, Amman.

Part Four

Aqaba Special Ecomonic Zone

4.1

The Aqaba Special Economic Zone

Introduction

In 2001, the Aqaba Special Economic Zone (ASEZ) was inaugurated. Being a liberalized, low-tax, duty-free and multi-sector development zone, the ASEZ is part of Jordan's assertive reform strategy to provide investors, from all over the world, with an attractive business environment.

Located at the crossroads of three continents, the ASEZ is a premium destination for investors and tourists alike. Situated at the head of the Gulf of Aqaba leading to the Red Sea, the ASEZ extends to the land borders of Israel and Saudi Arabia and embraces the territorial waters of Egypt, hence providing a strategic, comprehensive access to regional and international markets while promoting business opportunities and a high-quality lifestyle.

The Aqaba Special Economic Zone Authority

An administrative pioneer in the Hashemite Kingdom of Jordan, the Aqaba Special Economic Zone Authority (ASEZA) set out to bear the flare of progressive and transparent governance. It stands out as the prominent autonomous institution for the development and management of the ASEZ, offering integrated services and assistance to every business and corporation concerned. With its board of six ministerial-level commissioners, ASEZA is the first true decentralization model in Jordan. It is an inspiring symbol of modernism, committed to ever ensuring transparency through all its governing laws and regulations.

ASEZA: The one-stop-shop window

ASEZA aims at assisting investors with rapid and efficient support. It has created a special investor's one-stop-shop window that delivers all the services and tends to the business needs of investors. Furthermore, it has installed an electronically enabled Enterprise Registration and Permit System (ERPS), which has been awarded ISO certification, for labour, registration and permit issuance. Registering an enterprise in the ASEZ is therefore a swift and easy process guaranteeing direct and reliable steps towards full operation. Complementing its service-oriented approach, ASEZA personnel provide the highest-quality delivery services.

ASEZA operates a Customs Commission separate from the Jordanian National Customs. A business-friendly environment has been created in Aqaba in order to optimize profits, enhance a pleasant lifestyle and ensure efficient delivery of goods and services. In addition, ASEZA's simple corporate tax milieu contributes to minimizing any complexities of doing business while helping to maximize profits.

When established, ASEZA set a number of strategic goals including the wish to:

- create over 75,000 job opportunities and
- attract US $6 billion in investments by 2020.

ASEZA had already attained more than 115 per cent of its original goal by attracting more than US $6 billion in investment before the end of 2006.

The ASEZ golden opportunities

- No foreign equity restrictions on investment in tourism, industry, retail and other commercial services
- Regional multi-modal transportation hub with a full-service seaport and international airport
- Five per cent flat tax on net business income, except banking, insurance and land transport services
- No tariffs or import taxes on imported goods for individual consumption and registered enterprises
- No land and property taxes on utilized property for registered enterprises
- No foreign currency restrictions
- Full repatriation of profits and capital
- Streamlined labour and immigration procedures
- Multi-use commercial, tourist and residential environment
- Duty-free environment
- Exemption from social services tax

The crossroad to world markets

Jordan maintains privileged international trade relationships. Through-out the years, it has proved to be a trustworthy and dedicated partner, consolidating its position as a thriving liberalized trade and commerce pole. Various trade agreements underlie Jordan's growing objective of becoming the first liberalized environment provider in the region: the Jordan–US Free Trade Agreement, the Jordan–EU Association Agreement, the Qualifying Industrial Zones (QIZ) agreement and the Agadir Agreement. Moreover, Jordan's accession to the World Trade Organization (WTO) complements its quest for the establishment of a duty-free tax haven.

The ASEZ master plan: At the heart of modernity

In 2001, ASEZA adopted a comprehensive master plan that encompasses development activities in the zone for the promotion of portal, urban, tourist, commercial, industrial, logistics and other investment sectors. Extensive planning already covers five development areas: Aqaba Town, the Port Areas, the Coral Costal Zone, the Southern Industrial Zone and the Airport Industrial Zone.

According to the ASEZA 2020 master plan, investments in the zone are divided into three main activities:

1. 50 per cent in tourism
2. 30 per cent in services
3. 20 per cent in industries (13 per cent heavy industries, 7 per cent light industries)

Aqaba town: The oasis and beyond

On the edge of the desert, along the seaside, there rises an ancient city bursting with strategic tourism and investment prospects for the future. Modern architecture is to complement the old city's traditional elements, thus creating a unique cultural environment, and to provide new opportunities for investors. Tourists, residents and investors alike can relish the supremely laidback lifestyle. The beach is inviting and offers a dramatic view of the sea. The town enjoys a superb quietude amidst the fast pace of everyday life a rare feature blending past and present in scenic paths extending right through to Petra and Wadi Rum.

Port areas

The container port and industrial port will be expanded and some of their activities will be relocated. The general cargo operations in the main port will be relocated over time to the industrial port and the area will be redeveloped for tourism use, including a cruise ship and fast ferry terminal and a mixed-use hotel, retail, entertainment and residential development in an attempt to integrate the port with the city.

Coral coastal zone

Aqaba's other key tourism and residential development will be located in the southern coastal area, which includes Aqaba's coral reefs. Planning and development focus on minimizing the currently fragmented development parcels, protecting the beach and coral reefs, while encouraging private sector development to transform Aqaba's coral coastal zone into a new resort community with a marina, residential development, hotel and entertainment facilities all united with a continuous pedestrian promenade, which will run the length of the coast.

Southern industrial zone

A natural mountain buffer separates the coastal tourist area from the southern industrial zone, which is located close to the border of Saudi Arabia. The area will be expanded for future development for heavy agrochemical industries.

Airport industrial zone: Open opportunities

In addition to forming a strategic arm of Aqaba's transport hub, the airport industrial zone, located adjacent to King Hussein International Airport, will become the centre of light industrial and warehousing development. The airport will be expanded and will provide direct access to cargo and warehousing operations.

Modern infrastructure and services

Any successful international business relies on an integrated modern transportation network. Whether by air, sea or land, ASEZ offers a multi-functional system covering all business facilitation areas from ports, airports and highways to railroads.

The Port of Aqaba: An international harbour

The Port of Aqaba is the cornerstone of the historical waterfront city. It is the pivotal constituent of ASEZ's transportation network, offering up-to-the-minute services and facilities and providing international firms with consistently reliable staff and operational support. Benefits of the port services include the following:

- Large open and covered storage areas
- Electricity supply for refrigerated containers
- Storage areas for all types of bulk cargo
- Substantial storage capacity
- Efficient, fast and safe services
- Modern highways connecting Aqaba to other cities of Jordan and neighbouring countries

King Hussein International Airport: Open skies

While King Hussein International Airport offers passenger and freight transportation to Amman and international destinations, it fully characterizes Jordan's pursuit of exquisite relationships and preferential treatment for all partners. Located at the heart of the ASEZ, it operates under the 'Open Skies' policy. The airport accommodates all ranges of commercial aircraft, hence offering business opportunities in the following areas:

- Logistics
- Aviation services
- Trans-shipment
- Aerospace industries

Road and railway networks: Keeping closer

An 8,000-kilometre modern highway system stretches across the country, connecting Aqaba to bordering countries and Europe via Syria and Turkey. The Hijaz Railway also links Aqaba to other cities and areas with planned future extensions that will further increase Aqaba's accessibility.

Telecommunications: Connecting to the future

International firms and enterprises in the ASEZ can rely on a comprehensive telecommunications network that meets the highest world-class standards. ASEZ offers all business ventures and established companies the means to promote their projects and enhance productivity through modern infrastructure services. From advanced mobile communications networks to high-speed Internet connectivity and global satellite communication, ASEZ provides the ultimate set-up for fulfilling effective, easy and prosperous business partnerships.

Water, electricity and gas

- The ASEZ water supplies fall under the Aqaba Water Company's (AWC) management and policies. The AWC is the first government-owned company in the Arab world that runs according to private sector principles, once again manifesting ASEZA's unwavering commitment to governance and transparency.
- Natural pure water from the Disi Sandstone Aquifer does not require any treatment for domestic use. On the other hand, desalination represents a major investment opportunity as it is today a government priority.
- Electricity is to become Jordan's greatest asset. Aqaba's 650-megawatt thermal power station provides electricity to the ASEZ and the rest of Jordan.
- Natural gas is supplied to Aqaba through the El-Arish/Taba pipeline carrying gas from Egypt to Jordan, Syria and Lebanon. ASEZ's current and projected domestic and industrial demands are thus fully met.

Labour market flexibility

Jordan's advanced education system and high literacy rate serve its purpose of promoting a productive efficient workforce. Moreover, Jordan's flexible labour market offers businesses a 70 per cent margin for foreign employment while ASEZA provides the necessary visa procedures, work permits and residency permits for expatriate workers.

Serving the community

Community involvement is an integral part of the development process and the creation of a strong, sustainable and cohesive society as the community needs to be at the very centre of the decision-making processes. The local community of the ASEZ plays a vital role in ASEZA's efforts to turn the ASEZ into a world-class Red Sea business hub and leisure destination. One of ASEZA's major goals, in this regard, is to develop a self-sustaining capacity and to enhance community productivity.

Focusing on the future of the ASEZ local community through a human resource development perspective, ASEZA is mandated to develop policies and strategies for community social development in the fields of education, health, environment, low-income housing and poverty alleviation.

ASEZA has pledged to wholeheartedly fulfil its role in the community and to actively seek to integrate all its members. Dedication is what underlies its mission to facilitate life within the ASEZ and secure comfort and well-being.

Preserving a timeless haven

Rich in its cultural and natural diversity, Aqaba represents the perfect retreat for relaxation and exciting tourism activities. Accordingly, environmental and archaeological zones remain at the core of the master plan objective for the preservation of natural resources, within the construction frame. Several zones and reserves benefit from the required protection of Aqaba's cultural, archaeological, historical and natural heritage. Areas include the five environmental zones, coral reserves, archaeological reserves, natural area reserves and a beach protection zone. ASEZA strongly believes in ASEZ's inspirational status as a modern guardian of the ancient city of Aqaba.

ASEZ facts and figures

Over 5 years have passed since the zone was inaugurated, each year the zone has witnessed more and more developments in all aspects. In 2005 the ASEZ enjoyed another successful year. Economic indicators detected a qualitative and quantitative leap in all aspects. Over the past 5 years ASEZ has succeeded in achieving more than 115 per cent of its original goal, which was to attract US $6 billion by 2020.

- Air passengers totalled 167.672 in 2005, a 13 per cent increase when compared to 2004.
- Air cargo during 2005 was 1.5 million tonnes, a dramatic 187 per cent increase compared to 2004.

- Arab Bridge Maritime transported over 2 million passengers by sea on the Egypt/Nueibe'–Aqaba route in 2005, while a total of 59,000 vehicles were transported in 2005, a 24 per cent increase over 2004.
- About 431,981 tourists visited Aqaba in 2005 compared to 357,204 in 2004, a 20.93 per cent growth rate, with a 53.4 per cent room occupancy rate. The numbers of tourists that entered the zone in 2005 was double that 5 years earlier.
- In 2005 there was a 36 per cent increase in revenues generated from customs, income and sales tax as revenues collected reached 25,385,000 Jordanian dinars.
- A 65 per cent increase in the areas licensed for construction was recorded in 2005 compared to that in 2004. The total area licensed in 2005 was 487,633 square metres.
- Container handling saw a growth of 9 per cent in 2005 when compared to that a year earlier as total container handling reached 391,339 TEUs.
- Thirty-eight cruise ships docked in Aqaba port in 2005, an increase of 90 per cent over 2004.

4.2

The Aqaba Development Corporation

Introduction

The Aqaba Development Corporation (ADC) was launched in 2004 with the objective of unlocking the potential of the Aqaba Special Economic Zone (ASEZ) by accelerating its economic growth and development. Launched by the Aqaba Special Economic Zone Authority (ASEZA) and the Government of Jordan at the beginning of 2004, the ADC owns Aqaba's seaport, airport and strategic parcels of land as well as the development and management rights for these assets and key infrastructure and utilities.

ADC's mandate

The ADC is mandated to develop ASEZ by building or expanding infrastructure, creating business enablers for ASEZ and managing its key facilities. This will be achieved by attracting private sector developers and operators. The ADC also has the responsibility of implementing the ASEZ Master Plan in a manner that ensures integrated development and transforms Aqaba into a leading business and leisure hub on the Red Sea.

Private sector approach

A private shareholding company governed by a board of directors, the ADC is currently wholly owned by the Government of Jordan and ASEZA, each with a 50 per cent stake. The ADC is operated as a private sector organization and has secured a world-class multinational team to operate it, supported by a consortium of multi-disciplinary firms. Private sector participation in the development and management of ASEZ's strategic assets will be accelerated by the ADC either on a stand-alone basis or through public–private partnerships.

The business plan

ADC's objectives

ADC's main objective is to unlock Aqaba's economic potential by mobilizing private investment by packaging opportunities and leveraging public resources. To do this, the ADC has identified five main objectives to realize its mission:

1. Develop and manage ASEZ's strategic assets such as its ports and airports in accordance with sound business principles and practices to optimize private sector participation in their development and management
2. Develop and manage business-enabling projects and infrastructure to underpin and optimize private sector participation so as to accelerate ASEZ's economic growth and development
3. Undertake transactions that stimulate ASEZ's economy and promote the overall economic growth and development of ASEZ and the Kingdom of Jordan
4. Realize its business objectives on a viable and sustainable basis that not only realizes the economic and social development of ASEZ and the kingdom, but also generates adequate returns for ADC's shareholders and investors in the zone
5. Enable significant private sector management of the ADC and maximize private sector participation in all its deals

Project report

Transportation and infrastructure projects

1. Aqaba International Airport

The ADC established the airport company as a step forward in commercializing airport activities. The ADC seeks to provide Aqaba with a modern, fully equipped airport. King Hussein International Airport (KHIA) has adopted an open skies policy.

Jordan Aviation

The ADC and Jordan Aviation signed an agreement in which Jordan Aviation leased an area of land in KHIA to set up an aircraft maintenance centre for Jordan Aviation Aircraft. The total expected investment is around 3 million Jordanian dinars for a 70 m × 70 m engineering and maintenance hangar.

In addition, the ADC and Jordan Aviation signed an agreement granting Jordan Aviation self-handling rights for its aircraft and passengers at KHIA. In return, Jordan Aviation is to start daily regular flights from Aqaba to Amman and back.

Baddad Aviation

The ADC and the Baddad group signed an agreement to lease and invest 30,000 square metres of KHIA's land to construct buildings and hangers for aircraft maintenance, with a value of 15 million Jordanian dinars for the first stage of the project.

For this purpose, the Baddad group established Baddad Aviation, and signed East Line group, which manages Domodedovo Airport, Moscow, as technical operators. The new aircraft maintenance centre at KHIA will service Russian aircraft, especially the IL 62 and IL 76 models.

National Aviation Services

The ADC signed a 15-year contract with National Aviation Services (NAS) of Kuwait to undertake the development, management and operation of common-use air cargo services at KHIA. NAS will be responsible for establishing KHIA as a viable cargo hub, thereby enhancing services to current and future ASEZ-based enterprises and generating new air traffic at the airport. NAS will at the outset invest a minimum of 2.7 million Jordanian dinars to equip the facility and will hire approximately 40 staff initially, which will ultimately grow to about 100, predominantly local, personnel. NAS will also be responsible for marketing the facility and their services, and is expected to start work by the second half of 2006.

Ayla Flight Academy

Ayla Flight Academy will develop into the premier flight training organization in the Middle East, and help develop Aqaba's potential as a flight training hub for the Levant, by:

- providing rigorous training to professionally minded students
- utilizing brand new glass cockpit aircraft and
- making extensive use of the latest training techniques, including computer-based training and flight simulation.

2. Marine services

The ADC is seeking a private partner to operate the Marine Services at Aqaba Port through a joint venture. This tender comes within a comprehensive development plan, which the ADC has been implementing to rehabilitate and develop the port's facilities and the logistical and marine services in Aqaba from 2005 to 2010. The ADC previously launched an international tender 2 years ago, which attracted an international operator who won the tender to manage and operate the container terminal.

Marine services, consisting of vessel towage and manoeuvring along with managing pilot boats and other small harbour craft, represent essential ancillary services without which a seaport cannot safely function. The ADC is well aware that significant new investments are required, and new management, committed to providing the necessary skills enhancement to ensure improved performance, is essential. These factors mandate that the ADC look for well-qualified external partners. To enable the Port of Aqaba to have viable, productive and profitable marine services, the ADC is seeking a private sector investor/operator with the highest level of technical expertise and financial capabilities to manage, operate and re-equip Marine Services assets and activities at the Port of Aqaba, and also to re-equip, replace or otherwise bring up the standard of the current harbour vessels so that they are in class and suited to the present and anticipated needs of the port and vessels using the port.

The new investor/operator will be required to introduce advanced operating systems, recruit qualified Jordanian nationals to work at the port and provide employees with training both in Jordan and abroad. In addition, the investor/operator will be required to enhance safety procedures for ships, goods and passengers in line with international agreements. The ADC will soon announce the winner of this tender.

3. Main port relocation/redevelopment

Opportunity overview

Core to the ADC port programme is the relocation of the main port to the South Zone and redevelopment of the main port lands for predominantly commercial use. The ADC is developing a comprehensive approach to the business units presently located in the main port, which includes phosphate, roll-on/roll-off, general cargo, grain and small craft. Ownership and landlord responsibilities for the entire Port of Aqaba became vested in the ADC upon its creation. At the same time the ADC signed a management agreement with the Aqaba Ports Corporation (APC), whereby APC continues, for the time being, its role as day-to-day manager/operator of most of the port. A separate management agreement has been signed with AP Moller Terminals, which operates the container terminal on behalf of the ADC.

At the heart of ADC's strategy is realizing the vision of the zone's master plan by 2020. The plan earmarks Aqaba's main port for major waterfront redevelopment. The inner harbour will be transformed into a retail, commercial, residential and entertainment complex while the southern coastal zone, a nationally protected marine park, will develop as a tourist haven of sandy beaches, resorts, hotels, residential villas and marinas.

The relocation of the main port area will free up a prime waterfront development site in the fast growing city of Aqaba, where a significant amount of investments has poured in since it was declared as a special economic zone in 2001. That waterfront property will be developed into an urban tourism district, hosting a cruise terminal as well as hotels, villas, apartments, retails shops, restaurants and commercial centres.

This will also help extend the hotel area and the Corniche into one integrated tourist site on the northern shore of the Gulf of Aqaba. These developments, however, need to take into account Aqaba's pristine environment, particularly in the three port zone areas along the limited waterfront of Aqaba (27 kilometres).

To accomplish this, the first facility that should be constructed is a multi-purpose facility at the southern industrial zone. This facility will provide space to handle most bulk cargo from the main port and small shipments of bulk cargo that are currently loaded directly from ships to lorries. These small bulk shipments cause much of the dust seen at the port.

The construction of this multi-purpose facility will provide adequate space for tourism expansion for many years and still maintain space to handle cargo crucial to the Jordanian economy. This will also provide space for non-objectionable roll-on/roll-off cargo on land that is currently paved and requires no capital investment. The additional land is also needed for other development projects, such as a business incubator, being envisioned at the main Port.

Project status

The ADC is in the process of finalizing its overall port redevelopment and relocation strategy and expects to receive the full approval of the Board of Directors by end of this year. Therefore, no later than end of 2006 the ADC expects to be moving forward with a clear and detailed implementation programme for this multi-billion dollar project.

4. Sugar refinery

The ADC has invited companies to submit technical and commercial proposals to build and operate a sugar refinery on a long-term lease basis, as well as an associated marine facility on BOT basis as a receiving station for raw sugar.

5. Kuwaiti Jordanian Holding Company

The ADC signed a memorandum of understanding with the Kuwaiti Jordanian Holding Company (KJHC) to implement a number of infrastructure projects that will serve investments and existing and future projects in the ASEZ. A facilities management company and a utility company are to be set up as a joint venture between the ADC and KJHC by the first quarter of 2007.

6. Projects in the pipeline

Port activities such as a passenger/ferry terminal, phosphate terminal, oil jetty and industrial jetty are among the projects currently being packaged and will be announced as investment opportunities (BOT or ROT) or through a management contract.

- A new passenger terminal will be constructed in the southern port to free space for container terminal expansion and for relocation of activities from the main port.
- A long-term, on-land storage solution for oil will be developed in partnership with the Ministry of Energy and other stakeholders to ensure strategic storage capacity for the kingdom and to create a business case of interest to prospective private investors.
- A new Ro-Ro terminal will be designed and built adjacent to the container terminal expansion area, utilizing a portion of the site occupied by the present passenger terminal plus additional back-up storage area.

Major real estate projects

6.1. Labour housing

The ADC and the International Communication and Construction Consultancy Company signed an agreement to build a residential project on a 30,000 square metre plot of land for the engineers, construction workers and technicians of the construction phase of the Saraya Aqaba project.

The construction of the residential area will create 3,000 job opportunities during the construction phase of the Saraya Aqaba project. Estimated at worth around 5.5 million Jordanian dinars, the project started in mid-2006.

6.2. Saraya Aqaba

One of the major tourist and real estate development projects in Aqaba, Saraya Aqaba is set around an artificial lake and includes five-star hotels, sandy beaches, restaurants, entertainment facilities, convention centres and residential units. The project, with a total cost of US $810 million, represents a genuine partnership between the public and private sectors. It is scheduled to be completed in March 2009 and will provide around 3,000 jobs.

6.3 North and Back Road Logistics Parks – Warehouse Villages

Aqaba National Real Estate Projects Co (ANREPCO) is a new company established from a joint venture between the ADC and the National Real Estate Co (NREC) (Kuwait).The capital of this company is 26 million Jordanian dinars, ADC's share is 30 per cent, and NREC's share is 70 per cent.

6.4. Ayla Oasis

Ayla Oasis Tourist Project, which is under construction, is one of the largest tourism projects in the history of the kingdom. It is expected to provide 800 residential buildings, in addition to 1,500 rooms in four- and five-star hotels to be built over a period of 12 years. The total cost of this project is approximately US $1 billion, with a total area of four million square metres on the northern shore.

6.5. Yemeniya Heights Residential Development

This project encompasses a unique area with environmental considerations, located over a total area of 355,000 square metres near the coral reefs south of the city of Aqaba. The beach club will be developed by Al-Qabas Company for Real Estate Development to better serve the residents of Yemeniya. The club's area will total 50,000 square metres.

6.6. International Investment Arabian Group

The ADC signed an agreement with the International Investment Arabian Group (GAI) for the construction and development of a comprehensive residential city on 285,000 square metres of land north of Aqaba and costing 100 million Jordanian dinars. The residential city will be a new and unique model that will incorporate everything that a resident in Aqaba will require – high-quality housing, shopping centres and tourist and entertainment facilities. Green spaces will cover an area equal to two-thirds of the built-up land.

Part Five

The Tax and Regulatory Framework

5.1

Taxation in Jordan

Asem P Haddad, CPA Partner, Deloitte & Touche (Middle East), Jordan

Introduction

Most of the business laws and regulations of Jordan have been amended, revised and modernized during the last few years to attract direct and indirect foreign investments as well as national investments. Jordan has recently signed a free trade agreement with the United States and prior to that a partnership agreement with the European Union. Jordan also has qualified industrial zones (QIZs) whereby certain goods produced in such QIZs are eligible to enter the US market tax free or taxed at a reduced rate. Furthermore, Jordan is a member of the World Trade Organization.

Tax treaties

Jordan has signed comprehensive tax treaties with the following countries:

- Egypt
- France
- Tunisia
- Romania
- Turkey
- Indonesia
- Poland
- Malaysia
- India
- Canada
- Algeria
- Yemen
- Bahrain

- Syria
- Arab Economic Council Countries
- United Kingdom
- Lebanon
- Korea
- Kuwait

Corporate income tax

The income tax regime in Jordan is based on the self-assessment concept, whereby the resident taxpayers are required to complete and file an annual tax return and pay the declared income tax by 30 April of the following year.

Tax returns are subject to audit on a sample basis within 1 year of filing. Legal entities (companies) are taxed on net annual taxable income (taxable profits) generated in Jordan. The corporate tax rates range from 15 per cent to 35 per cent based on the industry of the legal entity. The following are the corporate tax rates for the different industries:

Banks and financial Institutions	35%
Insurance, money exchange, brokerage, telecommunications, trading and commercial services	25%
Mining, manufacturing, hotels and hospitals, transportation and construction	15%

Income generated from agricultural activities, farming, livestock and fisheries are exempt from income tax. Only 20 per cent of net income after tax of foreign branches and subsidiaries of Jordanian companies is subject to income tax in Jordan at a rate of 35 per cent. Fifteen per cent of net income from rent of property in Amman and 30 per cent of net income from rent of property outside Amman are exempt from income tax. Operating foreign companies (branch offices) are entitled to claim tax free up to 5 per cent of their net annual income earned in Jordan as head office-allocated expenses (branch office's share of head office expenses). Income realized from exported goods and certain exported services are exempt from income tax in Jordan in accordance with a cabinet resolution.

Incentives and fines

Taxpayers are granted incentives (discount) for early filing of income tax returns. Taxpayers, who file their annual tax returns by 31 January will receive a discount of 6 per cent of tax paid the discount is reduced to 4 per cent for filing in February and to 2 per cent for filing in March of the following year.

However, a fine of 2 per cent of tax due is imposed on each month of delay in filing the annual tax return with an upper ceiling of 24 per cent. Extension of the filing date is not allowable.

Furthermore, a late payment fine of 1.5 per cent is imposed for each month of delay in paying the income tax due, withholding tax and payroll taxes. This fine is not subject to any upper limit.

Capital gains

As a general rule, capital gains resulting from sale of property, land and securities are non-taxable for taxpayers other than banks and financial institutions. Banks and financial institutions enjoy a tax exemption of 25 per cent of capital gains.

Withholding taxes

- Employers are required to withhold income tax and social services tax due on employees from their monthly remuneration and pay them over to the income tax department on a monthly basis.
- A withholding tax of 2 per cent is required on amounts paid to resident service providers.
- Amounts paid to non-resident service providers including royalties, franchise fees and know-how are subject to a withholding tax of 10 per cent.

Dividends tax and investment income

In-cash and in-kind dividends, distributions of profits to partners as well as transfer of profits and repatriation of capital are not subject to withholding tax in Jordan. Furthermore, dividends and interest earned by individuals and legal entities 'other than banks and financial institutions' on securities, treasury bills and bonds as well as bonds and debentures are exempt from income tax. However, expenses and costs relating to exempted income are not allowable deductions provided that such costs and expenses do not exceed 50 per cent of the exempted income.

Interest earned on individual bank deposits as well as by non-residents is subject to income tax at a rate of 5 per cent. Interest on bank deposits of companies is taxed as a normal source of income at the same corporate income tax rate.

Moreover, only 25 per cent of dividends and interest earned by banks and financial institutions on securities, treasury bills and bonds as well as bonds and debentures are exempt from income tax.

General sales tax

Unless it is listed in the schedule of exempted goods and services, locally produced and imported goods and services are subject to sales tax in Jordan. The general sales tax (GST) rate is 16 per cent. Certain essential listed goods and services are subjected to a sales tax of 4 per cent. Sales tax paid on inputs used for the production of goods and the provision of services can be offset against sales tax charged on outputs (sales).

All taxpayers must register for GST if their taxable turnover in respect of goods or services exceeds the following threshold during 12 consecutive months:

1. 10,000 Jordanian dinars for manufactures subject to the special tax.
2. 50,000 Jordanian dinars for manufactures subject to the general tax.
3. 30,000 Jordanian dinars for service industries.
4. 50,000 Jordanian dinars for traders.
5. There is no threshold applied to importers. Therefore, all importers are required to register regardless of the amount of their imports unless such imports are exempted or intended for personal use.

Customs duties

Goods entering the kingdom shall be subject to customs duties prescribed in the customs tariff except for goods that are excluded under the provisions of this Customs Law or the provisions of the Investment Promotion Law, any concession Law or any international agreement.

The customs duties shall be either a percentage of the value of goods or a lump sum for each unit of the commodity. The fees of the tariff could be both a percentage and a lump sum for the same kind of goods, subject to a ceiling of 25 per cent. The customs value of the imported goods shall be the transaction value, which is the price actually paid or payable for goods, when bought.

Investment promotion law

Jordan has a very modern investment promotion law that provides attractive incentives to investors in different sectors. The exemptions are dependent on the geographical location of the project. Projects falling within the following sectors or sub-sectors shall enjoy the exemptions and incentives provided by the law:

• Manufacturing
• The agriculture sector
• Hotels and hospitals
• Maritime transport and railways
• Any other sector or sub-sectors the council of ministers decides to add

For the purpose of this law, Jordan is geographically segmented into three development zones – A, B and C – based on the degree of the economic development of each area in each of the sectors listed above, with A being the most developed and C the least developed area.

The following is a summary of exemptions provided under the law:

1. Exemption from Income Tax and Social Service Tax

Projects approved by the Investment Committee enjoy a 10-year exemption from income tax and social services tax at the following rates depending on the sector and the area in which the project is located.

	Rate
Projects in zone (A)	25%
Projects in zone (B)	50%
Projects in zone (C)	75%

Whereby a project is expanded, improved or modernized to increase production capacity, it shall receive an additional year of exemption for every increase in production of not less than 25 per cent, for a maximum of 4 years.

2. Exemption from customs duties

Imported fixed assets required for a project are exempted from customs duties and fees for a period of 3 years starting from the date of approval. Imported fixed assets needed for expanding, modernizing or developing a project are exempted from customs duties and fees provided that they result in an increase of a minimum of 25 per cent of production capacity.

Spare parts imported for a project are exempted from customs duties and fees provided that their value does not exceed 15 per cent of the total value of the fixed assets utilizing these spares.

Hotel and hospital projects are granted extra exemptions from customs duties and fees on their imports of furniture and supplies for the purpose of renovation, once every 7 years.

Free Zones Law

Jordan established a number of public and private free zones throughout the kingdom to facilitate its role as a regional hub. Goods may pass through these zones, exempt from customs duties and import fees. Facilities may also be leased in free zones at reduced rates.

Projects established in free zones enjoy the following exemptions and incentives:

1. Exemptions of profits from income tax and social service tax for a period of 12 years from the commencement of operations.
2. Remuneration of non-Jordanian employees working in a free zone is exempted from income tax and social services tax.
3. Goods imported into the free zone are exempted from customs duties, import fees and sales tax. Goods exported from the free zone are exempted from taxes and fees.
4. Exemption of products produced in the free zone for domestic consumption from customs duties and taxes is limited to the value of materials, costs and local expenditure involved in a product's manufacture, provided this value is approved by the Free Zone Committee.
5. Buildings constructed in the free zones are exempted from licensing fees and real estate taxes.
6. Freedom to repatriate capital invested and profits generated.
7. Ten per cent exemption of annual rent of land and structure for industrial projects.

Aqaba Special Economic Zone

Aqaba, the only Jordanian port on the Red Sea, has been designated as a special economic zone since 2000 according to a special decree legislated for this purpose. Projects in the Aqaba Special Economic Zone (ASEZ) are subject to tax laws and regulation other than those national tax laws and regulations applicable to projects located in other Jordanian territories. Projects located in ASEZ enjoy reduced income tax rates, reduced sales tax rates as well as other incentives.

Taxes on individuals

Individuals are liable to the Jordanian income tax on income derived or earned in Jordan, irrespective of residence. Income arising outside Jordan and originating from non-resident deposits in foreign currencies is not subject to tax, provided that the entry of such funds to the kingdom and the deposit abroad are made in accordance with the regulations and instructions of the Central Bank of Jordan. The tax jurisdiction is thus territorial, as in the case of corporate bodies. However, entitlement to personal allowances and some other relief is linked with residence.

A Jordanian citizen is regarded as a resident in Jordan if the individual spends at least 120 days in Jordan per year. A non-Jordanian is considered resident in Jordan if he or she spends at least 183 days in Jordan in a year. The days spent in Jordan need not be consecutive in either case.

Taxable income: This includes employment income and the other types of income that are taxable in the case of corporate bodies. Employment income: This comprises salaries, wages, allowances and any other benefits from any employment in Jordan, subject to an exemption of 50 per cent of the first 12,000 Jordanian dinars and 25 per cent of the remaining taxable income for private sector employees and 50 per cent for public sector employees. Subsistence allowances paid to private sector employees are not taxable provided that they are used for the purposes of the employment. Travel allowances not exceeding 10 per cent of the basic salary when incurred within the work centre and 20 per cent if incurred outside such centre are exempt with ceilings of 600 Jordanian dinars and 1,200 Jordanian dinars per annum, respectively. Entertainment allowances not exceeding 10 per cent of basic salary or 300 Jordanian dinars annually, whichever is less, are excluded from taxable income. If these limits are exceeded, the excess is taxable.

Allowable deductions: Residents may deduct the following personal allowances from annual taxable income:

Unmarried person	1,000
Married person	2,000
For each dependent child	500
For each dependent parent	500
For each dependent relative	200 (maximum 1,000)
For each son, daughter or close relative studying at university level and supported by the taxpayer	2,000
For each taxpayer where he or she is studying at university level	2,000

To claim a non-Jordanian as a dependent for tax purposes, the dependent has to be resident in Jordan. The costs of hospitalization and medications in Jordan incurred by a resident taxpayer on his or her own behalf or for the benefit of a dependent are calculated as given. Where medical expenses incurred outside Jordan relate to treatment not available in Jordan, or cover an operation in emergency conditions in accordance with the regulations, such expenses are acceptable provided the total amount does not exceed 10,000 Jordanian dinars per annum in Jordan and 15,000 Jordanian dinars outside Jordan.

Any amount paid by the resident for an emergency surgical operation performed outside Jordan that could not have been performed in Jordan, for him or her or for a dependent for whom he or she is legally responsible, according to the regulations, provided that the total amount exempt shall not exceed 10,000 Jordanian dinars per annum.

Rent payable by a resident taxpayer or his wife for his own accommodation in the kingdom, provided that the total amount exempted shall not exceed 2,000 Jordanian dinars per annum, is as given.

Interest of up to 2,000 Jordanian dinars per year on a loan applied by a resident taxpayer or his wife to acquire or build his own home.

Contributions to the Social Security Corporation and approved pension and savings funds.

Contributions to a medical insurance scheme.

Personal tax rates: The tax on taxable income of any person, except for companies, shall be charged at the following rates:

Slice of Taxable Income (per cent)	Rate of Tax Applicable to Slice (in Jordanian dinars)
0–2,000	
2,000–6,000	
6,000–14,000	
Over 14,000	

The maximum marginal rate for individuals is 25 per cent.

A social services tax is payable equal to 10 per cent of the income tax due.

Social security

Companies that hire five or more people (Jordanian or non-Jordanian) are required to subscribe to the social security scheme and, accordingly, pay 16.5 per cent of the total monthly salaries and benefits to the Social Security Department of which 5.5 per cent should be withheld from the employees' monthly remuneration, 11 per cent being the employer contribution.

The Social Security Scheme provides two types of insurance: insurance against work injuries and occupational diseases and insurance against disability, old age and death.

The insurance against work injuries and occupational diseases covers the medical care necessitated by the condition of the injured employee, such as the cost of medical treatment and hospitalization, daily allowances and the cost of rehabilitation, daily allowances for temporary disability, monthly salaries and fixed compensations, monthly salaries payable to the beneficiaries and funeral expenses.

Pension payments become payable to male employees at the age of 60 and to female employees at the age of 55 provided that they fulfil certain requirements set out in the law.

In addition to relieving the employer from compensating the employee for work injuries and occupational diseases, joining the social security scheme also relieves the employer from the end-of-service indemnity the employer is required to pay to the employee upon termination of employment as set out in the Labour Law. This means that the 11 per cent contribution of the employer covers end-of-service indemnities.

Upon leaving Jordan, foreign employees are partially reimbursed for their contributions to the social security scheme as follows:

- 10 per cent of their average annual wages for each year of service if the period of subscription to the social security scheme is less than 5 years.
- 12 per cent of their average annual wages for each year of service if the period of subscription to the social security scheme is more than 5 years and less than 10 years.
- 15 per cent of their average annual wages for each year of service if the period of subscription to the social security scheme is 10 years or more.

However, employees not subscribing to the social security scheme are entitled to end-of-service indemnity equivalent to 1 month's remuneration for every year worked multiplied by the latest average monthly remuneration.

The tax practice in Jordan

Tax returns are subject to audit and verification by the Income Tax Department on a sample basis within 1 year of filing. Furthermore, the Sales Tax Department makes occasional scheduled visits to audit taxpayers.

Payroll taxes are also subject to audit by the related departments and an annual payroll certificate needs to be obtained and presented to the corporate tax division. The corporate tax division usually matches the figures in the payroll certificate with the reported payroll expenses.

Although there are almost comprehensive tax-implementing regulations, certain areas are still discretionary and subject to discussion with the tax assessors. However, taxpayers have the right to object to a tax assessment and further appeal the assessment before the Income Tax

Court of Appeal until a fair and satisfactory resolution of the dispute is attained.

The Income Tax Law, the Companies Law, the Investment Promotion Law and other business-related laws and regulations are being revised and are expected to shortly pass through the legislative channels. The new tax law was expected to be enforced effective from 1 January 2007 but it had not passed by that date. It is unlikely the law will be applied retroactively once introduced.

5.2

Legal Environment in Jordan

Yousef S Khalilieh, Member Noor A Jundi, Associate and Shereen S Said, Associate Rajai K W Dajani & Associates, Advocates and Legal Consultants, Amman

Introduction

The Hashemite Kingdom of Jordan has been looked upon as a model for legal consistency. The Jordanian laws have consistently followed a certain trend, lending most Jordanian legislation an easy-to-follow character that is difficult to find in most other countries' legislations.

Although the country did not officially become independent until 1928, Jordan as the Emirate of Trans-Jordan enforced a body of Ottoman and British Mandate legislation, and kept them in force with only slight amendments until the period of legislative reform in the early 1950s, after the establishment of the Hashemite Kingdom of Jordan. At that stage, the constitution was first legislated and most other laws introduced following the same principles. This is one of the main reasons for the consistency of Jordanian laws. However, many important laws were legislated at a later stage such as the Civil Law, which was introduced in 1976.

The Jordanian constitution

The constitution was one of the first laws to be drawn up in the Hashemite Kingdom of Jordan, and although it was promulgated in 1952, it is frequently looked upon by other countries as a model constitution.

The constitution is divided into nine main chapters, each of which is vital to the political, economic and social life of most Jordanians. The first chapter discusses the system of government, making clear that Jordan is a parliamentary monarchy and expressing the importance of separation of the three main powers of the state.

The second chapter stipulates the rights and duties of Jordanians. Many important rights like freedom of speech and freedom of the press are specifically mentioned in this chapter, as is the declaration that all Jordanians are equal before the law no matter what their religion, colour or race.

The third, fourth and fifth chapters discuss the three main powers of the state, the authorities granted under these powers and the way in which they are separated. The fifth chapter states that the legislative power will comprise two chambers, the House of Deputies and the Senate. The members of the House of Deputies are sworn in by direct election, whilst members of the Senate are appointed by the king. In this chapter, the constitution also explains the method by which laws are legislated and amended, and gives executive authority, represented by the government, to legislate 'temporary laws' under certain conditions, which must later be ratified by parliament in order to become permanent. The constitution allows the government to legislate temporary laws only in the case when the parliament is not in session or the country is in a state of emergency.

However, it still grants the executive power the right to issue statutes that either explain the manner in which certain laws are to be implemented or deal with issues that either the constitution or specific laws stipulate must be organized by statute. A good example of this is the Statute of Civil Service, which the constitution itself provides should be organized by statute. The government also has the right to issue instructions or regulations that are lower in strength and value than statutes. These are usually used to organize the work in the governmental departments and to explain the way in which specific articles of laws or statutes in force shall be implemented or applied.

The sixth chapter talks about the authority of the judiciary and the way judges are appointed. The main article in this chapter declares that judges are independent and that no one shall have the right to influence their judgement. This chapter also discusses the different types of courts in the country, the main areas of jurisdiction for each type of court and the different stages of jurisdiction.

The seventh chapter discusses the financial and monetary matters in the country, how the budget is ratified and implemented and the process that must be followed for the budget to be reviewed and legalized.

The eight and ninth chapters of the constitution contain general provisions as well as directions applicable to amendment of the constitution and the conditions that allow such amendments.

In short, the constitution provides the main premises around which most of the other laws in Jordan are legislated. It is also considered the highest legislation in the country and if contradictions are found between the provisions of the constitution and those of other laws, statutes or regulations, those of the constitution have supremacy.

The Jordanian judiciary system

The Jordanian legal framework

Although Jordan was under the British Mandate for a considerable period of time, the kingdom follows the Latin Civil Law as its main judicial system. This stems from the Ottoman Empire – many laws of the period remained in force even after the empire's fall and were only amended slightly at first until the revolution of legislation, which started in the early 1950s.

Sources of jurisdiction

The Jordanian Civil Law (the 'code') was published in the *Official Gazette* on 1 August 1976 and came into force on the 1 January 1977. Article 2 of the code states that the sources of jurisdiction are to be followed in the order stipulated within the article. The first source is the law in its general sense. This includes laws enacted by parliament, the 'temporary laws', statutes and regulations. The second source is Islamic jurisprudence, which a court is supposed to follow if nothing related to the subject matter is mentioned in any part or section of the law. The third principle to be followed is legal precedence concerning the issues in question. When the court finds nothing in the above-stated sources of jurisdiction it is expected to use the general principles of justice.

On the other hand, in criminal issues Jordanian courts are bound to follow the Magna Carta principle, which states that neither crime nor punishment shall be applied if they are not specifically mentioned in the law. This means that courts in criminal matters are not free to return to as many sources as they deem necessary to govern the situation in question, as is the case in civil disputes, for they can judge only according to the law in force at the time of the trial. Deeds that are not considered to be crimes according to the law will not be punished.

In the administrative branch of the law, which is applied mostly by the High Court of Justice, the main principle for legislation is that there must be no penalty without legislation. This means that a court must not allow the administration to apply any penalties unless such punishments have been specifically stated by the law. In almost all other issues, the court discussing administrative issues has the right to return to the 'General Principles of Administrative Law', which means it has full authority to return to the sources it deems necessary to govern the situation in question.

However, as in most other civil law countries, Jordan considers precedence cases and legal jurisprudence as supplementary sources of jurisdiction. This means that although not obligatory, courts are allowed to search for answers for matters in question in earlier cases and sometimes writings of different authors on similar matters. However, this is mostly in theory because courts tend to follow the decisions of higher courts. This gives legal precedence a higher state of obligation than that stated in the law.

Types of courts in Jordan

The constitution divides the courts in Jordan into three main divisions:

1.   Regular courts
2.   Religious courts
3.   Special courts

Regular courts

This is the widest division of courts in Jordan and almost all disputes concerning civil, criminal and commercial issues are settled by them, unless the constitution or any other law in force specifically states that such a matter must be ruled by a religious or a special court.

The law that primarily addresses administration of the regular courts is the 'Law of Formation of Regular Courts, number 17, for 2001, which came into force on 11 June 2001. This law states that litigation must be in two stages and later stipulates the different types of regular courts in Jordan:

1. Magistrates' Courts

Magistrates' Courts are usually seen as the lowest level of regular courts in Jordan. They usually consist of just one judge and their jurisdiction is specifically mentioned in the law of civil procedures and the law of the Magistrates' Courts as being civil disputes not exceeding 3000 Jordanian dinars as well as some other specific small criminal issues.

In addition, Article 3 of the Magistrates' Courts Law grants such courts jurisdiction over a few more issues such as those concerning vacation of rented property or division of immovable real estate. This type of court is part of the first stage of litigation, which means that the courts in this phase have the right to discuss the matter in question on its merits and by law. Courts of the Second Stage of Litigation have the right to rule only if the First Stage Court erred in applying and implementing the law, unless otherwise specified by legislation.

2. First Instance Courts

First Instance Courts enjoy the highest level of jurisdiction and are sometimes said to have a 'general jurisdiction'. This means that any dispute that is not within the jurisdiction of the Magistrates' Courts or any other special, regular or religious court according to the law must be judged by the First Instance Courts. These comprise one judge in civil matters and two judges in the case of crimes not under the jurisdiction of the High Court of Felonies. In those cases where they are dealing with criminal issues for which the penalty is execution, life imprisonment or imprisonment for periods not less than 15 years, First Instance Courts must be made up of three judges. In some specific cases, the Courts of First Instance act as a Court of Appeal for decisions issued by Magistrates' Courts and other judgements that the law states should be appealed to them and not to the Court of Appeal. This type of court is also a part of the first stage of litigation.

3. Courts of Appeal

Article six of the Law of Formulation of Regular Courts establishes Courts of Appeal in Amman, Irbid and Ma'an. These courts have the authority to review decisions issued by the First Instance Courts, and judgements made by the Magistrates' Courts in instances where the law states that they should be reviewed by the Court of Appeal. These courts are usually formed of three judges although, in certain cases, a higher number of judges might be needed for the court to be in session. The Court of Appeal is almost always the second stage of litigation.

4. The Court of Cassation

The Court of Cassation is the most senior court in Jordan. Its location, according to the law, is Amman and it comprises five judges at a minimum and nine at a maximum. The Court of Cassation is a third stage court of litigation, which means that it has the authority to review a case only by reference to the law and not on its merits. It has jurisdiction to review judgements issued by the Courts of Appeal in civil disputes that exceed 10,000 Jordanian dinars. Claims under 10,000 Jordanian dinars may be heard with the specific permission of the cassation panel. In criminal matters, it has jurisdiction over judgements issued by the Courts of Appeal in felonies and on any other issues for which the law specifically mandates a review. Decisions taken by the Court of Cassation in its full formation are considered to be general principles of law that the lower degree courts in the kingdom are obliged to follow.

Religious courts

Article 105 of the constitution deals with the formation of religious courts in Jordan. It stipulates that religious courts are either sharia courts or tribunals of other religious communities. Sharia courts have jurisdiction over civil status for Muslims and *waqf* (religious tax) issues. The tribunals of other religious communities deal with the civil status of non-Muslims and are regulated by special laws relating to these communities.

Special courts

Special courts are those formed by special legislation as an exception to the general rule that grants jurisdiction to regular courts. Examples of such courts include the Court of Income Tax, the Court of Customs and the Highest Court of Felonies. Such courts are usually created in areas that the legislature deems should be governed by specialized courts with more experience and knowledge in specific matters. However, many of the decisions of the special courts, such as the Highest Court of Felonies, are subject to review by the Court of Cassation in the second stage of litigation. Some special courts have their own courts of appeal, such as the Court of Income Tax, most of whose decisions can be appealed before the Court of Appeals of Income Tax.

The different stages of legislation

The constitution provides a clear path for the introduction of new legislation in the kingdom, stipulating that the draft must pass through the four different stages of legislation before it can be considered an enforceable law. In cases of emergency requiring the government to issue Temporary Laws, such legislation must pass through almost the same procedure as the draft law in order to become a regular permanent law. However, statutes, which are issued by the Council of Ministers, and regulations, which are issued by administrators, do not need to pass through this procedure.

The first stage of legislation is the proposition, which is the stage in which the law is formulated and prepared before being passed to parliament to be voted upon. The government retains the right to propose that a certain law should be voted upon together with any 10 members of the House of Deputies or the Senate.

The second stage of legislation is the voting in regard to the proposal presented to parliament. The first chamber to discuss the draft is the House of Deputies. If the draft is passed there then it will be sent to the Senate for their decision. At this stage, if the Senate also passes the draft then it will be sent to the king for ratification. If the Senate does not pass the draft, it will be sent back to the House of Deputies with the amendments that the Senate recommends. If the House of Deputies agrees with the Senate on the amendments then the draft will be sent directly to the king for ratification. If not, then both chambers must meet in a joint session (in which the House of Deputies, which consists of twice as many members as the Senate, has an edge in the voting) to vote on the draft. If the draft passes a two-thirds majority vote, then the legislative procedure will be pursued.

The third stage of legislation is the promulgation or ratification by the king. This stage is usually considered to be the true birth certificate of the law that enables the head of the executive authority to exercise his power to introduce the new law. In any case in which the king does not ratify the law within 6 months, it is considered automatically ratified.

The fourth and final stage of legislation is publication of the law in the *Official Gazette*. By default, the law will be considered enforceable 30 days after such publication unless otherwise specified by the law itself.

Concerns

Jordan enjoys a very advanced legal system that has been undergoing substantial revision and modernization in recent years. Many of the old laws have been either amended or replaced to allow for the country to follow other advanced countries in providing the best legal protection for the country and its citizens. Some of the new or amended laws are the Companies Law, the Banking Law, several amendments concerning intellectual property issues, the laws of Civil and Criminal Procedures and the Landlords and Tenants Law. However, many of these await ratification by parliament.

5.3

Procedures for Handling Legal Disputes

Yousef S Khalilieh, Member Noor A Jundi, Associate and Shereen S Said, Associate Rajai K W Dajani & Associates, Advocates and Legal Consultants, Amman

Introduction

Legal disputes in Jordan are settled in one of two ways:

1. Through the competent legal authority in Jordan, as regulated and governed by several laws such as the Law of Civil Procedures No. 24 of 1988, the Law of Criminal Procedures No. 9 of 1961, the Law of Magistrates' Courts No. 15 of 1952 and the Law of the Formation of Regular Courts of 2001.
2. Through arbitration, upon the mutual agreement of the disputed parties, as regulated by the Arbitration Law No. 31 of 1997.

The competent legal authority in Jordan

The competent legal authority is represented by the courts, the system of which is hierarchical, whereby each court is bound by the *ratio decidendi* of a case decided by another court if it is lower in the hierarchy and will not be bound by it if it is higher. Courts in Jordan are divided into three types

1. Regular courts.
2. Courts of religious affairs
3. Special courts

Regular courts are represented by:

Magistrates' Courts that are specialized in hearing:

1. Small civil claims not exceeding 3,000 Jordanian dinars. The court judgement in these claims is only final if the total amount of the claim does not exceed 250 Jordanian dinars excluding evacuation of the leased premises claims.

2. Criminal claims such as offences and misdemeanours where 2 years of imprisonment would be the likely outcome.

First Instance Courts hear most of the civil and criminal claims outside the jurisdiction of the Magistrates' Courts, or any other claims referred to their jurisdiction by any applicable law. Furthermore, judgements issued from Magistrates' Courts in criminal claims may be appealed to the First Instance Court in regard to violations where the maximum penalty for the offences committed does not exceed imprisonment of 1 month and a fine of 30 Jordanian dinars.

The Court of Appeal, which is considered a second-degree court, has a presence in three districts, Amman, Ma'an and Irbid, and hears appeals against judgements issued by the magistrates and First Instance Courts.

The Court of Cassation is the highest judicial authority in Jordan and sets judicial precedents and hears civil claims exceeding 10,000 Jordanian dinars. Claims under 10,000 Jordanian dinars may be heard with the specific permission of the cassation panel. Furthermore, the said court may only hear claims with certain specified conditions as it does not examine the subject matter of a claim but just the legal issues.

All appeals related to administrative decisions issued by the public authorities in addition to violation of applicable laws and the constitution are heard by the High Court of Justice, which is located in Amman. All judgements issued by this court are final.

Courts of Religious Affairs hear matters of personal status, including marriage, divorce, inheritance and alimony. Persons of the same religion are subject to the appropriate religious courts, the Sharia Courts for Muslims and the Ecclesiastical Courts for Christians.

Special courts hear certain and specific cases such as those related to income tax, customs and state security matters. They are governed and regulated through separate laws and regulations such as those laid down for the state security court, the income tax court and the capital felonies court.

Arbitration

If a dispute is referred to arbitration, whether related to a civil or a commercial dispute between public and private persons, and regardless of whether the legal relationship is contractual or not, the arbitration will be based on the written agreement of the disputing parties, otherwise it is void.

The arbitration agreement may be prepared prior to or after the dispute is referred to court. Furthermore, unless otherwise agreed by the two parties or the arbitral tribunal, the arbitration must be conducted in Arabic. The arbitrating parties are free to agree on the place of arbitration, whether in the kingdom or abroad, but if they fail to agree on the place of arbitration, the arbitral tribunal will determine the location.

In general the arbitration procedures are very flexible and may be determined by the arbitral parties, including determination of the applicable law that will apply to the dispute, the time limitations for issuing the arbitral award and any specific conditions that will apply to the award.

Furthermore, the arbitration may be terminated by the following:

1. Issuance of an arbitral award terminating the dispute.
2. Issuance of a court order terminating the arbitral proceedings.
3. Mutual agreement of the arbitral parties.
4. Abandonment of the dispute submitted to arbitration by the plaintiff, unless the arbitral tribunal decides, at the defendant's request, to continue the arbitral proceedings.
5. A finding by the arbitral tribunal that the continuation of the arbitral proceedings has become ineffective or impossible.
6. Failure to reach the majority required for the issuance of the arbitral award.

An action to nullify an arbitral award must be raised within 30 days following the date on which the party against whom it was rendered was notified. Such action will only be admissible if the party requesting the nullity had not waived his or her right to do so before the issuance of the arbitral award.

When the above-mentioned period has lapsed, an application for the enforcement of the arbitral award will be submitted to the competent court along with the following documents:

1. A copy of the arbitration agreement.
2. The original award or a signed copy.
3. An Arabic translation of the arbitral award authenticated by an accredited authority if it was not originally issued in Arabic.

The competent court will examine the application without hearings and will order its execution unless it ascertains that:

1. The award violates public order in the kingdom. If that part in the award that includes such a violation can be separated from other parts of the award, the court may order the execution of the other part.
2. The award was not duly notified to the party against whom it was rendered.

The judgement enforcing any arbitral award is not subject to appeal. However, a judgement refusing such enforcement can be appealed before the Court of Cassation within 30 days of the date of notification of the decision.

Procedures for settling disputes

Any dispute arising in Jordan may be referred either to the courts or to arbitration. Where a dispute is referred to the courts, the legal procedures in civil claims are initiated by filing a written statement of claim to the competent court together with all court and stamp fees due. If filed with the Magistrates' Court, the written statement should be signed by either the plaintiff or his or her advocate.

The court fixes the date for hearing the claim and notifies the disputing parties. The judge hearing the claim will seek to conciliate between the disputed parties if the judge fails, he or she will hear the claim by examining all of the submitted documents and then hear the personal evidence of first the plaintiff and then the defendant.

The judge may decide to dismiss certain evidence, whether documentary or personal, if deemed unproductive or legally unacceptable. Thereafter, the court will hear the pleading of both parties and issue its final judgement in a public hearing. The judgement will state the names of the plaintiff and the defendant and their advocates, the subject matter and facts of the claim and the court's final decision.

The procedures implemented at First Instance Courts are initiated by filing a written statement of claim attached with a list of evidence, whether written or personal and signed solely by the advocate for the plaintiff.

The court will notify the defendant by providing him or her with the above-mentioned documents and the date fixed for the pre-trial hearing of the claim. The defendant will submit to the court his or her written statement of reply attached with the list of evidence, whether written or personal.

At the pre-trial hearing, the judge will hear evidence and examine all of the submitted documents. If some documents are missing, the parties will be requested to provide them to the court. In general, the pre-trial judge will try to solve the dispute amicably but if the disputing parties have no desire to reach a settlement, then the pre-trial judge will seek to simplify the matter by requesting the disputing parties to determine which issues are agreed upon and which remain subject to dispute.

When the pre-trial judge has completed the above-mentioned procedures, the claim will be referred to another judge, who will also examine the claim, hear the evidence of the disputing parties and dismiss certain evidence, whether documentary or personal, if it was deemed unproductive or legally unacceptable, and then, finally, hear the pleadings of each party. Thereafter, the court will issue its final judgement in a public hearing. The judgement shall state the names of the plaintiff and the defendant and their advocates, the subject matter and facts of the claim and the court's final decision.

Procedures implemented in regard to criminal claims are regulated by the Law of Criminal Procedures, which differ from those implemented in regard to civil claims, as they are filed with the public prosecutor who will initiate investigations and collect available evidence. Based on such investigations, the public prosecutor may either decide that the suspect is innocent or else issue an indictment. The matter will then be referred to the appropriate court, and an arrest warrant will be issued to hold the suspect for trial or, alternatively, to release him or her on bail. The trial will commence with the hearing of the statements of the public prosecutor and the advocate of the defendant. Thereafter, the court will hear the testimony of the defendant, the witnesses of the public prosecutor and those of the defendant. The court will examine their submitted written evidence and final pleadings.

Based on this, the court will issue its final judgement in a public hearing that will include all the details stated in the civil judgements in addition to the penalty imposed on the defendant, if found guilty, or his or her innocence due to lack of evidence or failure of the public prosecutor to prove the claim.

General conditions

In general, all court hearings are open to the public, unless the court decides otherwise because the subject matter of the claim is sensitive, personal or may affect public order. Furthermore, the court may prohibit certain people, such as teenagers, from attending hearings.

In civil claims, the judgement debtor will be responsible for payment of all court expenses and fees. In criminal claims, the court may exempt the judgement debtor from payment of the expenses and fees if the complainant acted in good faith when initiating the complaint.

All matters related to accepting or dismissing evidence submitted to a court in civil claims are subject to the Evidence Law No. 30 of 1952 and its amendments.

Claims may be heard either by only one judge, as in claims by Magistrates' Courts, or by more than one judge, as in some first instance claims. All Court of Appeal claims will be heard by at least three judges and Court of Cassation claims by at least five judges and as many as nine judges in cases of great importance.

Furthermore, any document submitted to court should be in Arabic. Any document submitted in any other language must be accompanied by an Arabic translation.

Practical situation regarding litigation

Due to the numerous and increasing number of claims filed with the courts and the limited number of judges, the litigation process in Jordan is very slow, each claim likely to take more than 1 year until it is finally settled. As a result, disputing parties usually resort to arbitration.

5.4

Intellectual Property Law

*Yousef S Khalilieh, Member Noor A
Jundi, Associate and Shereen S Said,
Associate Rajai K W Dajani &
Associates, Advocates and Legal
Consultants, Amman*

Introduction

Since Jordan became an official member in the World Trade Organization
(WTO) on 11 April 2002, the Jordanian parliament has been working
extensively on amending all the applicable legislation, laws and
regulations related to intellectual property rights, in order to conform
with and adhere to the standards and provisions of the WTO and its
agreements such as trade-related intellectual property rights (TRIPS)
and the Berne and Paris conventions.

Intellectual property rights are defined as the distinctive creations or
inventions of the mind, such as industrial designs, integrated circuits,
trademarks, geographical indications, copyrights and all rights related
thereto. In general, any inventor or owner of any of the above-mentioned
rights shall benefit (morally and/or materially) from his or her creation
or invention.

Due to the importance given to intellectual property rights in Jordan,
as well as in any other country, the Jordanian legislature passed several
laws and regulations including:

1. The Patent of Invention Law No. 32 of 1999 amended by the
   Temporary Law No. 71 of 2001 and Regulation No. 97 of 2001.
2. The Trademarks Law No. 33 of 1952 amended by Law No. 34 of 1999
   and its Regulation No. 1 of 1952 amended by Regulation No. 37 of
   2000.
3. The Protection of Layout-designs of Integrated Circuits Law No. 10
   of 2000 and the Regulation of the Protection of Layout-designs of
   Integrated Circuits No. 93 of 2002.

4. The Industrial Designs and Models Law No. 14 of 2000 and the Regulation of Designs and Models No. 52 of 2002.
5. The Copyright Law No. 22 of 1992 amended in 1998, 1999 and 2001 and lately amended by the temporary Law No. 78 of 2003.
6. The Geographical Indications Law No. 8 of 2000.
7. The Law of Unfair Competition and Trade Secrets No. 15 of 2000.

Competent authorities in Jordan

The authorities in Jordan responsible for the registration, implementation and protection of the rights related to the above-mentioned laws and regulations include the Ministry of Industry and Trade represented by the Department of Protection of Industrial Property, which is responsible for registering trademarks, patents, industrial designs and layout-designs of integrated circuits and the National Library Department, which is responsible for filing and certifying all literary works and for following up all crimes and violations related to computer and recording piracy.

The Copyright Law No. 22 of 1992 and subsequent amendments

The copyright law protects rights such as innovative literary, artistic or scientific works of any kind as well as works expressed in writing, sound, drawing, photography or movement. The protection provided encompasses the title of the work unless the title is a common term used to indicate the subject matter of the work. It also includes collections of literary or artistic works such as encyclopaedias, selections and collected data whether or not collected in a machine-readable form, in addition to their translation if translated into another language.

Provided that such collections represent innovative intellectual works, protection will also encompass selective extracts of poetry, prose, music or other such material, provided that the sources and authors of the extracts are specified in the said collections and that they do not infringe the copyright of any work that represents a part of these collections and is without prejudice to the rights of the original author.

All the above-mentioned works, whether published or printed in Jordan either by a Jordanian or by a non-Jordanian author, may be filed with the National Library Department free of charge. Works by Jordanian nationals published or printed outside but distributed inside Jordan may also be so filed. The filed copies must be identical in all aspects to the original work and must have the highest quality among the copies produced.

The protection of copyrights stipulated in this law shall be for the lifetime of the author plus 50 years after his or her death or, where there is more than one author, upon the death of the last surviving author. The 50-year period commences from the first of January of the calendar year following the actual date of death.

As for photographic and applied works of art, they are protected for 25 years from the assumed date of their production, which shall be the first of January of the calendar year in which they were actually produced. Other works such as cinematic and television productions, works whose author or rights holder is a juridical person, works that are published for the first time after the death of its author and works that do not bear the name of the author or carry a pseudonym enjoy the same protection. However, if an author revealed his or her identity during the protection period, the said period will begin from the death of the author and his or her works will be protected for 50 years from their deemed publication date, which will be the following first of January.

Furthermore, rights of the performers and producers of sound recordings remain in effect for 50 years, starting from the first of January of the calendar year following the year in which the performance or the production took place, and for 20 years for broadcast programmes that are transmitted by a broadcast or television organization commencing from the first of January of the calendar year following the year in which the programmes were broadcast for the first time.

It should be noted, however, that the Copyright Law stipulates that the non-filing of any work in the defined manner does not prevent a work enjoying the same protection.

The Trademarks Law No. 33 of 1952 and amendments

The Trademarks Law defines trademarks as any clear sign used or to be used by any person to distinguish his or her goods, products and services. Furthermore, the Trademarks Law also protects 'well-known' trademarks that are marks with a worldwide reputation on goods exported from their country of registration and that have acquired fame and reputation in the relevant sector among the consuming public in Jordan.

A registered trademark must be distinctive whether in words (Arabic or English), letters, numbers, figures, colours or other signs or any combination thereof and visually perceptible and should also not be similar or identical to any other registered trademark.

An application for the registration of a trademark must be filed with the Trademark Registrar at the Ministry of Industry and Trade on the form provided for that purpose. The registrar will examine the application and if it fulfils all the legal requirements and conditions will grant the applicant a preliminary acceptance for subsequent publication in the *Official Gazette*. Any person may submit, within 3 months of the date of such publication, an opposition to the registration of the trademark. The registrar, upon hearing both the applying and the opposing parties, if necessary, and considering the evidence, may decide whether and subject to what conditions registration may be permitted. The decision of the registrar may be appealed to the High Court of Justice within 20 days from the date of the registrar's decision. If no opposition was filed or the opposition has been rejected, the registrar will register the said trademark and issue a certificate to that effect following the collection of the prescribed fees.

The right of ownership for a trademark is for 10 years from the date of registration and may be renewed for another 10 years. Should the trademark owner fail to renew the trademark registration, within 1 year of the anniversary, it shall be regarded as cancelled and any third party may apply to have the mark registered in his or her name after the lapse of another year.

The Patent Law No. 32 of 1999 and amendments thereto

The Patent Law defines an invention as an idea in any of the fields of technology that relates to a product or a manufacturing process or both and solves practically a specific problem in any of the aforementioned fields.

Furthermore, any invention should meet the following conditions:

1. (a) It has to be novel as regards the prior industrial art and is unprecedented as regards disclosure to the public in any place in the world by means of written or oral disclosure, by use, or by any other way that allows awareness of the invention's content before the relevant filing date of the patent application or the priority of the application claimed under the provisions of this law.

(b) The disclosure of the invention to the public shall not be taken into account if it occurred 12 months before the filing date of the application or before its priority date, if any, and it occurred due to actions taken by the applicant or his or her predecessor or due to an abuse made by third parties against the applicant or his or her predecessor.

2. If it involves an inventive step that, having regard to the prior art relevant to the patent application, it would not have been obvious to a person having ordinary skill in the prior art.

3. If it is industrially applicable that it can be made or used in any type of agriculture, fishing, service or industry in the widest sense including handicrafts.

An application for the registration of a patent must be filed with the patents registrar at the Ministry of Industry and Trade, on the form provided for that purpose stating the detailed description of the invention. The description shall disclose the invention in a manner sufficiently clear and complete for it to be carried out by a person having ordinary skill in the art while stating the best mode for carrying out the invention known to him or her on the application date or the priority date.

The registrar will examine the application and if it fulfils all the legal requirements and conditions laid down, he or she will grant the applicant a preliminary acceptance prior to publication in the *Official Gazette*. Any person may submit, within 3 months of the said publication date, an opposition to registration of the patent. The registrar shall issue his or her decision in the case after hearing both parties but if neither of them wishes to give a statement, the registrar can adjudicate the case and notify both parties of his or her decision.

If no opposition is filed or if the filed opposition is rejected, the registrar will then issue the patent certificate subsequent to the collection of the prescribed fees. The ownership right of the registered patent shall be for 20 years from the registration date.

The Industrial Designs and Models Law No.14 of 2000

The Industrial Designs and Models Law has defined an industrial design as any composition or arrangement of lines that gives the product special form and appeal that may be used for industry or handicrafts including textile designs. As for an industrial model it is defined as a three-dimensional form whether associated with lines and colour or not, which also has a special form that may be used for industry or handicrafts.

An application for the registration of an industrial design or model must be filed with the Registrar of Industrial Designs and Models at the Ministry of Industry and Trade, on the form provided for that purpose, stating the kind of product and attaching drawings, photographs and other illustrative data embodying the design or model. The registrar shall examine the application and may invite the applicant to make adjustments to ensure fulfilment of all legal requirements and conditions, after which his or her decision to accept the application will be made subject to collection of the fees prescribed.

The ownership right of the registered industrial design or model shall be for 15 years as of its registration date and the ownership right of a layout-design shall be for 10 years as of the date of its first commercial exploitation anywhere in the world, provided that such period does not, in any case, exceed 15 years from the date of the creation of the layout-design.

Furthermore, any industrial design or model displayed by any creator at exhibitions, whether held in Jordan or abroad, will be temporarily protected pursuant to the procedures and conditions of the regulations issued in accordance with the provisions of the Industrial Designs and Models Law.

The Geographical Indications Law No. 8 of 2000

The Geographical Indications Law is based entirely on the TRIPS Agreement Articles 22 to 24, as it introduces the definition of geographical indication in addition to other special provisions relating to the protection of geographical indications for wine and spirits.

The Law of Unfair Competition and Trade Secrets No. 15 of 2000

The Law of Unfair Competition and Trade Secrets is based on the Paris Convention granting protection for unregistered trademarks that may confuse consumers whilst also stipulating the conditions for considering any information a trade secret. In general, unfair competition is defined as an act that is contrary to honest practice in industrial or commercial matters such as the following:

1. Acts that may create confusion with the establishment, the goods or the industrial or commercial activity of a competitor
2. False allegations in the course of trade of such a nature as to discredit the establishment, the goods or the industrial or commercial activity of a competitor
3. Indications or allegations that may mislead the public as to the nature, manufacturing process, characteristics, suitability for their purpose or the quantity of the products
4. Any practice that may discredit the reputation of a product, cause confusion in its external appearance or the way it is displayed or may mislead the public, in the course of announcing the price of the product or in the way of calculating it

Furthermore, the Trade Secret Law stipulates that any applicant requesting authorization for pharmaceutical or agricultural chemical products, similar to items already in production, may not rely on the data of the original before the lapse of the term of protection, which is 5 years.

Concerns

Jordan has not yet joined the Madrid Convention, which governs the protection of trademarks internationally, but is actively pursuing participation. Therefore, any registered trademark in Jordan is only protected locally but, if registered abroad, will be given a priority right from the date of registration in Jordan.

Furthermore, in order to encourage persons to register their trademarks in Jordan, no person shall have the right to file a lawsuit to claim damages for any infringement upon a trademark unless registered in Jordan. However, if a trademark is well known and not registered, then its owner may demand the competent court to prevent third parties from using it on identical or non-identical goods or services provided that such use indicates a connection between those goods or services. An application may be submitted to the registrar in order to cancel a trademark registered in Jordan by a person who does not own it after it was registered abroad.

5.5

Environmental Laws and Regulations

Subhi Ramadan, President,
Environmental Consultants Branch,
Ramadan Technical Services Co

Introduction

Environmental laws and regulations in Jordan cover technical, cultural and socio-economic impacts and are similar to those of developed countries. However, law enforcement is still weak, although improving. As to Jordanian standards and specifications (JSS), these have been prepared for essential goods and services and are increasing progressively in quality and quantity.

Jordan has signed many international environmental and trade agreements including a free trade agreement with the United States, some of which have environmental, socio-economic and labour components in addition to trade regulations.

Environmental laws, regulations, standards and specifications (ELRSS) are better organized and enforced in Jordan than in many neighbouring Arab countries, but remain less developed than those in Western countries. These ELRSS were derived from many well-recognized references such as the EPA of the United States, the World Bank, the World Health Organization and others, but have been tailored to suit Jordanian conditions.

Ministry of Environment

Environmental protection was initiated in Jordan in the 1960s. Laws and regulations were and still are scattered over many ministries. However, in 2003, a Ministry of Environment (MOE) was established in Jordan to replace a previous governmental organization that had been in charge of environmental affairs. Environmental Protection Law No. 1

of 13 Jan 2003 is the governing law in Jordan. The parliament approved it recently (2006), but it is still awaiting the king's approval, which is expected shortly. The previous Environmental Law No. 95 of 1995, which itself replaced earlier laws, is null and void, with the exception of the regulations that emanated from it until such time as these are replaced or cancelled. However, Aqaba Special Economic Zone (ASEZ), south of Jordan, has its own environmental laws and regulations 'Law No. 21 of 2001', which are similar to those mentioned above. A visit to ASEZ's site (http://www.aqabazone.com/ pages.php?localsite_branchname=Environment) is recommended.

The MOE is actively involved in all environmental affairs in Jordan, but will only gradually become fully responsible, as many aspects remain the responsibility of several other ministries. More information and details about MOE laws, regulations, projects and so on are available at the MOE website (http://www.moenv.gov.jo/english/index.php).

Practical aspects of environmental regulation

Local environmental experts in all fields are available in Jordan, who can perform and follow up on all Jordanian requirements. Accredited testing laboratories can also be found locally, although international, accredited laboratories' certificates remain acceptable in the kingdom.

Business in Jordan falls under three main categories: services, trading and manufacturing. Trading, whether import or export, is subject to ELRSS. Goods imported into Jordan must meet JSS or well-established international standards, where there are no JSS. Exported manufactured goods, on the other hand, must meet either the standards of the importing country or JSS, whichever is more stringent, if they are going to be sold in the Jordanian market. ELRSS and labour practices applied must also meet the terms of signed agreements between Jordan and the importing country or be in accordance with internationally signed agreements and, as a minimum, should meet the laws of Jordan. More information and detail about standards are available at the Jordan Institute for Standards and Metrology website (http://www.jism.gov.jo/).

Manufacturing in Jordan is an attractive activity and has many advantages and incentives. Environmentally, manufacturers must follow the above-mentioned trading rules as well as the following:

Before establishing an industry, the industry's owner must perform a comprehensive environmental impact assessment (EIA), in a form basically similar to that of the World Bank. The level of detail needed depends on the type and capacity of the industry. Industries are categorized (similar to categories of the World Bank) in accordance with the expected pollution emissions (quality and quantity) of the manufacturing process, with a minimum requirement of JSS regarding pollutants in addition to the management and monitoring requirements of the MOE. Standards are available in the field of drinking water, treated wastewater, air pollution and noise pollution, whilst other factors that have to be taken into consideration include solid and hazardous wastes, a public participation process and occupational health and safety. Any such EIA can be performed by Jordanian experts.

If financing for an industry is to be obtained from a foreign entity that requires an EIA, then the EIA has to meet that entity's environmental requirements in addition to those of Jordan. For example if a loan is obtained from the International Finance Corporation (IFC), then IFC environmental requirements have to be followed in addition to Jordanian requirements, with the stricter taking priority. Monitoring reports covering construction and operation phases of the project are required, as are annual monitoring reports. The yearly reports must include socio-economic impacts, in addition to emissions, for a category A project.

A comprehensive EIA report for a category A project includes scoping (stakeholders), public participation, detailed project description, analysis of alternatives, detailed baseline data, all environmental and ecological components, including marine studies if it is at the Aqaba shore, mitigation measures, monitoring (during construction and operation), policy, legal and administrative framework, an environmental management plan and the socio-economics of the project. Other categories require fewer details. Nevertheless, all depend on impact and emissions. The nature of the project itself is the deciding factor in terms of how it will be classified, as is the approvals obtained regarding the terms of reference of the EIA for the project.

Examples of categories/classification of projects

Category A: Refineries, power generation, ports, airports, large hotels, solid waste disposal, petrochemical industries, industrial cities, mining, steel production and cement industries.

Category B: Poultry, fish and livestock farms, large· excavations, desalination, special mining, storage of oil and gas, metals treatment, glass manufacturing and food processing.

Category C: Other smaller projects, parks and small hotels, treatment plants and small storage facilities.

It should be noted, however, that some projects do not require an EIA and these are defined on a case-by-case basis.

Sampling and penalties

Ministries and governmental organizations concerned with compliance with the regulations in place obtain samples of goods in order to check that they meet JSS requirements and also measure emissions to ensure compliance with ELRSS. Penalties are imposed in case of violations.

Part Six

Finance and Banking

6.1

Amman Stock Exchange

Jalil Tarif, Chief Executive Officer,
Amman Stock Exchange

Historical Background to the Capital Market in Jordan

The history of securities trading in Jordan can be traced back to the 1930s but it was not until 1976 that the Amman Financial Market was established to create a regulated trading market. More recently, as part of Jordan's move to upgrade its capital markets, a Securities Law was enacted in 1997, separating the supervisory and legislative roles from those of operating an exchange. As a result, the Amman Stock Exchange (ASE) was created along with the Jordan Securities Commission (JSC) and Securities Depository Center (SDC). The JSC supervises the issuance of and trading in securities and monitors and regulates the market. The SDC oversees clearance and settlement and maintains ownership records.

These three institutions replaced the Amman Financial Market, which had performed the dual roles of market operator and market regulator, serving the market's needs successfully for many years. But such an arrangement no longer complied with international practices hence the change.

Recently, a new Securities Law number 76 for the year 2002 has been issued, which authorizes the setting up other stock exchanges and allows the forming of an independent investor protection fund, stricter ethical and professional codes, and a more stringent observance of the rule of law.

The Jordan Securities Commission

The JSC regulates the issuance, primary offering and secondary trading of securities monitors the ASE and SDC and licenses and regulates entities conducting securities business (such as financial brokerage, investment management, financial advisory services, underwriting and custodial services) and their personnel. Its aims are to facilitate the dealing of securities in a sound environment and to protect investors.

The JSC's powers are vested in a board of five full-time commissioners, who are appointed by the Cabinet. Implementation of Commission decisions is the responsibility of the Chairman of the Commission, his delegate, or, in the Chairman's absence, the Deputy Chairman.

Financial services companies are subject to periodic inspection by the JSC and ASE Inspection Departments. The JSC Capital Market Monitoring Department monitors the market for insider trading, market manipulation and other breaches. It works closely with the ASE Listing and Operations Department, which pursues real-time monitoring of ASE trading, and the SDC Surveillance Department. JSC Disclosure Department monitors issuers' compliance with disclosure requirements.

Enforcement is primarily the responsibility of the JSC. It can suspend financial services companies, remove their licences and refer to the prosecuting authorities persons who carry on regulated activities whilst unlicensed or commit insider dealing or market manipulation offences.

The Amman Stock Exchange

The ASE was established in March 1999 as a non-profit, private institution with administrative and financial autonomy. It is authorized to function as an exchange for the trading of securities. The exchange is governed by a seven-member board of directors. An chief executive officer oversees day-to-day responsibilities and reports to the board. The ASE membership is comprised of Jordan's 59 brokerage firms.

The ASE is committed to the principles of fairness, transparency, efficiency and liquidity. The exchange seeks to provide a strong and secure environment for its listed securities while protecting and guaranteeing the rights of its investors. To provide this transparent and efficient market, the ASE has implemented internationally recognized directives regarding market divisions and listing criteria.

To comply with international standards and best practices, the ASE maintains strong relationships with other exchanges, associations and international organizations. The exchange is an active member of the Union of Arab Stock Exchanges, the Federation of Euro-Asian Stock Exchanges (FEAS), an affiliate member of the World Federation of Exchanges (WFE), an affiliate member of the International Organization for Securities Commissions (IOSCO) and a member of the Financial Information Services Division (FISD).

The ASE is charged with:

- Providing enterprises with a means of raising capital by listing on the Exchange
- Encouraging an active market in listed securities based on the effective determination of prices and fair and transparent trading
- Providing modern and effective facilities and equipment for trading, recording trades and publishing prices
- Monitoring and regulating market trading, coordinating with the JSC as necessary, to ensure compliance with the law, a fair market and investor protection
- Setting out and enforcing a professional code of ethics among its member directors and staff and
- Ensuring the provision of timely and accurate information of issuers to the market and disseminating market information to the public.

Market regulation and transparency are major priorities for Jordanian capital market institutions, where strict enforcement serves to enhance Jordan's reputation and attract foreign as well as domestic investment. The ASE works closely with the JSC to monitor trading on the exchange and regarding matters of surveillance. In this regard the ASE has introduced and passed a number of rules and regulations that govern its work and comply with international standards, such as: the ASE Internal By-Law, the Directives on Code of Ethics of ASE, the Directives on Disclosure Related to the ASE, Regulations for the Fees and Commissions of the ASE, Directives for Trading in Securities at the ASE, Directives for Listing Securities on the ASE, and the ASE Internal By-Law for Disputes Settlement.

Technological Development at the ASE

1. Electronic trading system & remote trading

The ASE's Trading System is a sophisticated electronic system that provides transparency and fairness of dealing for market participants, enhances liquidity and market depth and facilitates the market surveillance controlled by the ASE and the JSC. It is an automated, order-driven system that offers brokers immediate access to stock prices and orders and enables members to trade remotely, which improves dealers performance and provides brokerage firms and dealers in securities more flexibility and ease. Recently, the ASE has activated a new version of the electronic trading system (NSC V2+), which comes as part of the efforts to meet the increasing demand on the Jordanian Capital Market and in order to raise the capacity of the current electronic trading system to accommodate the increase in the daily trading volume, as well as the ASE's policy of preserving the safety of securities trading and safeguarding an equal treatment of those dealing in securities.

2. The Intranet

The Intranet that connects all the ASE members and its employees, supplies information and a correspondence channel for internal e-mail. It is an important step towards developing means of communication between its employees that saves time, effort and expense.

Recently, the ASE introduced and adopted new systems on the intranet. The first is the Domino.doc system which is used to archive documents issued by the ASE to its members that include brokers work reports, trading bulletins, announcements, disclosures, companies' financial statements and the ASE directives. The second is the Same Time system, which provides correspondence ability between the ASE and brokers and among brokers themselves. These systems replace the Outlook email system that was in use at the ASE.

3. Management Information System (MIS)

The MIS is an Oracle based and replaces an old Cobol and Access based system. It facilitates business within all the ASE departments

by ensuring swift reporting and enables members to have access to their reports in the shortest possible time. It also enforces surveillance by the ASE Listing and Operations Department and the JSC Surveillance Department, whilst offering the possibility of having immediate, during-the-session access to client reference numbers. Recently, the MIS was amended to accommodate the ASE needs. Also a new updated version of the market-monitoring program was released.

Also the ASE Installing new computers for all ASE departments, changing the monitoring systems and purchasing many servers in order to serve all the main systems at the ASE

4. Wide Area Network (WAN)

The ASE brokers, issuers, investors, data providers and other financial institutions are electronically connected to the exchange, depository and securities commission through a wide-area network (WAN), which links the stock exchange and depository to more than 130 market participants in Jordan who have electronic data dissemination screens (plasma screens) to view real-time changes in the market. Recently , the ASE upgraded the WAN to accommodate the increasing number of working brokerage firms.

5. Expansive data dissemination

Disclosure and dissemination of market information is a key priority for the ASE therefore, the exchange has made tremendous strides in its campaign to raise awareness and provide information about Jordan's Capital Market to the general public. The advancements include the adoption of the electronic trading system, and the development of other real-time displays of information.

Investors can access ASE information including listings and members' details through multiple channels from anywhere in the world. The ASE provides access to data 24 hours a day on its website at www.exchange.jo, which receives more than 120 million hits per month. Data vendors also provide ASE quotes and information such as that provided by REUTERS and BLOMBERG.

The ASE has begun publishing all issued announcements and disclosures received from listed companies on its website and on the main page of the Arabic version of the website. Latest news related to the ASE, the financial brokerage companies (ASE members), and the public shareholding companies, including annual, semi-annual and quarterly financial statements, preliminary financial data and any other material information that are disclosed by these companies and that could have an impact on securities prices, are also published.

In addition, share prices are displayed on Jordan Television on both the main Channel One and its satellite channel as well as on the specialized economic channel CNBC Arabia and many other satellite TV stations. Investors can also use mobile phones to learn about and follow up on share prices of listed companies through the SMS service and the 'JAVA' technology present on mobile phones.

The ASE Transferred its website host from the United States of America to the ASE premises in Jordan. The importance of this project lies in the fact that the whole site is in Jordan and on appropriate servers owned by the ASE, which provides it with full control over the website, and henceforth the ability to provide a better service for users and a rapid response to solve any problems that may occur.

A new program, Market Watch, is under testing to provide for more comprehensive live dissemination of ASE trading data.

6. Other developments

The ASE has recently introduced a new sector classification for companies listed at the stock exchange. The classification is in line with international standards and provides a clearer picture about listed companies in order to help investors make their investment decisions. The ASE also constructed a new index that is based on free float shares, which provides a better representation of the shares' prices movement in the market. This index is unbiased to large cap. Companies, thus limiting their impact on the index.

Pursuant to this classification, listed companies are classified in three major sectors: the financial sector that includes banks, insurance, financial services, real estate and investment companies the services sector that includes companies operating in the field of health care sector, education, energy, transportation, tourism and communications and the industrial sector that includes companies operating in the field of mining and extraction industries, engineering and construction, food and beverages, tobacco, textiles, leather and clothing, ceramics and electrical industries. These three major sectors are also divided into (23) sub-sectors, whereby companies that have the same operations and activities are placed in the same group.

Also the ASE developed a new index based on the free float shares, whereby the index is calculated using the market value of the free float shares of the companies and not the total number of listed shares of each company. This index is characterized by the fact that it reflects the shares prices movement in the market in a better way, and it is not biased to large market value companies. In addition, it provides small and medium cap companies a greater opportunity to influence the movements of the index. This index may be used as a base tool in forming financial derivatives. This index was given the base value of 1000 points as of the closing of the year 1999 and was calculated on a daily basis for the period 2000-2006. Moreover, the sector indices were given the base value of 1000 points as of the closing of the year 1999 and were calculated on a daily basis for the period 2000-2006.

In this context, ASE has signed an agreement with the Dow Jones Company to calculate a new index weighted by free-float shares, named "The Amman Stock Exchange and Dow Jones". The importance of this step stems from this company's international reputation in the field of financial markets indices. The index will be calculated through weighting by market capitalization of free-float shares for companies where a cap is set for the influence of any company on the index changes. This index may be used as a base tool in forming financial derivatives. This Index will be a composite one and will include most of listed companies, which will be selected based on a number of criteria related to the company's trading activity and liquidity, in addition to the company's market capitalization, revenues and profits.

As a result of signing this agreement, and in order not to confuse investors and users of the index, the ASE will adopt the index which will be calculated with Dow Jones as the only price index for stocks listed at the ASE. It will be disseminated on the electronic trading system and the ASE website as well as data vendors. ASE will continue to compute the sectors and sub-sector indices.

The ASE's Performance Overview

The ASE is one of the largest stock markets in the region, with a market capitalization as at the end of March 2007 of more than JD23.5 billion. The exchange currently lists 229 companies and has more than 770,000 investors. Up to the end of 2006 fifty percent of shares on the exchange are held by Jordanian corporate and individual investors. Arab investors own 34.3%, while non-Arab investors account for 11.2%, totalling 45.5%. The government, through the Jordan Investment Corporation, holds the remaining shares.

Foreign Ownership in ASE end of 2006)

The ASE has experienced tremendous growth in recent years and especially during 2005 and 2004. The share price index of the ASE reached an all-time-high during the trading session of 8th November 2005 when it reached 9348 points, a rise of 111% since the beginning of the year and closed at 93% rise in 2005. The accumulative volume also reached an all-time-high, trading for the year 2005 reaching JD16.9 billion or a 345% rise compared with 2004. The number of shares traded increased by 93% and executed contracts increased by 103% over the figures for 2004. The capitalization of the ASE for the year 2005 rose by 105% to reach JD26.7 billion, constituting 327% of GDP, a figure which is considered high comparable to those prevailing on international exchanges. During the year 2006, trading value declined by 15.8% to reach JD14.2 billion. The number of traded shares in 2006 rose by 59% compared to 2005 reaching 4104.3 million shares, and the number of executed transactions was 3.4 million compared to 2.4 million in 2005 an increase of 43.9%. The free-float weighted index dropped in 2006 to reach 3014 points, compared to 4260 points at the end of 2005 a 29.3% drop. The general index weighted by the market capitalization also dropped down to 5518 points at the end of 2006, compared to 8192 points at the closing of 2005 a drop of 32.6%. The ASE market capitalization by the end of 2006 was JD21.1 billion, a drop of 21.0%. The ASE market capitalization represents 233.9% of the GDP.

Market Capitalization of the ASE (million JD)

Clearing and Settlement

The Securities Depository Center (SDC) implements settlement on 'Delivery Versus Payment' DVP basis where trading contracts are settled electronically on T+2. The SDC assumes the role of a clearing house as part of implementing automated settlement. The transfer of ownership of deposited securities from the seller's account to the Buyer's account is conducted via book entry as a result of the daily trading files submitted by the Amman Stock Exchange to the SDC. Securities remain suspended in the buyer's account until the completion of the settlement process and full payment for their value. No transfer or pledge activity is permitted during this period.

The SDC undertakes the clearing process to calculate the broker's Net to Pay or Net to Receive in accordance with all the trading contracts executed by subtracting the total value of the broker's purchases of securities for the trading day from its total sales for that trading day.

Financial settlement is conducted between brokers, through the SDC, via money transfers from the brokers' accounts to the SDC Settlement Account at the Central Bank of Jordan which was adopted as the settlement bank. Subsequent to money transfers credited to the SDC settlement account, the SDC will transfer these amounts to the brokers which are Net to Receive and the SDC will transfer the ownership of the securities concerned from the seller's account maintained by his broker to the buyer's accounts maintained by his broker.

Taxation and Regulations Affecting Foreign Investors

There are no restrictions on the repatriation of the proceeds of the sale of securities, nor on the income arising from them. A 10% tax on distributed dividends was removed as of January 1, 2002 and there is no tax on capital gains.

Jordan has double taxation treaties with Egypt, France, India, Indonesia, Malaysia, Poland, Romania, Tunisia, Turkey, Yemen and collectively, the members of the Council of Arab Economic Unity.

According to the Non-Jordanian Investment Regulation No. 54 of 2000 issued pursuant to Article (24) of the Investment Promotion Law No. 16 of 1995, no ceiling exists on non-Jordanian ownership of companies listed on the ASE.

Prospective Developments

The Amman Stock Exchange embarked on a number of key projects in 2006 that ensure maintaining the lead the ASE has amongst Arab and regional stock exchanges. These projects can be summarized as follows:

- Application for a full membership in the World Federation of Exchanges (WFE).

- Upgrading of the technical infrastructure namely the electronic trading system, surveillance systems and increase the capacity of the ASE website.
- Improvement in on-line trading information dissemination by introducing new products such as launching the ASE Market Watch Application for investors as a corporate and retail product through Internet.
- Improved information dissemination by introducing new retails products.
- Introduce a new composite index in cooperation with International Index providers.
- Introduced Internet trading.

Market Statistics

Market size (as of 31th March 2007)

Listed companies	229
Market capitalisation	JOD23.5 m

Trading statistics

Trading floor (Equity)

	Volume	Value (JD)
1999	271.1m	389.5m
2000	228.4m	334.7m
2001	340.6m	668.7m
2002	461.8m	950.3m
2003	1008.6m	1855.2m
2004	1338.7 m	3793.3 m
2005	2582.6 m	16871.0m
2006	4104.3 m	14209.9m

Largest companies by market capitalisation as of end 2006

Position	Company	Value (JD)
1	Arab Bank	7604.2m
2	The Housing Bank for Trade & Finance	1637.5m
3	Jordan Telecom	1030.0m
4	Arab Potash	916.5m
5	Jordan Cement Factories	776.1m

Five most actively traded shares during 2006

Position	Company	Value traded (JD)	Volume traded (shares)
1	United Arab Investors	2290.3m	604.7m
2	Arab Bank	1717.9m	57.9m
3	Union Land Development Corporation	887.8m	270.7m
4	Taameer Jordan	680.8m	271.2m
5	Arab East Investment	668.3m	64.7

Main indices

ASE Share Price Index

The ASE has had a share-price index since 1980. In 1992 the index was revised and updated in co-operation with the International Finance Corporation of the World Bank. The index comprises the 70 most liquid companies from the first and second markets. The weight of each company in the index is determined by its relative percentage of the total market capitalization of the 70 companies. The ASE Share Price Index has a base value of 1000 and a base date of 31st December 1991. The index is divided into four sectors: banking, insurance, services and industrial.

The ASE also constructed a new index that is based on free float shares. This index was given a base value of 1000 points as of the closing of the year 1999 and was calculated on a daily basis for the period 2000-2006. Moreover, the sector indices were given the base value of 1000 points as of the closing of the year 1999 and were calculated on a daily basis for the period 2000-2006.

Year-End Share Price Index, P/E Ratios and Yields

Year	Index (JD)*	Market P/E	Dividend Yield (%)
1999	1673.5	14.30	2.88
2000	1330.5	14.82	3.64
2001	1727.2	15.34	2.70
2002	1700.2	12.97	3.21
2003	2614.5	21.75	2.36
2004	4245.6	31.11	1.74
2005	8191.5	44.20	1.65
2006	5518.1	16.75	2.32

* Weighted by the market capitalization

Securities Traded

Stocks, development bonds, corporate bonds, treasury bonds, rights issues and investment units.

Commission Rates and Other Client Costs

The main cost of dealing is commission. Commissions for trading in equities on the first and second of the ASE vary between 0.0054 and 0.0074 of value traded. The commission includes:

a) The brokerage firm's own commission, which is limited to between 0.004 and 0.006 of value traded and
b) Fees totaling 0.0014 of value traded payable to the key market authorities as to 0.0005 (JSC), 0.0005 (ASE) and 0.0004 (SDC) and levied by the broker on their behalf.

Commissions on bonds traded on the ASE vary between 0.00045 and 0.00095 of value traded. As with equities, this will comprise the brokers' commissions (between 0.0003 and 0.0008 of value traded) and fees payable to the key market authorities.

Brokers receive commissions calculated on the basis of the market value of both buying and selling transactions of the security, according to the following table:

Security traded	Lower limit	Upper limit
Shares+Rights	JD5.4 per thousand	JD7.4 per thousand
Bonds	JD0.45 per thousand	JD0.95 per thousand
Investment units	JD2.0 per thousand	JD2.2 per thousand

Trading Hours

Business hours

Office hours	Sunday-Thursday, 08:00-16:00

Official trading hours

Time	Market	Pricing Group	Session Stages
9:30 am to 9:35 am	Bonds	Continuous	Pre - opening

9:35 am			Opening
9:35 am to 9:55 am			Trading
9.30 am to 10.00 am	First + Second Market	Continuous	Pre - opening
10:00 am			Opening
10.00 am – 12.00 noon			Trading
12:00 noon – 12:15 pm	Block trades		

Banking Regulations and Supervision in Jordan

Faris Sharaf, Deputy Governor, Central Bank of Jordan

Market structure overview

Much like in other countries in the MENA region, banks dominate Jordan's financial sector. Jordan's banking sector is large relative to GDP, though it remains concentrated. The ratio of bank assets to GDP reached a high of 228 per cent in 2005, and the number of operating banks in Jordan rose to 23 by that year's end. The sector includes 13 Jordanian commercial banks, 2 Jordanian Islamic banks and 8 foreign banks. There are three specialized credit agencies that deal with agricultural credit, rural and urban development and industrial development. The banking sector is highly competitive and most banks provide a full range of consumer, commercial and investment banking services.

Banking sector aggregates (2005)

Number of Banks	23
Total Assets/GDP (nominal)	228.1%
Total Credit/GDP (nominal)	83.9%
Total Deposits/GDP (nominal)	145.4%
Return on Equity	20.9%
Capital Adequacy Ratio (BIS)	17.6%
Non-performing Loans (net of provisions)	1.4%

Credit to the private sector grew by over 30 per cent in 2005 because of a surge in demand. Consumer loans represented approximately 33 per cent of the 7.6 billion Jordanian dinars in total outstanding credit facilities in 2005 whereas trade- and industry-related loans accounted for an additional 34 per cent. The main area of growth has been in retail and personal banking, especially in credit card and mortgage financing. Retail credit, including credit for stock purchases, saw a 58 per cent increase over that in 2005. Mortgage financing has been increasing in line with the increase in real estate prices and demand. As a result, the percentage of mortgage loans to GDP has increased from 2 per cent in 1997 to over 8.8 per cent in 2005. The ratio of non-performing loans from year-end 2002 through 2005 has declined from 17.1 per cent of total loans to 6.5 per cent on a gross basis and 7.8 per cent to 1.4 per cent based on net of provisions. Non-performing loans in absolute terms also fell over the same period. These market factors have led to an increase in banking sector profits by over 290 per cent from 2001 through 2005 while return on equity has increased from 9 per cent to 21 per cent over the same period.

The regulatory framework

The Central Bank of Jordan (CBJ) has been vested under law with the sole responsibility for regulation and supervision of the banking system. Anyone engaged in 'banking activity' is required to comply with the provisions of the Banking Law of 2000. 'Banking activity' has been defined in the law as 'accepting deposits from the public and using these deposits in full or in part to grant credit, or for any other activities designated by the Central Bank as banking activities pursuant to special orders issued for this purpose.'

The permissible activities of banks are defined in Article 37 of the Banking Law, which outlines the financial activities a bank may practise, subject to its licensing by the CBJ:

- Accepting deposits of various types
- Granting all types of credit, including financing commercial transactions
- Providing payment and collection services
- Issuing and administrating instruments of payment, including bank acceptances, debit and credit cards and travellers' checks
- Dealing in, selling and purchasing money and capital market instruments for its own account or for its customers' accounts
- Purchasing and selling debts with or without the right of recourse
- Financing through leasing
- Dealing in foreign exchange at forward and spot markets
- Management of security issues and underwriting, distribution of and dealing in security issues
- Providing management and consultative services for investment portfolios and investment trustee services, including the management and investment of funds for others

- Management and safekeeping of securities and precious items
- Providing financial agent or adviser services
- Any other related banking activities approved by the CBJ in special orders issued thereby for this purpose

Banks are permitted to set up subsidiaries to undertake non-banking activities like securities and insurance businesses with the prior permission of the CBJ, but their supervision is left to the functional supervisor.

Licensing criteria

In order to facilitate a healthy financial system, and to define precisely the population of institutions to be supervised, the arrangements for licensing banking organizations and the scope of activities governed by licences are clearly defined. The Banking Law of 2000 unequivocally gives the CBJ the authority to license banks and the right to set criteria and reject applications for establishments that do not meet the standards set. Clear and objective criteria reduce the potential for political interference in the licensing process.

The licensing process, at a minimum, consists of an assessment of the banking organization's ownership structure, directors and senior management, its operating plan and internal controls and its projected financial condition, including its capital base.

The CBJ, as the sole licensing authority, determines whether that new banking organization has suitable shareholders, adequate financial strength, a legal structure in line with its operational structure and management with sufficient expertise and integrity to operate the bank in a sound and prudent manner. Licensing regulations, as well as supervisory tools, are designed to limit the number of bank failures and the amount of depositor losses without inhibiting the efficiency and competitiveness of the banking industry by blocking entry to it. Both elements are necessary to maintain public confidence in the banking system.

Corporate governance

There is a broad recognition by the banking sector of the need to enhance corporate governance standards. A number of initiatives, some market-led and other spurred by the CBJ, are under way. However, key issues remain to be addressed. While Jordan's banking sector is large relative to GDP, it is closely interlinked with many historical business relationships. This has created an environment conducive to overlapping and blurred lines of responsibilities for owners, boards and management.

Recognizing some of the governance challenges in the system, the CBJ embarked on a number of initiatives to strengthen banking governance. In 2004, the CBJ issued *Bank Directors' Handbook on Corporate Governance*, drawing on the BIS Corporate Governance Guidelines, which provides a set of recommendations to the banking sector. The CBJ is now making these recommendations more binding. The CBJ has asked all banks to prepare plans for compliance with Basel II, which has prompted banks to undertake more formal evaluations of their internal systems and controls, mapping of operational risk and management of credit and other risks. In addition, the CBJ's regulations on internal control, loan classification, asset/liability management and compliance, among other areas, require that prudent credit granting and investment criteria, policies, practices and procedures are approved, implemented and periodically reviewed by bank managements and boards of directors.

Banking supervision

The supervisory system in Jordan contains a mixture of off-site and on-site inspection, periodic reporting and ongoing discussions with banks' senior management and their boards of directors.

An essential part of the CBJ's supervisory system is the independent evaluation of a bank's policies, practices and procedures related to the granting of loans and making of investments, and the ongoing management of the loan and investment portfolio. During on-site examinations, which are conducted using CBJ in-house resources only, examiners have direct access to the books and records of the financial institution being examined. This enables examiners to make a fair and realistic assessment of the condition of the institution in various risk areas. The evaluation of the financial soundness of the institution is achieved by assessing (1) CAMELS (Capital Adequacy, Asset Quality, Management, Earnings, Liquidity, and Sensitivity to Market Risk), (2) ROCA (Risk Management, Operational Controls, Compliance and Asset Quality) for foreign bank branches and (3) adherence to statutory prudential limits in each of these areas.

In order to ascertain the prudence of the practices and procedures adopted by a bank, an assessment is made of its risk management policies and systems as well as its adherence to them. The practices and procedures adopted are outlined in the examination manual and are designed to reveal the extent to which the financial institution is employing adequate measures to ensure the safety and soundness by effective identification, measurement and control of risks that are inherent in the banking operation.

The CBJ requires banks, through loan loss provision regulations, to have mechanisms in place for continually assessing the strength of guarantees and appraising the worth of a collateral. A loan is classified as substandard after 90 days, doubtful after 180 days and a loss after 360 days. For non-collateralized loans (or the part of the loan that is not covered by the collateral) the following provisions are required:

- Substandard: 25 per cent
- Doubtful: 50 percent
- Loss: 100 per cent

Returns are filed on a daily, weekly, monthly, quarterly, semi-annual and annual basis. Data reported to the CBJ cover numerous areas including on- and off-balance sheet assets and liabilities, profit and loss, capital adequacy, liquidity, large exposures, non-performing loans, sectoral distribution of credit, loan loss provisioning, market risk and deposit sources.

The CBJ requires banks to make periodic disclosures of information that are timely, accurate and sufficiently comprehensive to provide a basis for effective market discipline. The reliability of disclosed information should be assured by sound internal control and risk management systems, and complemented by effective external and internal audits.

The banks are required by law to maintain their accounts in accordance with internationally recognized accounting principles and to prepare its financial statements comprehensively to reflect the actual financial position of the bank and its branches and subsidiaries with due compliance with the requirements specified by the CBJ in this regard. In addition to adopting the most recent internationally accepted accounting standards, the CBJ sets asset valuation rules that are consistent, realistic and prudent and loan loss provisions that reflect realistic repayment expectations.

Anti-money laundering

More than ever before, the topic of anti-money laundering (AML) has taken on increasing importance in Jordan. The risks posed by money laundering and terrorism financing to the reputation and integrity of financial systems are being recognized widely across the world, and in Jordan.

To date, the CBJ is the only supervisory authority that has taken concrete steps to put in place a substantive AML regime in Jordan. Such policies are meant to promote high ethical and professional standards in the banking sector and prevent a bank from being used, intentionally or unintentionally, by criminal elements. This includes strict 'know-your-customer' rules and procedures that banks are required to carry out, tough record keeping requirements and reporting of any suspicious transaction to the dedicated unit at the CBJ. The CBJ inspects compliance with AML regulations as part of its annual on-site inspection procedure, and has the authority to use its general sanctioning powers under the banking law in case of non-compliance.

A draft AML law is currently being considered by parliament that broadly addresses a number of aspects of money laundering prevention, detection and repression. This law is meant to bring Jordan up to date with international standards. It will address the main weaknesses of the Jordanian system by criminalizing money laundering specifically, introducing a financial intelligence unit (in the Egmont Group sense), and strengthening cooperation amongst different government agencies.

Continuous upgrading

The CBJ aims to build a solid foundation of prudent capital regulation, supervision and market discipline, and to enhance risk management and financial stability. Banking supervision is constantly being strengthened, and most prudential standards are in line with international best practice. The CBJ is upgrading banking supervision in several areas, including reviewing the applicable laws and regulations with a view to making them more responsive to the emerging needs. Other areas that are being addressed are mainly with regard to strengthening the regulatory framework for good governance and efforts for banks to improve risk management and disclosure practices. These steps would further improve Jordan's compliance with the Basel Core Principles, and ensure successful migration towards Basel II observance.

The CBJ's vision is to have an efficient and competitive banking system in Jordan that meets international standards of best practices in risk management and corporate governance, complies with applicable laws and regulations and satisfies the credit needs of the domestic economy thereby supporting economic development of the kingdom.

Part Seven

Marketing

7.1

The Media and Advertising

Suleiman Matouk, Ideal JWT

At the end of 2006 advertising expenditure had reached between US $210 million and US $220 million. At the current rate of growth, advertising expenditure is expected to exceed US $620 million by 2010.

Less than 3 years ago Jordan had its first privately run radio station, Fann FM. Today, there are more than eight privately owned and run radio stations – Rotana (Arabic), Sawt El Ghad (Arabic), Mazaj (Arabic), Mood (English), Play (English), Beat (English) and Ahlen (English) – all of which are on FM, and in addition, of course, are the government owned and run radio stations in both Arabic and English.

Over the past couple of years the number of daily newspapers has grown from four to more than seven *Al Ra'i, Ad Dustour, Al Ghad, Al Arab Al Yawm, Al Anbat, Adiyar* and the English daily *Jordan Times* are but a few.

The past few years have also witnessed the birth of many new magazines. Today the list contains, amongst others, *Laylina, Anti, Milh wa Sukar* (Salt and Sugar), *Baiti*, in addition to *Sharqiyat* all of which are in Arabic. The English list contains *Living Well, Home, Jordan Business, Jo, Venture, Viva, Couples' Life, Luxury, Skin, Nox, Where 2 Go, On Campus, Luxury, Our Values* and *I* magazine.

The second half of 2004 and 2005 witnessed a boom in the stock and real estate markets. In addition, and with the completion and the official opening of the state-of-the-art King Hussein Bin Talal Convention Center at the Dead Sea, Jordan became one of the leading hosts of conferences, meetings and exhibitions, be they political or commercial. Many regional real estate companies are now focusing on developing the market in Jordan, introducing large housing and commercial projects. In addition to skyscrapers now being built in Amman, Aqaba also has a fair share of huge projects such as the Saraya Aqaba project, Ayla and Tala Bay. Furthermore, a large plot of land in the heart of the AlAbdali area in Amman is now being turned into a modern downtown with office buildings, apartment buildings, shopping areas and streets exclusively for pedestrians. This boom in the real estate market and the influx of large size regional real estate development companies have positively affected the advertising industry in the past 18 months by raising the advertising spend to new levels.

The media scene in 2007 is expected to go through additional major changes. For one, the long-awaited, and only, privately owned TV station, Al Ghad TV (ATV), is expected to be launched. A second licence for a satellite station was recently awarded. This should in turn strengthen the TV spend as it will no longer be restricted to the government-owned and -run Jordan TV.

Another sector of the media is going through drastic changes. This is outdoor media. All through 2006, the Greater Amman Municipality had been reconsidering this sector due to the adverse effect all the outdoor signs have on the skyline of the capital. To address this a committee to beautify Amman was commissioned to review the licensing procedures and the control of outdoor adverting. Its recommendation, which should be implemented as of January 2007, has been to restructure the outdoor media licensing procedure by not renewing many of the outdoor sign licences. The effects of this are now being felt, but the actual effects on the industry at large is yet to be seen.

As has been the case in previous years, in terms of advertising spend figures, the newspapers are still top of the list at more than US $150 million, or 77 per cent of the total market spend on advertising as per IPSOS-STAT figures for the period from January to November 2006. Second on the list is TV, with a little over US $12 million, or 6 per cent, followed by outdoor (US $11.9 million), radio (US $10.3 million), and magazines (US $9 million). No figures are yet available for the electronic media.

Despite the difficult times the region has been facing, Jordan has been able to maintain a stable and safe environment attracting many regional investments. This in turn has been felt in the advertising industry through the continuous growth in the advertising spend figures over the past several years, which is also expected to carry through in the near future. Some new international agencies joined the up-wave by opening offices in Amman in the past couple of years. Today, the main international and regional advertising agencies with a presence in the Jordanian market include Grey, Horizon FCB, JWT, Leo Burnett, Lowe Pimo VDV, Memac-Ogilvy, Publicis-Graphics, Saatchi & Saatchi, TBWA, and Team Y&R.

Part Eight

Living and Working

8.1

The Jordanian Labour Law

Yousef S Khalilieh, Member Noor A Jundi, Associate and Shereen S Said, Associate Rajai K W Dajani & Associates, Advocates and Legal Consultants, Amman

Introduction

The Jordanian Labour Law No. 8 of 1996 (the law) was published in the *Official Gazette* on 16 April 1996 and came into effect exactly 2 months later. Matters relating to employment contracts are in general regulated by the Civil Law No. 43 of 1976.

Practice

The law organizes the rights and duties of both employers and employees and applies to any natural person who performs work for an employer in Jordan in return for wages, whether the work is on a permanent, temporary or seasonal basis. However, the law does not apply to the following:

1. Civil servants
2. Municipal employees
3. Domestic servants
4. Gardeners, cooks, agricultural employees and persons employed in similar occupations

The law prohibits, under any circumstances, the employment of juveniles who have not attained the age of 16 or the employment of anyone under

18 years of age in hazardous or exhausting circumstances or for work
that endangers the health and the safety of juveniles.

Contract of employment

The relationship between employees or a labour union, on the one hand,
and employers on the other, is regulated either by an Arabic written
contract of employment executed in at least two copies or by a verbal
agreement that can be proven by legal methods.

A written contract regulating the relationship between an employee
and an employer can be for a fixed duration, which expiries upon the
expiry of a specified period (limited employment contract), or for a term
that is not fixed (unlimited employment contact).

The law requires that every employer employing 10 employees or more
must maintain internal regulations for his or her establishment that set
out the hours of work, the daily and weekly rest periods, work offences
and the penalties and consequences thereof, including the method of
termination of employment, and any further details that are relevant to
the nature of the work in question, provided that the said regulations do
not violate the provisions of the law. Such internal regulations are
subject to the approval of the Minister of Labour and are applicable from
the date of approval.

Wages

A committee formed by the council of ministers on the recommendation
of the Minister of Labour and comprising representatives of both
employers and employees fixes the minimum wages payable in Jordanian
dinars for specific jobs and professions.

Subject to the relevant minimum fixed wage, all wages must be
stipulated in every contract of employment, but if not, an employee is
entitled to receive a wage applicable to work of the same nature, if any.
Otherwise, the amount payable will be based on the wage customarily
paid in that field or, where there is no point of reference, the court will
estimate the amount due in accordance with the provisions of the law.
All wages must be paid within a maximum period of 7 days from the date
of entitlement.

Wages and other amounts payable to an employee, his or her heirs or
those entitled subsequent to his or her demise will be considered as
having a first class general lien preceding all other debts including taxes,
fees and other rights payable to the government and debts secured by
real estate mortgages or in-kind securities.

Probation period

Under the law, an employee may be placed under probation for the first 3 months of his or her employment, during which period an employer may terminate the service of the employee without having to give him or her notice or even pay any gratuity. In the event that the employee's services continue after the expiry of the probation period then the employment contract will be unlimited. The full probationary period must be included when calculating a total period of employment.

Working hours

An employee may not work more than 8 hours per day or 48 hours per week, although the employee may distribute the number of maximum working hours within the week as long as it shall not be more than 11 hours per day.

Nevertheless, an employer may require that an employee performs work for more than the daily or weekly working hours, in which event the employee is entitled to receive an overtime wage for every hour at a minimum rate of 125 per cent of his or her ordinary wage. Also, if an employee works on his or her weekly rest day, a religious feast or during official holidays, the person is entitled to receive a minimum wage for the work of at least 150 per cent of the standard wage.

Vacations and leaves

The law grants an employee 2 weeks' fully paid holiday per year as annual leave, unless a longer period is stipulated in the work contract. If the employee has been employed by the same employer for a period exceeding 5 consecutive years then he or she is entitled to 21 days' fully paid holiday annually, unless a longer period is stipulated in the work contract.

An employee shall also be entitled to 2 weeks' sick leave fully paid per year provided that he or she has been working for 6 months in any year of employment. This period may be extended for another 14 days fully paid if the employee is hospitalized or with only half his or her usual salary if the leave was on the recommendation of a medical committee.

Female employees

The law grants female employees certain special privileges, including an entitlement to maternity leave with full pay for a total period of 10 weeks. Additionally, female employees who work at an establishment that engages 10 employees or more have a right to leave without pay for a maximum period of 1 year in order to devote her full time to looking after her children.

Termination of contract

A contract of employment can be terminated by mutual agreement, the expiration of its specified work or if the employee dies or is disabled by a disease that prevents him or her from working and such fact is evidenced by a medical report.

However, and with due observation of the above, an employer is prohibited from terminating the contract of a pregnant working women as of the sixth month of her pregnancy or during her maternity leave of an employee who is on conscription or reserve service during such service or of an employee when he or she is on an annual or sick leave, on leave granted for the purpose of labour, culture, pilgrimage, or during his or her mutually agreed-upon leave to serve on a full-time basis for a working syndicate or to join a recognized institution.

The law grants an employee who works for an unspecified duration, who is not subject to the provisions of the Social Security Law and whose employment is terminated for any reason whatsoever the right to receive end of employment compensation at the rate of 1 month's salary for each year of his or her actual employment. For periods of employment of less than 1 year, he or she shall be paid on a proportionate basis. The salary in such cases will be the last salary the employee received. In case the employee worked on the basis of commission or by piece, then the salary shall be calculated by taking the average monthly income that he or she earned during his or her final 12 months.

In addition to end of employment compensation, the employee is also entitled to the benefits granted to him or her by any savings scheme, pension fund or similar scheme that the employing establishment has provided.

In order to ensure an employee's rights and to enhance his or her career, the law compels an employer to provide, on termination of the contract for any reason whatsoever, a service certificate stating the name of the employee, the type of work and his or her dates of joining and terminating the employment. At the same time the employee is obliged to return to the employer all papers and tools in his or her possession belonging to the employer.

Furthermore, employees in any profession or occupation may establish their own Labour Union to oversee their interests to ensure due application of the provisions of the law.

Jurisdiction

In case of unfair dismissal, the law entitles any employee the right of recourse to the courts. If the court decides that the employee was unfairly dismissed then it may rule either that the employee return to his or her work or that the employer pay compensation to the employee, including the payment of a month's notice and all the other entitlements due to the employee pursuant to the law and employment contract, provided that such compensation is not less than 3 months' salary and not in excess of 6 months' salary, calculated on the basis of the last salary the employee received.

The law provides for a Wages Authority, which entitles the employee to challenge the wages he or she was receiving prior the termination of employment, provided that such action is brought within a period not exceeding 6 months from the date of termination.

Decisions issued by the Wages Authority shall have the force of court judgements and may be appealed to the Court of Appeal within 10 days of being issued, provided that the value of the judgement exceeds 100 Jordanian dinars.

Any labour dispute other than those relating to wages fall within the jurisdiction of the Magistrate's Court and any judgement issued by them may be appealed to the Court of Appeal within 10 days of issue.

All claims submitted to the Magistrate's Court are exempted from the payment of fees including those for execution of the decisions that it passes. No labour-related dispute may be heard by any court after the lapse of 2 years from the date on which the cause of action arose.

Furthermore, the provisions of the Labour Law do not affect any of the rights granted to employees by any other law if that law gives the employee better rights than those granted to him or her under the provisions of the Labour Law.

Every condition in a contract or agreement, whether concluded before the law or subsequently, under which any employee waives any of his or her rights under the law shall be considered null and void.

Non-Jordanian employees

It is not permissible to engage any non-Jordanian employee except with the approval of the Minister of Labour and on condition that the work delegated to such employee requires experience and ability that are not readily found among Jordanian employees or where the number of employees so qualified in Jordan does not meet domestic market demand. Priority for employment of non-Jordanians must be given to Arab experts, technicians and employees.

A work permit must be issued by the Ministry of Labour prior to the recruitment or engagement of any non-Jordanian employee for which the employer must pay a fee for issue and subsequent renewal.

Conclusion

The law in Jordan is in harmony with the rules and regulations of international and human rights labour agreements and is deemed to grant employees fair and special privileges. When issued the law was considered to be a modern model ensuring stability and equity of the rights of employees.

8.2

Living and Working in Jordan

Mark Timbrell, Resident Manager,
InterContinental Hotels Group, Amman

Overview of the country

'Diverse' is the adjective that always springs to mind when looking for a word to describe Jordan. One can drive from the Syrian border in the north to Aqaba in the south in about four and a half hours, a distance of some 400 kilometres. So Jordan is not a big country by world standards, but packed into this fascinating kingdom is a history of mankind that dates back thousands of years. The main archaeological record starts at Beidha, some 15 kilometres from Petra David Attenborough in one of his series referred to it as the first ever recorded settlement of humans. Dating back 15,000 years Beidha marks the point where man gave up hunting and gathering in favour of farming and a settled village life the very first village of all villages that led to towns and then to cities.

Since that time, Jordan has been central to the emergence of civilization and of course religion. One can still drive around today and see signs to Moab and Edom, those violent kingdoms mentioned in the Old Testament of the Bible.

History, archaeology, ecology, geography and climate are the words that give meaning to the diversity referred to. Millennia ago, Egyptians, Assyrians, Hittites and others criss-crossed the area now called Jordan, trading and warring. But it wasn't until the arrival of the Greeks in about 330 BC, the rise of the Nabatean Culture in the south and the later occupation by Rome in the 1st century BC that the archaeological evidence becomes obvious to the untrained tourist eye. They left behind them the awe-inspiring sites of Petra, Jerash, Umm Qais, Pella and the Citadel of Philadelphia – modern-day Amman – as well as many more.

In about AD 30, Jesus Christ was baptized at Al Maghtas in Jordan, 'Bethany beyond the Jordan' referred to in the book of John 1:28. Christianity spread and the Roman Empire split. The Eastern 'Byzantines' embraced Christianity and they left much of their evidence in the beautiful church mosaics seen in abundance across the country today, particularly at Madaba, Mount Nebo, Umm Ar Rassas, Petra and elsewhere.

Next came the Ummayids bringing with them Islam and leaving behind a wholly new style of architecture whose best examples are known today as the Desert Castles, such as Qasr Amra and Qasr Kharaneh. The zealous crusaders came to Jordan in the 12th and 13th centuries in a vain attempt to establish Christianity by the sword and both sides left behind fine examples of mediaeval military construction at Kerak, Shobak and Ajloun.

Finally came the Ottoman occupation that ended with the Arab Revolt and the creation of the modern day kingdom of Jordan. Still running today on special request are the original steam locomotives and carriages of the Hejaz railway made famous in 'Lawrence of Arabia' – the ones that got away!!

Fifteen thousand years of extraordinary history crammed into a few sentences! That's because this isn't a history of Jordan – instead it should be a whetting of the appetite for anyone thinking of settling here for a few years or longer. There is so much to do and see, one need never have a boring weekend.

Most of the 'favourite trips' mentioned below tend to capture a little bit of all of this history, together with the other dimensions of climate, ecology and geography. A good starting point is a visit to Iraq al Amir – a small palace building dating back to the 2nd century BC, which a French archaeologist reconstructed in the 1960s. Apparently, he came to the site and made replica pieces of all the stones – then he returned to France and spent a couple of years reconstructing the palace as a model. When he had completed the model as best as he could, he returned to Jordan and repeated the whole thing in real life! The 'Qasr' is only a short drive from West Amman, about 20 minutes, in Wadi Elsir. It is a lovely spot, especially in springtime, very green with lots of pretty flowers.

It is fascinating to be walking in the very land where the stories of the Bible's New Testament are set. One can do an absorbing full day 'biblical tour' from Amman provided an eye is kept on the time. Leave town at about 9 am and head for Qasr Mukkawir, located off the King's Highway, south of Madaba. It takes about 1 hour and 20 minutes to get there. It's great to go in springtime and at the end of March: once off the 'highway', one can usually see the rare black iris growing in the fields and on the roadsides. If the iris is not to be seen, because it only blooms for a variable 2-week period, there are plenty of other beautiful wild flowers to see – mainly from February to April. Mukkawir has fabulous views, stands in magnificent isolation and is great for an exhilarating short walk. It was the palace of Herod the Great where it is alleged that

Salome danced and demanded from Herod the head of John the Baptist – what a piece of history!

Madaba is on the way back to Amman and boasts some of the best Byzantine Mosaics. There is the museum there (try to find the 'secret garden') as well as the famous 'Map of the Holy Land' inside St. George's Church. Try combining a trip to Madaba with lunch at Hareth Jdoudna: it is a renovated traditional family house with an open courtyard and it is particularly pleasant to sit out in the shade from spring to autumn.

Along from Madaba, Mount Nebo is about a 10- to 15-minute drive. Make sure to go when the weather is clear as from this point one can see for miles across the Jordan Valley to the West Bank. This site is purported to be the place from where Moses saw the promised land of milk and honey. The Dead Sea shimmers far below, with Jericho and Jerusalem in the distance – it's pure magic!

From Mount Nebo, take the road immediately down to the Jordan Valley and on to the Baptism site. It will take another 40 minutes or so. At first glance at the Baptism site, it certainly is not as impressive as Petra or Jerash, largely because one is not being bombarded by large numbers of well-preserved ruins. Instead, although the archaeological evidence is all around, the Baptism site is more of a 'feeling'. It is a sense of realization that in this place, almost 2,000 years ago, Christ was baptized and one of the world's biggest religious movements started. Here in Jordan at Bethany beyond the Jordan.

Pope John Paul II opened this site in 2000 and it would be no surprise if in years to come this 'park' became the number one attraction for tourism in Jordan. Beware it can get extremely hot in the valley during the summer months, 40°C plus, and so it is best to visit from October to the end of April.

Whilst Amman shivers in winter, the Jordan Valley can be 10°C to 12°C warmer. Only a 45-minute drive to the Dead Sea from Amman but one is transported from winter to spring or spring to summer, without passing through airport lounges or facing custom formalities! One can relax in the luxury of any of the ever-increasing numbers of Dead Sea Hotels. Plenty of swimming pools, stunning views, good restaurants, great spas and, of course, the unique experience of being at the lowest point on earth and floating in the mineral-rich waters of the Dead Sea. It's a real treat to save up for and a decadence to take advantage of when in Jordan! Useful tip there are a lot less flies in spring than in autumn.

If staying overnight between May and September, it's worth considering combining the visit with a fun outing to Wadi Mujib. You need to arrange a guide in advance through the Royal Society for the Conservation of Nature (RSCN) and they will take you on a guided tour up the gorge. You need to be quite fit for this one, and have a sense of adventure. Arrange to be there early at 7–7.30 am and there will not be any disappointment!

During the summer, a weekend away at the nature reserve in Wadi Dana is great fun. One can stay at the small guesthouse, or, better, camp. The campsite is run by the RSCN and almost everything is available (tents, blankets, clean bathrooms, etc). The view from here across the Wadi Araba is spectacular, the site is very well managed and clean and a guided tour can educate one about the flora and fauna of this unique reserve. Depending on one's energy levels, the walk can take hours and keen bird watchers will love it! Try not to go during a public holiday period as it can get quite crowded and ruin the isolation that this wonderful location can provide.

For jolly campers, camping in Wadi Rum is an absolute must. To enjoy an overnight stay to the maximum it's best to team up with at least two other vehicles – including someone in the group who has been here a few times before and knows their way around! Take your own kit, including a four-wheel drive-off road vehicle, and follow the rules and advice given by the rest house in Rum village. April to October or even mid-November is the season – on a clear moonless night the stars are amazing, it is pure enchantment. Watch 'Lawrence of Arabia' before going, it will enhance the experience.

There are plenty of good guidebooks to read on all the options and it is well worth planning trips to make sure all the best are covered whilst resident here. Some useful organizations to be in touch with are the Friends of Archaeology, the Humane Centre for Animal Welfare and the Hash, all of which organize walking and hiking trips and will ensure one meets up with Jordanians and expatriates who have a sense of discovery and adventure.

Living in Amman

Most expatriates are based in West Amman, which is a very smart part of town. Finding your way around is relatively easy as the map of this area is quite clear when it comes to the main roads. Finding friends' homes for the first time is not so easy as there is no such book as an A–Z! West Amman is growing rapidly and frankly it would have to be updated every 6 months to keep up. Areas of open ground 6 years ago are now residential neighbourhoods. Luckily most invitations come with map attached!

Settling down and making friends is easy. Obviously, the children make friends at school but those who arrive without kids will find many activity groups full of welcoming faces, both expatriate and Jordanian. These associations and societies range from the more formal such as rotary clubs and business associations (Jordan/British, Jordan/French, etc) to the less formal such as British Ladies, American Women,

Scandinavian Speaking Ladies as well as societies like the Friends of Archaeology, and the ubiquitous Hash.

Excellent schooling is available from kindergarten through to graduation. The International Baccalaureate achieves excellent results and is reckoned to be one of the best in the Middle East. British and American curricular are available as are the French and obviously Arabic. The International Community School caters to children from 4 to 16 years, covering the UK curriculum and has in the region of 40 nationalities. It is renowned for accepting and assimilating non-English-speaking children rapidly into the school and community. All schools have fleets of buses to transport children to and from home. Most expatriate schools also have very active parent teacher associations and to a large extent the schools provide the majority of extra-curricular activities with clubs, outings, sports and so on.

West Amman has a good and increasingly upmarket selection of shops, cinemas, activity centres and sports clubs, offering golf, tennis, squash, swimming, horse riding and so on. Of course, Amman is not far away from the scuba diving centres in the Red Sea and many take the opportunity of being in Jordan to get their PADI certificate.

There are several excellent supermarkets now located near the 7th Circle intersection, nothing international as yet, but in 2007 Carrefour will be open. Almost everything is available from both Europe and the United States but some imported items can be a bit expensive. There has been a massive improvement over the past 5 years in this field and it looks set to continue. In addition there are some speciality shops and, yes, there is a pork butcher you may be surprised to learn about. Some supermarkets stock alcohol and this is also available at 'off licences' around town. Jordan has quite a developed brewing and distilling industry and local beverages are of course much less expensive than the imported ones. In recent years there has been quite a hike in taxes on such luxuries, so it is expensive. Be aware, however, that alcohol is not permitted for sale during Ramadan and some religious holidays. Recently, some very modern and extensive shopping malls have been opened. The largest is Mecca mall, big by any standard, and it contains cinemas, bowling and many of the major brand shops and fast food outlets – beware it gets fully packed on the weekends in particular. For those who enjoy shopping areas as opposed to big malls, the district of Sweifiyah between the 6th and 7th Circles is fast becoming a shopper's paradise with high-end and mid-range clothing and shoe shops.

Good standard accommodation in West Amman is readily available and finding somewhere to live is easy through the real estate agents. It can be quite expensive but equally you can find excellent deals. A moderate three- to four-bedroom stand-alone villa can be as much as 20,000 Jordanian dinars per year but you can also find good three-bedroom apartments in a block for as little as 7,000 Jordanian dinars (unfurnished) if you search long enough. Neighbourhoods are generally quite quiet but as anywhere it is worth making sure you are in a good area before committing yourself. Oh! And check the neighbouring land is not vacant as I can guarantee that as soon as you move in the builders will start to excavate for a new house or apartment block. Also, it is worth checking the capacities of your water tanks. Most apartment buildings come with a 'guard' who is usually non-Jordanian and takes on the role of a Mr Fix-it, taking care of arranging your gas bottles and diesel deliveries as well as useful extras such as washing the car twice a week and so on. All for a relatively low shared cost with other tenants.

Getting around Amman is easy, there are plenty of cheap taxis (just make sure the driver puts the meter on before you set off!) but be prepared to have to direct the driver if you are not travelling to a major hotel or shop. You can find the driving a challenge or relatively easy, it very much depends from where you are coming. The road and traffic system has been significantly upgraded in recent years and is certainly above average in the region. Traffic police are particularly hot on speeding, wearing seat belts in the front and not using mobile phones whilst driving.

For driving a hire car, you do not need a Jordanian license and your own licence will be accepted. Hire cars start at about 22 Jordanian dinars per day for a category A. If you buy your own car (vehicle tax is quite high if you are not exempted), then a Jordanian licence is necessary. A written test and a short drive around the block with an examiner is all that is needed but this can take two half days and it is best to take a friend or colleague who speaks Arabic with you.

A large majority of Jordanians are Muslims, about 94 per cent, with a roughly 6 per cent Christian minority. All religions are well tolerated and there is a wide selection of churches in Amman representing many different denominations from the Catholic, Orthodox and Anglican churches.

Hospitals are plentiful and in fact Amman is recognized as a medical centre in the Middle East. Most doctors have trained in the United States, the United Kingdom and Europe and many patients come to Jordan from around the region for relatively low cost treatment.

In conclusion, Amman is a modern city with a good municipal management and infrastructure. Water is scarce in the region but is well supplied and should be conserved as much as possible. Most houses and apartments have large reserve tanks and if there is a shortage, a tanker can easily be arranged at short notice. It is a relatively quiet city and great for families.

Meeting and working with Jordanians

Jordanians receive foreigners with genuine warmth and friendliness and they are very careful to separate the individual from the policies of one's government. More than in most other countries in the world, the people one works with will offer invitations to visit their homes or to join them for an outing or for a drink. Don't be surprised if in a group most of the conversation ends up in Arabic this may be a little disconcerting but there is no bad intention. Despite the excellent level of English generally encountered, it is worth remembering that in social gatherings, Arabic is a Jordanian's first language and therefore the best medium for general chit-chat, joking and storytelling.

Better, as an expatriate, learn some Arabic words and expressions as Jordanians are very proud of their culture and language and an expatriate's interest to communicate in their language is very well received.

If planning to stay in Jordan for a year or more it is very worthwhile learning about the ethnic and religious mix of the country. At first glance the unaccustomed eye would miss one of the most interesting aspects of Jordan. There is quite a class structure and it can be helpful to know who are the movers and shakers, who is related to who and which family names come from where.

Don't be fearful of making a 'faux pas' by wishing Happy Easter to a Muslim or Happy Eid to a Christian. Certainly in West Amman, no one gets the slightest bit offended. Two phrases in Arabic that can be used over any of these periods to anyone are *'kul am wa-inta bkhair'* and *'Eid Mubarak'*.

Working in Jordan can be challenging due to cultural differences and either one will enjoy it and feel it very rewarding or, alternatively, one may find it very frustrating. Working with people of a different culture and with different values inevitably means one works either with or against the flow. Respecting local practices and culture is the most fundamental factor for understanding in the workplace.

For example, it is important to realize that the extended family is very much a part of local life for most, if not all, employees. There are times and periods when there is enormous family pressure on people to be present or to visit relatives. Of course there are events such as weddings and funerals that need no further understanding – however, in Jordan the period of condolences (3 days) may need to be observed, especially if the deceased relative is close, and Eid holidays are important gathering periods. If someone is well known and loses a relative, attendance at the condolences is expected. A visit of no more than half an hour together with other colleagues is highly appreciated.

Greetings can vary in different circumstances but generally the handshake with the right hand is the most common. However, an exception to be aware of is that some conservative Muslim ladies will not shake hands with men at all. If uncertain, it is best to nod, smile, extend a verbal greeting and watch to see if their hand is extended before making a move. It will be noted that men greet each other with kisses this is usual if both men are related or are friends.

When invited out to dinner at a restaurant or to someone's home, take a small hostess gift such as an arrangement of flowers or a box of chocolates this is essential etiquette in Jordan.

Hotels and restaurants

In early 1995 there were just three international chain five-star hotels in Amman and none in Petra, the Dead Sea or Aqaba. Now 10 years later there are 10 hotels competing in Amman, 5 in Petra, 2 at the Dead Sea and 2 in Aqaba. This explosion in supply was largely due to the business confidence generated by the 1994 Peace Treaty with Israel. Investors saw a golden opportunity in a country with tremendous regional tourism potential (Jordan, Palestine, Syria, Lebanon, Israel and Egypt) and a growing economy supported by European and American aid. From 1998 to date, this increase has resulted in both benefits and drawbacks.

On the plus side, the new products offer customers brand new facilities and new services at very competitive prices by international standards. Unfortunately and inevitably the available pool of quality trained staff has been diluted in recent years and it will probably take a year or two at least to get back the equilibrium. Although there is only one new project in Amman for 2004 and Petra is at capacity, investors now see the Dead Sea and Aqaba as the golden growth opportunities over the coming 5–10 years. Prime examples of these would be the 320-bedroom, beachfront intercontinental resort in Aqaba in early 2005 and a 450-unit holiday inn resort on the shores of the Dead Sea by 2007.

The recent Iraq crisis has provided a welcome boon for the hotels. Good supply, excellent rates and world-class conference facilities combine to place Amman firmly on the map as both a business centre for this region and a gateway to the huge Iraqi market with its pent-up demand. Clearly, opportunity is showing its face finally and all hoteliers are keeping their fingers crossed. Many have said in the past, 'All these hotel rooms! Who's going to fill them?' Well, already there are periods of excellent high demand and if all pieces of the puzzle stick together, business will be good for everyone.

Of course all these new hotels have also brought with them a whole new array of restaurants and bars offering different themes and cuisines. In recent years there has been a massive improvement in the availability and supply of all sorts of new food products from the United States, Europe and the Far East. His Majesty has taken a personal interest and supported the five-star hotels' executive chefs in the efforts to streamline the import of fresh products with a limited shelf life. Amman may not yet be on the same level as other big cities in the region like Dubai or Beirut, but it is catching up fast. In addition to this the local farmers are now experimenting with new fruits and vegetables, so variety is also improving considerably.

Good restaurants in Jordan are not just confined to the hotels. There are plenty of stand-alone restaurants. Competition is fierce in this arena and many establishments do not last the course. There are not that many customers and every proprietor is subjected to the fickleness of Ammanites who tend to favour the new. However, a few places have stood the test of time and the reasons for their success vary. It can be the quality of the food and service but equally important are the ambience and the ability to attract the 'in crowd'. Some of the current names of 'independents' likely to be heard are the Blue Fig, Whispers, Romero and Fakhreldine.

Residential Property Market

Alma Alic, Abdoun Real Estate, Amman

Introduction

Situated in the heart of the Middle East, Jordan is the meeting point of three continents: Europe, Asia and Africa. Elements of history and modernity blend together in the capital Amman, where one moment one can be wandering back in time at the ancient Citadel Hill and the next driving through the urban and contemporary streets of Abdoun.

Jordan is often seen as a liberal and accessible face of the Middle East and as one of the most promising emerging markets in the region, with rising income levels and increased interest from foreign investors. Jordan's vision of a thriving market includes a future that caters to the needs of the people and promotes business and investment opportunities in the region.

Foreign nationals are allowed to purchase property in Amman, one of the fastest growing cities in the Middle East and home to almost a third of the Jordanian population, although as of this time most choose to rent from local landlords.

Practicalities

When renting, it is important that a prospective tenant produces a valid copy of his or her passport. Other permits are not essential at the outset, as most landlords are well aware that it takes time to obtain residence and work permits in Jordan. Landlords do, however, require full personal and employment information about the client and in some cases will require a guarantee letter from the prospective tenant's company. A lease can be issued in a company's name against a letter stating the property will be for the exclusive use of the named employee and his or her family, although landlords tend to prefer to contract with the individual living in the property. This is for two reasons: First, the rent cannot be increased while the contract is with the same tenant. Second, properties rented by companies can sometimes be used by many different short-term employees who tend to neglect their temporary homes.

Housing allowances vary according to the status of the employee and can range from a basic allowance for unfurnished or semi-furnished accommodation to a fully furnished all-inclusive package. With this information in hand, the renter or his or her company should approach a reputable company agent, who will help locate a suitable property. The property market in Jordan, unlike some other countries in the region, is not a free-for-all: some real estate agents have exclusive property management agreements for defined properties and buildings, which are only listed and shown by those agents. Other properties are listed by all agencies and available through any of them.

To assist the agent in selecting a property it is absolutely essential that the renter provide clear information as to what is required. For example:

- What budget is available?
- What sort of accommodation is required, a villa or an apartment?
- Is the property to be furnished, semi-furnished or unfurnished?
- Should the property be a ground floor, rooftop or mid-floor residence?
- Should it be a free-standing or a semi-detached house?
- How many bedrooms or bathrooms are required?
- Should the property be in a specific area of town?
- Should the property be in or out of town?

Once a suitable property has been found, a quick decision is needed, and often payment of a deposit pending availability of the full sum due, as availability changes daily.

In Amman, a majority of the expatriate community live in Abdoun, a newly developed area considered to be the most modern neighbourhood in the city. The people living in this area include families from all over the world who nearly all speak English. Other residential localities include Swafiyah, Al Rabia, Jabal Amman, Shmisani and Dair Gbar.

Financial and lease information

Residential leases are usually for a term of 1 year renewable under the same terms and conditions for a similar period, with the annual rent payable in advance. Landlords prefer multi-year occupants, and are usually willing to compromise on the rent they charge for such clients. All contracts are signed under Jordanian law and are unbreakable with any amount paid in advance being non-refundable, unless the agreement contains a diplomatic clause.

Residential leases can also be on a monthly basis but such rentals cost about 20 per cent more. Leases are automatically considered renewed for another term unless notice of termination has been given by each party in writing 2 months prior to the date of expiry. Real estate agents act as intermediaries between landlords and tenants, where necessary, but all leases are made to protect the interests of both parties. Once a lease is signed, both parties and the real estate agent involved retain an original copy.

Payment terms

As mentioned, most landlords prefer an annual rent payable in advance on the signing of a lease and as a result tend to waive the requirement of a refundable deposit equal to 1 month's rent and a security deposit of the same amount. However, some landlords will accept 3 or 6 months' rent in advance, and are prepared to negotiate payment terms on an individual basis. In addition, a government tax equivalent to 2 per cent of the annual rent is payable by all the tenants, except those entitled to a tax exemption such as diplomats.

A real estate agent's commission payable by both the landlord and the tenant is usually 5 per cent of the annual rent for the first year and 1 per cent of the annual rent for any renewal. For short-term rentals, most of the real estate agents ask 10 per cent of the rental amount as commission. Government sales tax of 16 per cent is applied to the amount of the commission paid.

Extras

Rental prices usually do not include water, electricity, telephone, maintenance bills or the salary of the caretaker of the building, which are all paid monthly by the tenant.

Foreigners are required to pay a deposit of US $400 to have a telephone line installed in their name. An average water bill is US $70 every 3 months, and tenants should make sure that the premises being rented have sufficient water storage, as there is a water shortage problem in Jordan. Electricity bills during the summer months come to approximately US $100–150 a month for an apartment that has three ACs, the actual figure being dependent on their usage. In winter, electricity costs about US $70 a month. Every apartment building has a caretaker whose salary is approximately US $40 a month paid directly to him by each tenant.

The landlord is responsible for maintaining the premises and all technical installations, but he or she bears no responsibility for damage caused due to the negligence of the tenant. There is a separate clause in every rental contract referring to maintenance issues, and all responsibilities are always stated in writing prior to signing by both parties.

Approximate average rental prices in Amman

Abdoun

Flats/villas	Two bed	Three bed	Four bed	Five bed
Unfurnished	800	1,200	1,600	1,800
Semi-furnished	1,000	1,400	1,800	2,000
Fully furnished	1,200	1,600	2,000	2,200

Other districts including Swafiyah, Al Rabia, Shmisani and Dair Gbar

Unfurnished	500	800	1,000	1,500
Semi-furnished	750	1,000	1,200	1,700
Fully furnished	850	1,300	1,400	1,900

All prices are in Jordanian dinars 1 Jordanian dinar = US $ 0.708 approximately

In quoting these prices it should be noted that all rentals are affected by:

- The age and condition of the property
- Market availability
- The property's proximity to schools and shopping areas
- The presence of a garden, terrace or swimming pool

It should be noted that the prices of four- and five-bedroom units refer mainly to houses rather than flats, due to shortage of independent or semi-detached units for rent. Major increases, however, have not been seen in apartment rentals as many new buildings have been constructed providing an increased level of such accommodation.

A large number of gated communities and towers are being built in Amman's suburbs, with estimated completion times of 2008 or 2009. It is uncertain as yet how these will affect the rental market, since the areas of construction are not in districts where expatriates tend to reside.

Commercial Property Market

Alma Alic, Abdoun Real Estate, Amman

Introduction

Since 1992 Jordan has implemented a significant number of laws and initiatives designed to improve the business environment. Under the leadership of King Hussein and then King Abdullah, Jordan has demonstrated its commitment to economic reforms, including reforms of the customs, taxation and investment laws, which have significantly improved Jordan's business climate. As a result Jordan is becoming an increasingly attractive market for global trade.

Amman, the capital city, is the focus of the Jordanian economy, being the centre of government activity, commerce, services and manufacturing. It is being transformed into an international centre attracting substantial inward investment. Amman's thriving business community has created a city of opportunities as continued privatization and the economic growth forecast stimulates and accelerates the pace of both domestic and international investment.

The main business areas in the city are located in west Amman close to a number of roundabouts and crossroads along Zahran Street, the main road from downtown to the Queen Alia International Airport. These road intersections are commonly referred to as circles, numbered one to eight from downtown outwards towards the west.

As the city has grown, the commercial centre of Amman has moved to the west, with the main business district today being close to the third and fourth circles and expanding outwards to Shmeisani. Many former residential properties in this area have almost overnight been converted to commercial use.

This shift is reflected in a number of major new commercial developments. Largest and most significant is the project led by Abdali Investment and Development near to the Shmeisani area (see article on 'The Regeneration of Downtown Amman'). The commercial centre of

Amman is likely to shift in the direction of this new development, with many companies seeking to be located close to Abdali.

Other significant commercial development is taking place in the areas of Mecca Street and Wadi Saqra, where many commercial buildings are currently under construction with completion dates in the middle of 2007.

Another huge impact on commercial properties in Amman will be created with the construction of Jordan Gate. Jordan Gate – the first phase of the Royal Metropolis project – will be a futuristic development comprising two high-rise towers connected by a multi-storey podium. Built on an area of around 28,500 square metres, these buildings will together encompass a built-up area of approximately 220,000 square metres.

Jordan Gate will feature executive offices, modern conference facilities, an ultra-luxurious five-star hotel and an array of retail outlets. The development, at 6 Circle in Amman, will occupy the highest point in the city and on anticipated completion of the first phase in 2008 will be visible from every part of the capital.

International businesses are entitled to own their premises but nevertheless the market is characterized by widespread leasing activity. Indications are that the leasehold sector comprises 75 per cent of commercial demand.

At the moment (late 2006), there is a shortage of commercial properties on the rental market. Due to the major construction, we are expecting a wide range of availability at the end of 2006 and beginning of 2007 for leasing, including a significant number of good-quality office properties.

In the past couple of years, the commercial rental market in Amman has increased about 20–30 per cent. Consulting a representative from a reputable real estate agency is strongly recommended to ensure that a company attains the property required on the best terms.

Commercial lease structures

There are no standard lease formats in use within the commercial sector and therefore leases vary considerably depending upon the landlord and the managing agents, but a majority of leases are short term, ranging from 1 to 5 years. It is not uncommon for a real estate agent to negotiate lease clauses until common ground has been reached between landlord and tenant. In some cases such negotiations expand to the rental price, although this is less likely in prime office buildings.

Payment terms

Rent is usually paid yearly in advance on the signing of the lease although in some instances this can be negotiated to 6 months in advance. Since the rent is paid in advance, it is not a common practice to leave post-dated cheques or deposits with a landlord.

Service charges

Service charges are common for all commercial office space, vary between 10 per cent and 20 per cent of the rent and are always paid in advance in addition to the rental price. The charge usually covers the maintenance of the building, security and cleaning of common areas. The tenant is usually responsible for all the other bills within the leased office space (such as for electricity and water).

Agency fees

Both the landlord and the tenant have the obligation to pay 5 per cent of the first year's rental value by way of brokerage fees. If the contract is renewed both the lessor and the lessee pay 1 per cent of the rent for each subsequent renewal. A sales tax of 16 per cent is applied to commissions.

Fitting-out works/tenant improvements

A landlord will usually allow a rent-free period for fitting-out works to be undertaken by a new tenant. This rent-free period will have to be negotiated at the start of the contract but usually allows for a couple of months of fitting-out work provided that the landlord has agreed to the fitting-out proposals. The landlord, utilizing nominated maintenance contractors, can often give assistance with building or fitting-out works. All improvements undertaken by the tenant become the property of the landlord at the end of the lease unless agreed otherwise.

Termination or renewal procedures

Depending on the lease expiration clause, a tenant is usually obliged to inform a landlord in writing 2 months prior to the expiration date of the lease term of his or her intentions. Early termination of a lease by a tenant can be a problem since the rent is paid in advance and is not, in most cases, refundable. Early termination of the lease can be possible if there is a diplomatic or a similar clause stating that the tenant has the right to terminate the contract if the company is leaving Jordan and ceasing all operations in the country. If neither party gives notice, Jordanian law dictates that the contract is automatically renewed for another similar term subject to the same terms and conditions without any new lease actually having been signed.

Dilapidation procedures

The tenant and the landlord will inspect the premises on delivery of a termination notice and, as the tenant is obliged to leave the premises in good condition, fair wear and tear excepted, he or she is expected to compensate the landlord for any direct damages or losses to the leased premises resulting from negligence or misuse. Any work needed has to be completed before acceptance of termination of the lease by the landlord.

Transport and parking

Taxis are abundant in Jordan and operate on a meter system, while public buses run on limited routes but are not usually used by expatriates. Still, the car is the primary mode of transport in Amman and, as a result, car ownership is high, which is reflected in the volume of traffic on the roads and the overly congested parking facilities. Parking spaces are limited and arrangements must be incorporated into the initial lease contract in order to secure adequate parking. The lease will state the number of free parking spaces available, depending on the size of the leased property, but the tenant may want a separate agreement for additional parking spaces as needed and if available. Most of the newly constructed commercial buildings are being built with two underground floors for parking, and thus parking should not be such an issue.

Rentals

Rentals are usually quoted on a per square metre basis, but lease agreements usually state both the floor area and the annual rent. Approximate commercial rental rates in Amman as of mid-September 2006 are as follows.

Office Type	Rent per Square Metre per Year (Jordanian dinars)
Prime Commercial	100—150
Secondary	70—100
Tertiary	50—70

1 Jordanian dinar = US $0.708.

Appendices

Appendix 1

USEFUL ADDRESSES AND CONTACT DETAILS

1. Accountants and Auditors (Certified Public Accountants)

Saba & Co	Telephone:	462 2163
Deloitte & Touche (Middle East), Jordan	Fax:	4654197
PO Box 248,	E-mail:	ahaddad@deloitte.com
Amman 11118, Jordan		knabulsi@deloitte.com
		nkhoury@deloitte.com
Khleif and Co (Correspondent of KPMG)	Telephone:	5685409
Ommayya Street, Block No 66, 2nd floor,	Fax:	5681748
Amman Commercial Complex,	E-mail:	kpmg@nol.com.jo
Abdali, PO Box 830430, Amman, 11183,		
Jordan		
Ernst and Young,	Telephone:	5526111
PO Box 1140,	Fax:	5538300
Amman 11118, Jordan	E-mail:	Amman.office@jo.ey.com
	Website:	www.ey.com
BDO National Brothers Group	Telephone:	5515036, 5515038
Wadi Saqra,	Fax:	5538618
Al Mirad Building, 2nd Floor,	E-mail:	bdo@nets.com.jo
Al Rabieh, PO Box 1219,		
Amman 11118, Jordan		

2. Advertising Agencies

Memac Ogilvy Mather, Jordan	Telephone:	5524287
	Fax:	5532487
Idea JWT, Jabal Alweibdeh	Telephone:	4653013
Horizon FCB, Tla AlAli	Telephone:	5519606
Intermarkets Advertising, Jabal Amman	Telephone:	4622571
M & C Saatchi, Sweifieh	Telephone:	5885883
Publi Graphics	Telephone:	5660160
Publicis Graphics, Madina Munawara Street	Telephone:	5528174
TBWA / Jordan, Shmeisani	Telephone:	5525545

3. Banks (In Amman only)

Arab Bank, Shmeisani	Telephone: 5607115, 5607231,
Arab Banking Corporation, Abdali	Telephone: 5668549, 5664183
Arab Jordan Investment Bank, Shmeisani	Telephone: 5607126
Bank of Jordan, Khalda	Telephone: 5534169
Cairo Amman Bank, Wadi Saqra	Telephone: 4616910, 4639321
Capital Bank, Amman	Telephone: 5694250
	Website: www.efbank.com.jo
Citibank, Shmeisani	Telephone: 5675100
Egyptian Arab Land Bank, Queen Nour Street	Telephone: 5650180
HSBC Bank Middle East, 5th Circle, Jabal Amman	Telephone: 5518090
Industrial Development Bank, Shmeisani	Telephone: 4642216
International Arab Islamic Bank, Gardens	Telephone: 5694901
Islamic International Arab Bank, Downtown	Telephone: 4643270
Jordan Gulf Bank, Shmeisani	Telephone: 5603931
Jordan Investment and Finance Bank, Shmeisani	Telephone: 5665145, 5692470
Jordan Islamic Bank, Shmeisani	Telephone: 5677377
Jordan Islamic Bank for Finance and Investment, Abu Alanda	Telephone: 4732001
Jordan Kuwait Bank, Abdeli	Telephone: 5629400, 5662126
Jordan Ahli Bank, Jabal AlHussain	Telephone: 5673984, 4642391
Philadelphia Investment Bank, Salaf AlSail	Telephone: 4619235, 4647437
Societe Generale Bank, Shmeisani	Telephone: 5695470
Standard Chartered, Shmeisani	Telephone: 5655315
The Housing Bank for Trade and Finance, PO Box 7693, Amman, 11118	Telephone: 5667126, 5607215, 5607315 Fax: 5678131, 5691675
Union Bank for Savings and Investment, Shmeisani	Telephone: 5607011

4. Business Consultants

BDO National Brothers Group, Wadi Saqra Street, Al Mirad Building, 2nd Floor, Al Rabieh, PO Box 1219, Amman 11118	Telephone: 5515036, 5515038 Fax: 5538618 E-mail: bdo@nets.com.jo
Khleif and Co (Correspondent of KPMG) Amman Commercial Complex, 2nd floor, Abdali, PO Box 830430, Amman 11183, Jordan	Telephone: 5685409 Fax: 5681798 E-mail: kpmg@nol.com.jo
Ernst and Young, PO Box 1140, Amman 11118, Jordan	Telephone: 5526111 Fax: 5538300 E-mail: Amman.office@jo.ey.com

| Audit and Consult Consortium (Dweik and Co), Jabal Amman | Telephone: 4651931, 4648866
Fax: 4648866
E-mail: auditcon@dweik-acc.com
Website: www.dweik-acc.com |
| Abbasi Consultancy (Abbasi Group – Nexia International) | Telephone: 5660709
Fax: 5676901
E-mail: abbasiandco@index.com.jo
Website: www.abbasi-cpa.com |

5. Hotels

This is a non-inclusive list of some of the leading hotels in Amman.

Amman Marriott Hotel, Shmeisani	Telephone: 5607607 Fax: 5670100 Website: www.marriotthotels.com
Crowne Plaza Amman-Amra 6th Circle, Jebel Amman	Telephone: 5510001 Fax: 5510003 Website: www.interconti.com
Four Seasons Hotel, 5th Circle, Jebel Amman	Telephone: 5505555 Fax: 5505556 Website: www.fourseasons.com
Grand Hyatt Amman, Hussein bin Ali Street, Jebel Amman	Telephone: 4651234 Fax: 4615037 Website: www.amman.hyatt.com
Hotel Intercontinental Jordan, Queen Zein Street, 3rd Circle	Telephone: 4641361 Fax: 4645217 Website: www.interconti.com
Le Meridien Amman, Shmeisani	Telephone: 5696511 Fax: 5667137 Website: www.lemeridien-amman.com
Le Royal Hotel, Amman, 3rd Circle, Jebel Amman	Telephone: 4603000 Fax: 4603002 Website: www.leroyalhotel-amman.com
Sheraton Amman, 5th Circle, Jebel Amman	Telephone: 5934111 Fax: 5934222 Website: www.Sheraton.com

6. Useful Telephone Numbers

Local Telephone Directory Enquiries	1212
International Telephone Directory Enquiries	1214
Telephone Problems	139
Traffic Bureau – Operations	190
Rescue Police	191

Capital Police	192
Directorate of Public Security	196
Amman Municipality Fire Department	198
Ambulance and First Aid	199
Customs Department	4623186
Amman Chamber of Commerce	5601742, 5666151
Amman Chamber of Industry	4643009/4644747
Jordan Businessmen Association	5677426
Traffic Collisions	4639141
Highway Police	5343402
Royal Court	4637341
Electricity Emergency (Amman)	4750981/2
Industrial Cities	4022101
Free Zone	4029641
Aqaba International Airport	03-2012111
Queen Alia International Airport, Amman	06-4452000
Flight Information	06-4452700
Royal Jordanian Flight Information – Marka	06-4453200
Civil Airport	06-4891401

7. Airlines – Telephone Numbers

(All in Amman – code – 06)
(Source: Yellow Pages Tourism, 2006)

Aeroflot	5663150
Air Canada	4625535
Air France	5100777
Austrian Airlines	5660449
British Airways	5828801
Cyprus Airways	5620264
Egypt Air	4612004
Emirates	4615222
Etihad	4680100
Gulf Air	5620264
Iberia	4625197
KLM	5100760
Kuwait Airways	5690144
Lufthansa	5601744
MEA	4603500
Olympic	5664877
PIA	4625981
Qatar Airways	5679444
Royal Jordanian	5607300
Saudia	5521007
Swissair	4642943

| Turkish Airlines | 4641710 |
| Yemen Airways | 5652713 |

Appendix 2

USEFUL INFORMATION

1. Currency

The local currency is the Jordanian dinar (JD), which is made up of 1000 fils (or a 100 piasters). Currency notes occur in denominations of 50, 20, 10, 5 and 1 Jordanian dinars. Coins are to be found in denominations of 5, 10, 25, 50, 100, 250, 500 fils and 1 Jordanian dinar. The dinar is pegged to the US dollar and the approximate rate of exchange is 1 Jordanian dinar = US $1.42 (December 2006).

2. Credit cards

All major credit cards are accepted by hotels, restaurants, hire car companies and the larger stores. They may also be used in the increasing number of ATM machines in the country.

3. Health

No specific vaccinations are needed for Jordan, unless entry is being made from countries where cholera and yellow fever are prevalent when an inoculation document must be presented on arrival, although some doctors advise preventative injections against polio, tetanus, typhoid and hepatitis A. The taking out of health insurance prior to travelling to Jordan is recommended.

Local medical services are generally of a high standard, with most doctors being bi-lingual in Arabic and English as medical science is taught in English. Large well-equipped hospitals are to be found in Amman.

Pharmacies are to be found throughout the country offering a wide range of products, which tend to be expensive. It is recommended that people with special requirements should bring their medication with them.

4. Water

Tap water is generally safe to drink in Jordan especially in the major towns and cities but bottled water is readily available for those who prefer it. Water is a very scarce resource in Jordan and so visitors are asked not to cause unnecessary wastage.

5. Clothing

Businessmen are recommended to wear a suit and tie to meetings even though their hosts might be more casually attired. Businesswomen should wear long skirts or trousers and should always cover their shoulders and arms.

In the summer light clothing is recommended but Amman, in particular, can be cold in winter and so warmer clothing as worn in northern Europe and the United Kingdom is suggested, including overcoats and/or raincoats.

During Ramadhan, the month of fasting, conservative attire is recommended for both men and women.

6. Alcohol

Alcohol is served in most hotels and restaurants in Jordan's main cities. It may be purchased also from supermarkets and shops. Locally produced beers and wines are found, as is Arak, an Ouzo-like drink consumed with water and ice.

7. Working hours

Banks

Amman

Sunday to Thursday: 08.30 am to 3.00 pm
Closed on Fridays, Saturdays and public holidays
ATMs are increasingly to be found available 24 hours a day and usually accept Visa and MasterCard

Aqaba

Sunday to Thursday: 8.30 am to 2.30 pm

Commercial Offices

Sunday to Thursday: 9.00 am to 6.00 pm (but some take a 2-hour lunch break). Some Christian businesses may be closed on Sunday

Shops

Hours are flexible with some open 9.30 am to 1.00 pm and 2.30 pm to 6.00 pm and others, especially smaller stores, 8.00 am to 8.00 pm, maybe with a mid-day break.

Government

Amman

Sunday to Thursday: 8.30 am to 2.00 pm
During Ramadhan all working hours tend to be reduced

Aqaba

Sunday to Thursday: 7.30 am to 2.30 pm

Aqaba Special Economic Zone Authority

Sunday to Thursday: 8.00 am to 4 pm (there is also a customer support hotline operating 7 days a week)

8. Local time

Local time is GMT +2 between October and March and GMT +3 from April to September.

9. Car rental agencies

There are a plethora of local car rental firms. The following are the contact details of the local franchises of international companies (all are in Amman – Code 06):
Avis – 569 9420
Budget – 569 8131
Europcar – 565 5581
Hertz – 553 8958
National – 560 1350
Payless – 552 5180
Sixt – 585 8773
Thrifty – 568 4771

10. Departure tax

A departure tax, at variable rates, is payable in local currency on departure from the country. Non-Jordanians pay 5 Jordanian dinars whether leaving by land, sea or air, whereas Jordanians pay 8 Jordanian dinars if departing by land 25 Jordanian dinars by air and 6 Jordanina dinars by sea.

11. Electricity

220 V AC, 50 Hz. Wall plugs are European rounded two-pin and British rectangular three pin.

12. Jordanian embassies overseas

Algeria, Algiers
   Telephone: +2 132 692 031
   Fax: +2 132 691 554
   E-mail: jordan@mail.wissal.dz
Australia, Canberra
   Telephone: +61 262 959 906
   Fax: +61 262 397 236
   E-mail: pesy@anteract.net.au
Austria, Vienna
   Telephone: +431 405 1025
   Fax: +431 405 1031
   E-mail: jordanembassy@aon.at
Bahrain, Manama
   Telephone: +973 1729 1109
   Fax: +973 1729 1198
   E-mail: jordanemb@batelco.com.bh
Belgium, Brussels
   Telephone: +322 640 7755
   Fax: +322 640 2796
   E-mail: jordan.embassy@skynet.be
Brazil, Brasilia
   Telephone: +5561 248 5407
   Fax: +5561 248 1698
   E-mail: emb.jordan@tba.com.br
Canada, Ottawa
   Telephone: +1 613 238 8091
   Fax: +1 613 232 3341

Chile, Santiago
  Telephone: +562 228 8091
  Fax: +562 228 8783
  E-mail: jordanemb@terra.cl
China, Beijing
  Telephone: +8610 653 23 926
  Fax: +8610 653 23 283
  E-mail: joremb@public2.east.net.cn
Egypt, Cairo
  Telephone: +202 348 5566
  Fax: +202 360 1027
  E-mail: jocairo@ie-eg.com
France, Paris
  Telephone: +33 101 557 47 373
  Fax: +33 101 557 47 374
  E-mail: amb.jor@wanadoo.pr
Germany
  Telephone: +228 354051 / 2
  Fax: +228 353951
Greece, Athens
  Telephone: +301 677 5618
  Fax: +301 674 0578
  E-mail: jorembl@internet.gr
India, New Delhi
  Telephone: +9111 465 3099
  Fax: +9111 465 3353
  E-mail: jordanemb@ndf.vsni.net.in
Indonesia, Jakarta
  Telephone: +6221 520 4400
  Fax: +6221 520 2447
  E-mail: jordanem@cbn.net.id
Iran, Tehran
  Telephone: +9821 205 9703
  Fax: +9821 205 1872
Iraq, Baghdad
  Telephone: +9641 541 2892
  Fax: +9641 541 0343
Israel, Tel Aviv
  Telephone: +972 375 17 722
  Fax: +972 375 17 712
  E-mail: jordanl@bezegint.net
Italy, Rome
  Telephone: +3906 862 05 303
  Fax: +3906 860 6122
  E-mail: embroma@tiscalnet.it

Japan, Tokyo
  Telephone: +813 3580 5856
  Fax: +813 3593 9385
  E-mail: emb-jord@giganet.net
Kuwait, Kuwait
  Telephone: +965 253 3271
  Fax: +965 253 3270
  E-mail: joremb@qualitynet.net
Lebanon, Beirut
  Telephone: +961 592 2500
  Fax: +961 592 2502
  E-mail: jorem@dm.net.lb
Libya, Tripoli
  Telephone: +21821 360 0236
  Fax: +21821 361 4762
  E-mail: jordanembassy@excite.com
Malaysia, Kuala Lumpur
  Telephone: +603 452 12 684
  Fax: +603 528 8610
  E-mail: jordanembassy@po.jaring.com
Morocco, Rabat
  Telephone: +212 7 751 125
  Fax: +212 7 758 722
Netherlands, The Hague
  Telephone: +31 704 167 200
  Fax: +31 704 167 209
  E-mail: jordanembassy@wanadoo.nl
Oman, Muscat
  Telephone: +968 692 763
  Fax: +968 692 762
Pakistan, Islamabad
  Telephone: +9251 823 459
  Fax: +9251 823 207
  E-mail: ordanem@comsats.net.pk
Palestine Authority, Gaza
  Telephone: +9707 282 5134
  Fax: +9707 282 5124
  E-mail: jorrep@hallv.net
Qatar, Doha
  Telephone: +974 483 2202
  Fax: +974 483 2173
  E-mail: jordan@qatar.net.qa

Russia, Moscow
  Telephone: +7095 299 4344
  Fax: +7095 299 4354
  E-mail: emjordan@dol.ru
Saudi Arabia, Riyadh
  Telephone: +966 1 488 0039
  Fax: +966 1 488 0072
South Africa, Pretoria
  Telephone: +2713 342 80 267
  Fax: +2713 342 7847
Spain, Madrid
  Telephone: +34 913 191 104
  Fax: +34 913 082 536
  E-mail: jordania@teleline.es
Sudan, Khartoum
  Telephone: +249 11 475 090
  Fax: +249 11 471 038
  E-mail: joremb@sudanmail.net
Switzerland, Bern
  Telephone: +41 313 840 404
  Fax: +41 313 840 405
  E-mail: jordanie@bluewin.com
Syria, Damascus
  Telephone: +963 11 333 4642
  Fax: +963 11 333 6741
Tunisia, Tunis
  Telephone: +216 1 780 875
  Fax: +216 1 780 461
  E-mail: emb.jordan@planet.tn
Turkey, Ankara
  Telephone: +312 440 2054
  Fax: +312 440 4327
  E-mail: omar@superonline.com
United Arab Emirates, Abu Dhabi
  Telephone: +971 2 444 7100
  Fax: +971 2 444 9157
United Kingdom, London
  Telephone: +44 207 937 3685
  Fax: +44 207 938 8795
  E-mail: lonemb@jordanembassy.com.uk
United States of America, Washington DC
  Telephone: +1 202 966 2664
  Fax: +1 202 966 3110
  E-mail: hkjembassy@aol.com

Uzbekistan, Tashkent
   Telephone: +9987 127 42 479
   Fax: +9987 120 66 44
   E-mail: jordanuz@online.ru
Yemen, Sana'a
   Telephone: +967 1 413 276
   Fax: +967 1 414 516
   E-mail: jaysem@y.net.ye
Yugoslavia, Belgrade
   Telephone: +3811 136 91 950
   Fax: +3811 136 91 091

13. Foreign Diplomatic Missions in Jordan – Telephone Numbers

All embassies are located in Amman (Dialling Code 06)
   (Source: Yellow Pages Tourism, 2006)

Algeria	4641271
Australia	5807000
Austria	4601101
Bahrain	5664149
Belgium	5932683
Bosnia & Herzegovina	5856921
Brazil	4642169
Bulgaria	5529391
Canada	5203300
Chile	5923360
China	5515151
Czech Republic	5927051
Egypt	5605202
France	4641273
Germany	5930367
Greece	5672331
Hungary	5925614
India	4622098
Indonesia	5538911
Iran	4641281
Iraq (Liaison Office)	4623175
Israel	5524680
Italy	4638185
Japan	5930486
Korea	5930745
Kuwait	5605139
Lebanon	5929111
Libya	5693102

Malaysia	5902400
Mauritania	5855146
Morocco	5921771
Netherlands	5930525
Norway	5931646
Oman	5686155
Pakistan	4622787
Palestine	5677517
Philippines	5923748
Poland	5512593
Qatar	5607311
Russia	4641229
Saudi Arabia	5924156
South Africa	5921194
Spain	4614166
Sri Lanka	5820611
Sudan	5854500
Sweden	5901300
Switzerland	5930417
Syria	4641076
Tunisia	5674307
Turkey	4641251
United Arab Emirates	5934781
United Kingdom	5923100
United States of America	5906000
Yemen	5923771

14. Entry formalities

Single entry visas are available on arrival at Queen Alia International Airport and at Aqaba International Airport for most nationalities at a fee of 10 Jordanian dinars. Entry to Jordan by land necessitates the obtaining of a visa in advance from a Jordanian diplomatic mission abroad. They are also available from Jordanian diplomatic missions overseas, from which multiple entry visas may also be obtained at a cost of 20 Jordanian dinars. Contact with a Jordanian embassy overseas is strongly recommended prior to travel to ensure the existing regulations have not changed.

Visas obtained from Jordanian consulates are valid for 3–4 months from the date of issue. Tourist visas are valid for a stay of 1 month initially but can be extended for up to another 2 months. After that date a visitor must exit and re-enter the country, or undergo immigration procedures. If a visa has not been properly renewed before leaving Jordan then a fine will be payable at the point of exit.

Anyone planning to stay in Jordan for more than 2 weeks must register at the nearest police station (this usually undertaken by the hotel in which the traveller is staying).

15. Language

Arabic is the official language of Jordan with English also being widely spoken.

16. Weights and measures

Jordan uses the metric system. Land is frequently measured in terms of the dunum (donum), which approximates to 1,000 square metres.

17. Public holidays

1 January	New Year's Day
30 January	Birthday of His Majesty King Abdullah II
1 May	Labour Day
25 May	Independence Day
14 November	Birthday of His Majesty the late King Hussein
25 December	Christmas Day

In addition are the following Islamic holidays with their likely dates in the Gregorian calendar in 2007 (for each subsequent year each Islamic holiday will occur approximately 11 days earlier against the Gregorian calendar). Also mentioned is the approximate date of the start of the fasting month of Ramadhan

13 September 2007	1st Ramadhan 1428
13 October 2007	Eid al Fitr
20 December 2007	Eid al Adha
10 January 2008	1st Muharram 1429

18. Taxis

Taxis are prolific and inexpensive. Yellow taxis may travel only inside cities and require special permission to move outside. Beige taxis can travel between and inside cities. White taxis operate as service (shared) taxis on defined routes. Major hotels have taxi stands but charges are higher than taxis hailed on the street.

19. Telephone dialling codes

The international code for Jordan is 962

Local codes within Jordan are:
06 – Amman.
03 – Aqaba, Karak, Maan, Petra and Wadi Mousa.

02 – Ajloun, Jerash, Irbid, Mafraq and Um Qais.
05 – Dead Sea, Jordan Valley, Madaba, Salt and Zarqa.

20. Tipping

Tipping is not essential but always appreciated.

21. Travel between Amman and Aqaba

In addition to taxis and self-drive cars there are two other possibilities for travel between Amman and Aqaba – by plane and by express coach. Royal Jordanian operates a daily night-time flight in each direction, both of which necessitate overnight stays in order to fulfil one's business, and Jordan Express Tourist Transport Company (JETT), the cheapest manner of travel by far, makes a number of 4-hour journeys daily in each direction by double-decker coach.

22. Security

It is strongly recommended that advice on security is sought from British and other government sources prior to making any journey to Jordan. Although a generally peace-loving country there is potential for terrorist attacks and so care must be taken of one's personal security during any visit.

23. Some cultural considerations

- Jordan is predominately a Muslim country and so it is strongly recommended that both men and women dress conservatively.
- Public displays of affection should be avoided although local people of both sexes may be seen kissing others of the same sex on each cheek. Handholding by friends of either gender is often seen and is generally acceptable.
- The freedom to practise their faith by religions other than Islam is protected.

Appendix 3

Contributors' Contact Details

Abdali Investment & Development PSC

P.O. Box 925309, Amman 11190, Jordan

Tel:	962-6-468 0084
Fax:	962-6-468 0087
E-mail:	abdali@abdali.jo
Website:	www.abdali.jo
Contacts:	Jamal Itani, Chief Executive Officer
	Luna H.Madi, Marketing Manager

Abdoun Real Estate

Abdoun Almouhtaseb Center, P.O. Box 830625, Amman 11183, Jordan.

Tel:	962-6-5920605
Mobile:	079-5530007
Fax:	962-6-5932605
E-mail:	wael@abdoun.com.jo
Website:	www.abdoun.com.jo
Contacts:	Wael N Aljaabari – General Manager.
	Alma Alic Aljaabari.

Abdullah Jonathan Wallace

P.O. Box 30121,
Budaya,
Bahrain

Tel:	973 17 693 503
Mobile:	973 3677 0407
E-mail:	Abdullah@al-anqaa.com

Amman Chamber of Industry

P.O. Box 1800, Amman 11118, Jordan.

Tel:	962-6-4643001
Fax:	962-6-4647852
E-mail:	aci@aci.org.jo
Website:	www.aci.org.jo
Contact:	Juma Abu-Hakmeh – Director General.

Amman Stock Exchange

P.O. Box 212466, Amman 11121, Jordan.

Tel:	962-6-5664081
Fax:	962-6-5664071
E-mail:	info@ase.com.jo
Website:	www.ase.com.jo
Contact:	Jalil Tarif – Chief Executive Officer.

Aqaba Development Corporation

Chamber of Commerce Building
   P.O.Box 2680, Aqaba 77110 , Jordan

Tel:	962-3-2039100
Fax:	962-3-2039110
E-mail:	info@adc.jo
Website:	www.adc.jo

Aqaba Special Economic Zone

P.O. Box 2565, Aqaba 77110, Jordan.

Tel:	Customer Support Hotline:	962-3-962-3-2035757/8
	Investor Services Directorate:	962-3-203575718
Fax:	Investor Services Directorate:	962-3-2091035
E-mail:	info@aseza.jo	

Capital Investments

P.O. Box 940982, Amman 11194, Jordan.

Tel:	962-6-5200 330
Fax:	962-6-5692872
E-mail:	research@capitalinv.jo
Website:	www.capitalinv.jo
Contact:	Ali Al-Husry, Chairman and CEO
Website:	www.aqabazone.com

Central Bank of Jordan

P.O. Box 37, Amman 11118, Jordan.

Tel:	962-6-4630301
Fax:	962-6-4616400
E-mail:	faris@cbj.gov.jo
Contact:	Faris Sharaf , Deputy Governor

Environmental Consultants Branch, Ramadan Tech. Services Co.

P.O. Box 851223, Amman 11185, Jordan.

Tel:	962-6-5929067
Fax:	962-6-5934267
E-mail:	saramadn@nol.com.jo
Contact:	Subhi A. Ramadan – President.

Free Zones Corporation

P.O. Box 20036, Amman 11118, Jordan.

Tel:	05/3826000 – 05/3826429
Fax:	05/3826430
E-mail:	frez@free-zones.gov.jo
Website:	www.free-zones.gov.jo
Contact:	Mahmoud Qutaishat – Director General.

IDEA JWT

P.O. Box 910437, Amman 11191, Jordan.

Tel:	962-6-4653013
Fax:	962-6-4627207
E-mail:	suleiman.matouk@ideajwt.com
Website:	www.ideajwt.com
Contact:	Suleiman I. Matouk – Managing Director.

Intercontinental Hotels Group

Intercontinental Jordan, P.O. Box 35014, Amman 11180, Jordan.

Tel:	962-6-4641361
Fax:	962-6-4645217
E-mail:	mark_timbrell@icjordan.com
Website:	www.ichotelsgroup.com
Contact:	Mark Timbrell – Resident Manager, Intercontinental Hotel, Amman

Jordan Investment Board

P.O. Box 893, Amman 11821, Jordan.

Tel:	962-6-5608400/15 – Ext. 102
Fax:	962-6-5608427
E-mail:	mazen@jib.com.jo
Website:	www.jordaninvestment.com
Contact:	Dr. Maen Nsour – Chief Executive Officer.

Jordan Investment Trust PLC

P.O. Box 911447, Amman 11191, Jordan

Tel:	962-6-550 8888
Fax:	962-6-550 8899
E-mail:	ahmad.tantash@jordinvest.com.jo
	dalia.adawieh@jordinvest.com.jo
Website:	www.jordinvest.com.jo
Contact:	Ahmad Tantash, Chairman and CEO
	Dalia D. Adawieh, Manager, Marketing Department

Jordan Tourism Board

P.O. Box 830688, Amman 11183, Jordan.

Tel:	962-6-5678444
Fax:	962-6-5678295
E-mail:	info@visitjordan.com
Website:	www.visitjordan.com
Contact:	Mazen K. Homoud - Director General
	Omar Alfanek, Economic Researcher

Marwan A. Kardoosh

Director of Research,
    Jordan Center for Public Policy, Research and Dialogue,
    P.O. Box 830825, Amman 11183, Jordan

Tel:	962-6-592 3676/7/8/9
Fax:	962-6-592 3368
E-mail:	kardooshm@yahoo.com

Ministry of Industry and Trade

P.O. Box 2019, Amman 11181, Jordan

Tel:	962 6 562 9030
Fax:	962 6 569 9464
Website:	www.mit.gov.jo

National Electric Power Co.

P.O. Box 2310, Amman 11181, Jordan.

Tel:	962-6-5818230
Fax:	962-6-5818336
E-mail:	ahiyasat@nepco.com.jo
Contact:	Dr. Ahmad Hiyasat - Managing Director.

Natural Resources Authority

P.O. Box 7, Amman 11181, Jordan.

Telefax:	962-6-5826705
Mobile:	962-77-498015
E-mail:	dr_zsalem@nra.gov.jo
Website:	www.nra.gov.jo
Contact:	Dr.Ziad S.Hamarneh – Director of Projects Development and Investment
	Eng. Issam Qabbani - Head of Petroleum Studies

Rajai K.W. Dajani and Associates

Jordan Tower Building, Shmeissani, P.O. Box 5590, Amman 11183, Jordan.

Tel:	962-6-5680111
Fax:	962-6-5680333
E-mail:	ykhalilieh@dajanilaw.com
Website:	www.dajanilaw.com
Contacts:	Rajai Dajani – Advocate, Senator, Member of International Court of Arbitration - Paris.
	Yousef Salim Khalilieh – Advocate
	Noor A. Jundi, Associate
	Shereen S. Said, Associate

Saba & Co.,
Deloitte & Touche (Middle East) – Jordan

P.O. Box 248, Amman 11118, Jordan.

Tel:	962-6 4622163
Fax:	962-6-4654197
E-mail:	knabulsi@deloitte.com
	ahaddad@deloitte.com
	nkhoury@deloitte.com

Sana Abdullah

Journalist,
P.O. Box 137, Amman 11821, Jordan.

Tel:	962-6-5828603
Mobile:	962-77-308599
E-mail:	upiamman@go.com.jo

The Philip Dew Consultancy Limited

SSi House,
  Fordbrook Business centre,
  Marlborough Road,
  Pewsey, Wiltshire SN9 5NU

Tel:	44 1672 563 784
E-mail:	philipdew@dewconsult.com
Website:	www.dewconsult.com